The Quest

The Quest

Jim Kochanoff

Adventure Books

Copyright © 2020 James Kochanoff
All rights reserved
ISBN: 9798689265230

No part of this publication may be reproduced, distributed or transmitted in any form or by any means, including photocopying, recording, or other electronic or mechanical methods, without prior permission of the author, except in case of brief quotations embodied in critical reviews and certain other non-commercial uses permitted by copyright law. For permission requests, write to the author at www.adventurebooks.ca

Names, characters, places and incidents are a product of the author's imagination. Locales and public names are sometimes used for atmospheric purposes. Any resemblance to actual people, living or dead, or to businesses, companies, events, institutions, or locales is completely coincidental.

Dedicated to my wife Avai for her time and effort to review my work. The characters in this book appreciated her work.

The book is also dedicated to my mother-in-law Santha Ram who died in May 2006. Her kindness will not be forgotten.

Acknowledgments

I would like to thank my two families, Stan and Peggy Kochanoff—Satha Ram for their love and support during my life.

I thank my friend Michael Bayer who assisted me with marketing this book with a one-sheet and cover design. He would always drop everything to help me and never charged a cent.

I thank my friend Zita Hildebrandt who provided a final edit of my book. Her assistance was very much appreciated.

To my friend Alain Bolduc, whose magnificent sketches brought life to the story's characters. He is truly a talented artist.

Foreword

Fists and Fantasy does not take place on earth but on a world where different rules apply. Their technology may be centuries behind our world, but their magic and brute strength are a great equalizer. In the book's setting, humans are in scarce supply and don't have a critical role in the world. Because travel is difficult, communities tend to be isolated and suspicious of anyone not from their region or race. The world is not well mapped and travelers encounter many difficulties and strangeness on their journeys. There is a common language amongst the beings of this world but different dialects have developed over the centuries, making communication sometime difficult.

Yet despite the differences, there are more similarities between our worlds than may first be evident. There is greed, there is hate, and there is love. Creatures will fight for what's right and steal for what they believe is theirs. The land may be different, the residents strange, the rules may not make sense, but emotions are the same no matter where you live.

Sit back and enjoy the adventure!

He was dreaming.

It was so real. He held it in his hands. It glowed and pulsed in his grip. The power soared throughout his body. He looked directly into its light. It was ancient and magical, it belonged to him. But as quickly as that thought entered into his head, he sensed the presence of the others. He could not see their features but he knew that they would take it away from him. His concentration broke and the gem suddenly disappeared from his hands. Shocked at his loss, he screamed and woke from his sleep.

His dream had become a nightmare.

1

A Fool and His Money

A great distance away, another nightmare was beginning.

"No returns," the little man uttered, and was rewarded with a large hand that wrapped around his neck. He gurgled a few words of protest while a bead of sweat dripped down his large nose. It hung for a moment on his nostril before sailing through the air, splattering on the plank floor. The large, calloused hand squeezed tight around his windpipe. The little dwarf's world was vanishing from view.

"My money now or this will be your last breath," the voice whispered as the little man dangled high into the air. Burbon saw his toes well above the tavern's floor.

Wealth always has a price, he thought, *and sometimes pain is the payback.*

Earlier that evening; Burbon trudged carefully through the streets, evading mud puddles and animal waste. He headed towards the tavern; an old customer had stopped into town. It was always against his better judgment to conduct business after hours. *Trade during the day, eat and drink by night. May the two never cross paths.* But his greed for money was too much for him to resist.

The suns were setting as he pushed open the wooden door into the town's only pub, the Cross 'n' Arms. The tavern was busy with most patrons drinking and singing. The tavern's inhabitants included trolls, warriors, elves, and creatures that defied any category. No matter a being's origin, the common vice of alcohol brought them all together. Burbon stepped into the chaos like someone who belonged here.

He was small by any creature's standards and had a large handlebar mustache to add size to his stature and it gave him a dramatic flare. He wore his favorite weathered vest over durable clothes and his kilt came

to his knees to expose his legs. His small sword rested on his belt, always ready for use.

Burbon was a master salesman; he could determine your needs and assess how much you would be willing to pay for it. He was persuasive and relentless. He sat down at the end of a dirty table.

"A mug of ale for me, Solvana," he yelled to a bar wench.

"Right away, Burbon," she replied with a smile. She leaned over a keg and poured a draught. "Is it business or pleasure tonight?" she asked and handed him a mug of ale. The liquid cascaded over the brim to drip onto the table.

"With you around, it is always a pleasure," he charmed.

"You're such a flirt, Burbon," she replied and headed back to the bar.

Beautiful girl, if only she were shorter, he thought. His concentration was broken as his client entered the pub and walked over to his table. Vokel was an ugly troll with a wandering eye that always made you feel uncomfortable. He was not much taller than Burbon, but was a lot wider, his girth spilled over his belt. Yet he always has a knack for finding interesting objects for Burbon to buy. Tonight's acquisition was no different.

"Ah a pint is what I need. Thank you, Burbon," Vokel commented as he downed the drink before Burbon has had a chance to put it to his lips. Burbon shook his head and raised his hand for another ale.

"Now what is so important that you can't come to my store during regular business hours?" Burbon asked. Vokel wiped the foam from his chin.

"I am leaving tonight, taking the overnight carriage to Ritel. Trust me; you will like what I have to offer."

"This better be a legitimate sale, I won't be buying stolen merchandise like the Fiefton affair." Burbon pointed at Vokel with his finger.

"A misunderstanding, dear friend." Vokel was offended. "One that was cleared up long ago." Vokel pulled out a leather bag and untied the drawstrings. The well-worn leather revealed an amber jewel. A lantern's light caught the oval shaped gem creating a rainbow of brilliant colors. Burbon stroked his chin.

"Such a noble piece, why part with such a beauty?"

"I need some money for a…business transaction," replied Vokel. Burbon looked at him with some amusement.

"Been gambling again on nextars, have you, Vokel? When will you learn that those races are rigged?" Burbon commented.

"Nothing like that, I am just in need of some currency. Now, do you want to give advice, or do you want to buy it?"

"Well, let's take a closer look." Burbon took out an eyepiece to examine the amulet. He saw Vokel's head magnified by the gem's face. As he examined, he noticed two sides were perfect, but the other half has a broken edge as if it was part of much larger stone.

"Although beautiful, the gem is obviously flawed. Not sure I can find the right buyer for this. I'll pass." Burbon pushed the stone back across the table. Vokel smiled back. Over the years he has grown accustomed to Burbon's bargaining style.

"Look again, I'm sure you can come up with a fair price," Vokel pushed the gem back to Burbon who examined it from all angles.

"I will give you forty bright stones for this piece. Nothing more, even that price is generous." Vokel spat on the floor in disgust.

"You want more?" Burbon questioned. "But this is highway robbery. You may as well tie my hands behind my back and take my money."

"That can be arranged," Vokel snarled.

"What?"

"Nothing."

"I want fifty pieces," Vokel says. Burbon spat his mouthful of ale on the table.

"Fifty? Are you mad? Forty-three, no higher."

"Forty-seven or I get up and leave."

"Forty-five or I spill the rest of this beer over your head," Burbon smiled.

"Deal," Vokel smiled back and tossed the amulet stone over to Burbon. Burbon took a number of metal coins from his pocket and placed them on the table in front of Vokel.

"Well my friend, it's lucky that I am in a charitable mood tonight. Let's drink on it. Solvana! A round of ales for my friend and I."

As Burbon raises his mug, a shadow darkened over the table. A large hand knocked Burbon's mug to the floor. Burbon looked up, way up, to see a stranger with yellow eyes. *A familiar face perhaps, a farmer from outside the district?* He peered around and saw the empty seat where Vokel had sat. The farmer regained his attention.

"You are a thief and a liar. The seeds you sold me never grew. I want my payment back. NOW!"

The events of the evening flew by in an instant. *Time to stop thinking about how I got here and find a way out.* Burbon considered his last words carefully before he passed out.

"No returns may have been too harsh. If I could have the merchandise back, I could refund your money," Burbon croaked as he was dropped to a nearby table. He slowly felt his lungs fill with air again.

"Those seeds are in the ground, I did exactly as you instructed," he pointed with a dirty fingernail as his yellow eyes glowed with intensity. "They never grew. They are worthless, like you." Several men behind the farmer laughed in unison. He had not come alone.

"I'm sure you must be mistaken," Burbon replied, "but if you can wait until business hours tomorrow, I would be happy to refund your money." He backed up towards the exit of the tavern.

"The only mistake was dealing with a cheat like you. I will show you what I do to cheats!" The farmer walked towards Burbon as the rest of the bar watched in anticipation.

"Can't we talk about this? Maybe I could interest you in a recent acquisition?" Burbon inched closer to escape.

"Hold your filthy tongue! I will not be cheated a second time." He put his face closer to Burbon. The farmer drew his sword and put it to the trader's neck. Burbon gulped as the blade felt cold against his throat. Burbon closed his eyes.

The farmer's sword was knocked away and rattled on the floor. Burbon stared in relief at a large warrior staring down at the farmer. Clad in metal armor, he stood close to seven feet tall. A large broadsword was strapped to the length of his massive back. A metal helmet with a sharp serrated blade runs the ridge of his skull. The warrior was built like an impenetrable wall.

"You will leave this creature alone!" he commanded. A chair fell to the floor as the table of four farmhands stood up to circle him. The warrior smiled and his fists tightened, anticipating the upcoming brawl. Two farmhands leapt at the warrior smashing him into the next table. The others rushed over to assist.

The farmer picked up his fallen sword and turned toward Burbon. The trader jumped above the table to avoid the blade. He stared at the crowd of patrons who watched the fight. He pointed his arm dramatically in the air and yelled at the farmer.

"You have insulted my livelihood! You have tarnished my good name! I will teach you to treat me with respect." Burbon leapt onto the shoulders of a nearby patron and grabbed the wooden chandelier above him. He swung on the chains over the farmer's head. The farmer slashed his sword and missed Burbon again.

"Stand still, so I can hit you!" cried the farmer as Burbon landed on another table and drew his small blade. Even standing on the table, Burbon still has a height disadvantage. Burbon ducked as the farmer's sword swung through empty air.

Burbon stopped suddenly and in a dramatic tone exclaimed, "I am the greatest swordsman my family has ever seen. In a family of twenty, no one has defeated me!" Their swords clashed and Burbon's blade was knocked out of his hand. He shrugged his shoulders and backed away.

"I didn't say anyone in my family was any good."

A large farmhand swung his fist at the face of the warrior. His hand was caught inches before the warrior's face and was rewarded by the sound of breaking fingers. The farmhand grimaced as his hand was bent backwards and the pain forced him to the floor. Another farmhand smashed a chair over the back of the warrior.

"I don't like surprise attacks," the warrior replied as his free hand punched the trembling farmhand in the face sending him sailing into the bar.

The farmer swung again and Burbon dodged narrowly under the blade. He jumped off the table and crawled between the farmer's legs. Burbon knocked a small pouch off of the farmer's belt and several tiny objects fell to the floor. Burbon examined one and turned it in his hand. He looked up at the farmer in amazement.

"You tried to cheat me! You never planted the seeds!" Burbon yelled. The farmhands stared down and picked up several of the seeds, realizing the farmer's lie. They grabbed the farmer and roughly pulled him towards the door. The farmer stumbled and fell face forward into a patron's soup. The tension in the bar broke as everyone laughed.

"Get him out of here," directed Solvana, "and don't ever come back!" The remaining farmhands scurried out of the tavern after the farmer. Burbon walked up to the warrior and extended his hand.

"Thank you, sir. To what do I owe the honor of your aid?"

"Fate has smiled in your favor tonight, little man. The honor is mine. Something told me that I should help you," replied the warrior crumpling a piece of paper in his left hand.

"That's very cryptic for someone who talks with his fists. Are you going to get all mystical on me?" Burbon waved his fingers in the air as if to cast a spell.

"Ha, Ha! You are funny. You remind me of my father," he returned his broadsword to his back. Burbon was surprised.

"A small guy like me reminds you of your father?"

"You may be small in stature, but you are large in character. That trait my father also shared."

"Shared? Did something happen to him?"

"I left home and served for many years during the wars, fighting for what I believed was just. But upon my return, I found my home empty and my father gone without a trace. No one could answer for his disappearance. Now I search throughout the land in hope of finding him."

"A noble cause, my friend. I hope that you find him. I am Burbon the Trader. And you are?"

"Stonewall...a mercenary. If people bother you again, I will help you - for a price." The mention of money made Burbon laugh.

"I'll try to make the effort of not getting trouble."

"Farewell," bided Stonewall. He tossed a piece of paper to the floor and stepped through the swinging doors of the tavern. Burbon bent down and picked up the discarded paper. He unrolled it, a fortune that came with fate cookies. This one read: SAVE A MAN IN TROUBLE AND EMBARK ON AN INCREDIBLE ADVENTURE.

"What you got there, honey?" remarked Solvana passing by Burbon with a tray of ale. Burbon smirked.

"Nothing," he said and crumpled the paper. "Just a silly fortune."

2

Fate and Misfortune

Many leagues away, a looming shadow crossed a blackened landscape, scorched dead trees dotted the terrain. This part of the world was isolated, the land rocky and mountainous; few beings lived here. In the distance, a huge castle rested alone on the horizon. A flying beast entered into one of the stone towers and landed in a bone-lined nest hidden in the corner of an antechamber. It circled its nest, checking for intruders before it finally rested. Its beak gnawed on a half-eaten bone. A drop of water fell from the ceiling into its eye, disturbing its meal.

The castle was poorly lit with only pockets of flame illuminating its hidden corners. The rock walls ancient and weathered. Rain eroded small holes where rodents tunneled, looking for food. The castle rooms were cold; the fires provided little heat from the elements. A throne made of jagged rock rested against the far wall of the antechamber. Footsteps echoed in the hall as a misshapen servant hunched forward to the throne. He was careful to keep his eyes cast to the floor so to never directly face the figure on the throne.

"The amulet has been seen near a village in the backlands," he whispered. The figure returned his gaze but makes no acknowledgment of having heard him. The servant continued. "Arrangements have been made for shadow thieves to capture the gem. There are no signs of the others that you fear." Moments later he realized his mistake, but before he could back away, the figure stood up from the throne and flung the servant's body against the wall. The servant slid to the ground before the next onslaught.

Fear! I fear no one! The voice crackled like electricity through the servant's brain. The telepathic blast almost caused him to pass out, much more powerful than any physical pain. It had been years since the prince had spoken aloud; all commands penetrated the servant's brain, like a knife slicing its food.

"My apologies, Prince. I know not what I say!" the servant cringed.

When the stones are combined, its magic will control this land. I have wallowed in this miserable place for too long. My time has come to leave. His face came out of the shadow, his helmet covering his gruesome features. The servant's body was on the verge of convulsing from the telepathic power.

My dreams will no longer haunt me. Find that amulet!

Sunshine reflected off the frosted glass window of Burbon's Curiosity Shop. His name stenciled on the glass. On a window shelf a menagerie of items were scattered from faraway lands. Dust abounded on the shelves around the strange objects in the store. As dusk darkened the street, Burbon closed the door to his store while saying goodbye to his last customer.

"Good night, bring your money again," he laughed. He picked up a broom and sweep the debris near the door out into the street. He absent-mindedly patted his stomach. *It is time to fill this belly of yours. There will be more money to make tomorrow.* He placed his broom in the corner of his shop. "Goodnight my treasures," and gave a final look around. He blew out a lamp and closed the store door behind him. The amulet that Burbon purchased days ago sat in a glass display by the door. For a moment Burbon thought it pulsed red, exhibiting some interior life. He looked again and realized that it is just his imagination.

He walked down the street ready for a meal at the inn. He passed an alleyway and missed something slithering in its darkness. The figure had no definite form, but its presence could be felt by anyone venturing too close. It used the darkness of the alley walls and moved to the front window of Burbon's store. The amulet pulsed red again on the store shelf. The shadow stopped and peered into the window. Ever so quietly, it slid under the door and flowed along the floor. The shadow moved over several items before coming to the amulet. The amulet pulsed a final time and then darkness obscured its form. Moments later, the darkness disappeared and all that was left was the empty holder where the amulet had lay.

Hours later Burbon waddled out of the tavern and patted his full belly.

Another successful day, another delicious meal. What could go wrong? Suddenly he shivered as a coldness passed by him.

Maybe I'll go by the store before heading home. He turned around and crashed into Stonewall's waist. Burbon fell onto his back on the street. He shook his head while looking up.

"You gave me a scare, warrior, you are quiet for a large man," Burbon remarked. Stonewall extended his hand.

"I'm sorry, my little friend. I was heading to the Inn tonight when you stumbled into me. Is something wrong?" Burbon brushed the dirt off his tunic.

"I'm not sure. I have a strange need to revisit my store tonight. Call it a store owner's instinct."

"The winds are foul tonight," Stonewall smelt the air while stating his conviction.

"That's quite a nose you have. Can you tell when it's going to rain?" Stonewall doesn't return Burbon's quick smile.

"Don't jest my friend. Our world is no longer a safe place to travel. There are bad times ahead. The darkness in the south continues to grow."

"That's a wives' tale, Stonewall. You're as bad as the old women who weave tall tales to children to prevent wandering."

"And when is the last time you left this village?"

Burbon hesitated. "Actually, most of my business is selling to the villagers."

"Take it from someone who has traveled this land of ours," stated

Stonewall. "The world is fragmented; forces beyond this village are working against the common good."

"Save your tales for the campfire, warrior. I've got a business to run." He walked down the narrow street while looking at the Stonewall's serious face. "Come on, you can guard me as I walk back to my store. Maybe I can sell you something?"

"Not unless you sell armor for one my size," he said while falling into step. Burbon's little legs ran to keep pace with Stonewall's large steps.

Minutes later they arrived at the store. Burbon inserted the key into his door. He sensed something was wrong upon entering and scanned the shelves.

"Hhhmmmm...the Orson Crown is still here (he blew the dust off), as is the Eye of Amagar (he turned it slightly towards the wall to hide a flaw) the Staff of Rondone, here...oh no! The amulet I purchased is gone! Why would only that be taken?"

"Maybe there is more to that amulet than meets the eye," offered Stonewall. "What did it look like?" Burbon grabbed several items from the shelf.

"Well, the amulet was a big as this iron sphere and as shiny as this glass figure," Burbon pointed to a small statue. "It was amber in color, like honey."

"Sounds ordinary enough. Are you sure you didn't misplace it? Seems like there are more valuable things in this store to steal," Stonewall handled a pouch of gems. Burbon took the pouch out of his hand.

"I'm certain. Someone took it. No one steals from Burbon the Trader, no matter how small the item! Chances are the thief will try to sell it nearby within a day. But where and to who?" Burbon scratched his chin. "In this town, it could be a lot of people. I need someone who can find the truth."

Stonewall looked down at Burbon with hidden knowledge. "Burbon, do you believe in fate?" he asked.

"Fate? Are you going to give me a fortune from a fate cookie?"

A flicker of anger registered on Stonewall's face.

"There are some things in this world that take faith in order to happen."

"I believe in things that I can hold in my hands." Burbon hit his cash register.

"There is more to our world than counting money."

"Easy for someone to say who has very little of it." Burbon shuffled the money though his finger making sure of none was stolen.

"No, Trader. You are plentiful in wealth but poor in faith."

"Depends on what faith would get me."

"Would you believe in faith if I could find someone to help you?" Stonewall asked.

"I'll believe anything as long as it gets my amulet back."

"I have met someone in this town who can help you, Burbon. She knows and hears all. You must meet the Seer!"

A wooden sign dangles from a storefront that says *Madame Zahara, Fortune Teller—I Know and See All!* Burbon stared in disbelief.

"This fraud is the Seer? Your head is thicker than your neck. You dragged me here?"

"Watch and listen. Learn to believe," commanded Stonewall.

"Watch and listen? I'm listening to your mad ideas and I'm watching you waste my time."

Burbon opened the door for Stonewall. "After you. Let's give my money away."

They walked inside to a dark room illuminated by a few flickering candles. Strange shapes hung down from the ceiling; Stonewall ducked his head beneath them. A beaded doorway led to another room. A table sat in the middle on a large rug with several chairs. The air smelt of sweet incense. On top of the table was a cube sitting on a small mount. Light shapes danced in its interior like a lava lamp.

Burbon heard the sound of footsteps. A woman walked through the beaded doorway. Madame Zahara was a stout woman of many years, only slightly taller than Burbon. Two wild eyes that seem to move independently of each other framed her gray-mattered hair.

"Fortunes told, palms read, free tarot card reading after four visits," she prattled off. "How can I help you gentlemen?"

"We have come to talk to the Seer," stated Stonewall.

"And what's your business with him," she asked nonchalantly. Burbon stepped in front of Stonewall.

"I have some questions to ask him, but you probably already know that," Burbon said factiously. Madame Zahara ignored his comment and went to a nearby shelf, opening a bottle of a strong-smelling liquid. She smiled at Stonewall.

"You have brought a disbeliever with you, warrior. That will cost extra," she chuckled and drank the liquid.

Burbon was at the end of his patience and turned to Stonewall. "We're wasting my time, I'm leaving." Burbon walked back to the entrance.

"Not so fast, unbeliever." Zahara put her arm out, preventing Burbon from leaving. Her strength was considerable despite her age.

"I sense you have lost something. Do you wish to recover it?" she asked Burbon.

Surprised, he looked at Stonewall. "Did you…?"

"I said nothing to her," he replied.

"All will be explained at the séance. Please have a seat." Zahara motioned to both men to sit around the table.

One of her eyes watched Burbon with apparent interest. "If I am able to reach the Seer, what is it that you need to know?" asked Zahara.

"I need to find the whereabouts of an amulet that was stolen from me. I can describe it if you like."

"No need. The Seer will contact your mind and see the object. I must link my mind with the Seer, and I will need your help. The Seer needs to feel your life energy. That and your belief in him will cause him to appear."

"If this Seer can get my amulet back, I'll believe in anything," Burbon jested. His humor was lost on Zahara.

"Then let us begin!" she stated. Zahara began chanting in tongues. The cube swirled with activity; flashes of color sparkled through its interior.

"Neat trick," Burbon whispered to no one in particular. Suddenly the wind blew through an open window and tiny sparks popped off of the cube.

"Ooooddaaallllaallleeyy, oooddaaallleeey," she yelled. Her eyelids flickered and her body trembled. Burbon was repulsed as if she was contagious. Suddenly Zahara's body went limp and she sunk back in her chair. Stonewall moved towards her with concern.

"Is she...?" Burbon jolted back in his seat as beams of light shoot out of the cube in all directions. The brightest beam from the cube shone onto Zahara's forehead causing her eyeballs to roll back into her head. Only the whites of her eyes were visible. Her body became ramrod straight as if frozen into a statue. A deep man's voice issued from her throat.

"I am the Seer. I know why you are here." Burbon raised one eyebrow studying Zahara to try to determine her trickery.

"And I know why you are here - to fleece me of my money," Burbon added dryly.

"Don't waste time. I can only possess this vessel for a short period." Sparks from the cube flashed red. *"Perhaps you don't want to know the whereabouts of the amulet?"* Burbon looked at Stonewall who was rapt with interest.

"You have my attention. Where can I find it?" Burbon asked. The cube cackled with blue flame.

"I can tell you, but be warned. The knowledge will change your life. This amulet is very powerful and is wanted by the most evil of forces. If you go after it, you can never go home again.

"Rubbish!" Burbon slammed his fist on the table, unfazed by the threat. "I paid good money for that amulet and I want it back. Enough of your dramatics, tell me where I can find it!"

"You shall have your wish. Tomorrow at dawn, in the caverns north of this village, there will be an exchange for your amulet. The exchange will deliver the amulet back to its true master. Once you enter the cave, there is no turning back."

"Anything else?" Burbon puzzled with the directions.

"Remember the number three." Smoke swirled through the cube resembling a storm. *"May the gods have mercy on your souls."* Light disappeared back into cube and a breeze rushed through the room. Zahara shook her head as if waking from a long sleep. One of her eyes travelled around the room before resting its gaze on Burbon.

"Where am I? Did the Seer arrive? What did he tell you?"

"To go to the caves outside of the village." He gazed at Zahara straight into her eyes. "For your sake, this better not be part of some trickery." Burbon turned to Stonewall. He was not accustomed to asking for help. "Stonewall, will you come with me?"

"You pay and I will lead the way." Stonewall pledged.

Burbon puffed up his chest, ready to take on danger. "What are we waiting for? We have preparations to make!" Burbon ran for the door.

"Wait! There is more..." Zahara gestured.

"What do you mean?" inquired Burbon.

"This isn't free. Five bright stones, please," Zahara held her hand out as Burbon reached into his vest pocket.

Burbon yawned as the sunlight shimmered over a craggy mountain summit. "Ungodly hour," murmured Burbon hiding behind a huge rock. He scratched at his tunic, trying to shake the dirt off of his clothes.

"Yet you are as committed as ever," replied Stonewall. He looked down from their outcropping above the cave's mouth. From their vantage point, they have a wide view of the cave entrance. No one could enter the cave unseen.

"Why would they make a transfer here?" Burbon asked.

"These caves go directly through the mountains and can save a traveler many days of effort, if one knows the way."

"And you know the way?" Burbon asked.

"I do not. The Seer is correct, we must be extremely careful after entering the caves, one can get lost very easily and die of starvation."

"Thanks, that's uplifting." Burbon heard the sound of hooves hitting the roadway. "Look over there," he pointed down the hill. A creature on a lone horse approached. Both men hunched down to avoid detection.

They peered through the cracks of the rock and watched the shadowy creature jump down from the horse. It looked around and then slithered into the cave.

"Nothing's going to stop me from getting back my possession," as Burbon rose.

A hand dropped onto Burbon's shoulder. Both he and Stonewall whirl around to face a tall female archer. Her long narrow elfin ears stuck over her black headgear. A quiver of bolts was strapped on her back with a cross brace of leather over her chest to hold it in place. A small sword was strapped to her leg, but it was her hand that got Burbon's attention. She pointed her crossbow with a bolt ready to loosen directly into Burbon's chest.

"First, you have to deal with me," she snarled.

3

The Third Way

The archer's finger was poised to release a bolt at Burbon's heart. Stonewall reached for his sword.

"I wouldn't do that. Your armor may stop my bolt, but the little one will die before you can stop me," the archer stated. Stonewall remained motionless.

"Who are you and what do you want?" Burbon was more frustrated than angry, knowing that his prize was rapidly disappearing.

The archer's crossbow wavered for a moment. "I am Taro. I have been traveling for weeks to reclaim an item very precious to my family. The trail went cold weeks ago, until I followed a thief to a nearby village. Then I followed him here and I saw the two of you from below. I wanted to be sure this wasn't an ambush." Burbon relaxed and held his arms out towards Taro.

"We are on the same side. I am here to retrieve something that is mine as well. My name is Burbon and—"

"I am Stonewall!" The warrior eased the hold on his sword.

"We will lose them if we don't move. We can help each other," Burbon offered.

"That remains to be seen," she said, but she lowered her crossbow. "We go together but I will have first call on the stolen goods."

"Agreed!" Burbon shook her hand. Stonewall turned towards the mountain entrance.

"We must go!" he jumped down the embankment towards the entrance. He knocked small pebbles down to the ground. Burbon and Taro followed in his path.

Burbon passed the rider's mount. It ignored the three of them and munched on a clump of grass. As Burbon entered into the mouth of the cave, the darkness made him shiver. Taro scratched magnesium from an arrowhead against the wall and the flash ignited a wooden branch. The light flickered along the rocky interior; sediment streaked the walls. Water dripped down, echoing through the cave. Beyond the sound of the drips, the cave was deathly quiet. The passageways were narrow, but the ceiling was high, many times Stonewall's height

"Where could he have gone? He was right in front of us. When I get my hands on that thief, I'll thrash him within an inch of his life. Nobody steals from me," Burbon ranted. "I'll..."

"Does he always talk so much?" Taro asked Stonewall.

"No, this is his quiet time," the warrior replied.

The light revealed a large iron ring hanging on the wall. Burbon reached up to touch it.

"Watch out, those rings can open passageways or traps," warned Taro. Burbon's hand jumped off the ring.

"How do you know?" asked Burbon.

"These caves are a common place for gobtrolls to hide their goods. They are littered with a maze of passageways that wind through the mountains. They use them to transport goods."

"Gobtrolls! If I meet one of those ugly beasts, I'll smash its hideous head. I thought those ugly cave dwellers only lived in the south?"

"They live throughout our land and not only in caves, trader," replied Stonewall. "Their heads are almost the size of your body and their mouths could swallow you whole. I hope you have the fists to fight one if we come across one of their nests."

"They don't scare me! I dare one of them to show themselves!"

Suddenly, a creature with red eyes and teeth flew by, almost colliding with Burbon. Taro sliced the winged beast and its pieces fell to the cave floor. Burbon clutched his chest.

"It was just a bat," replied Taro.

"Are you okay?" Stonewall was concerned.

"I'll let you know as soon as my heart starts up again. Oh, there it goes." Burbon gave his chest a few taps. Something splashed from the ceiling and caused Stonewall to slowly look up.

"I think we are being watched," he commented.

"I don't see anybody up ahead," said Burbon.

Stonewall scanned the rock wall. "I don't think they are in front of us. They're…"

Taro's makeshift torch flickered on the ceiling illuminating the face of a gobtroll braced in the stalactites.

"……Up!" he pointed.

Several gobtrolls dropped down to the cave floor, their ugly green faces snarling at the trio. The trolls were almost as tall as Stonewall was wide. Their heads were hideous and oversized for their bodies with sickly yellow eyes. Their large teeth jutted out in an under bite in their massive jaws. They dressed the same, in black tunics with metal spikes on their wrist and shoulders. Their boots sported an evil point on the heels, ready to inflict pain.

"It's a trap! Hope you elves know how to fight!" Burbon yelled to the archer. She evaded the swing of a mace and kicked the creature between the legs. The gobtroll shrieked and slumped to floor.

"I'm the last one you need to worry about." A spear sailed through the darkness narrowly missing Stonewall's head. He charged forward and picked up two gobtrolls and slammed them into each other. They staggered, bumped into each other, and fell face forward to the ground.

Burbon drew his small sword as a gobtroll approached. The creature leapt at Burbon and forced him into a dead-end. Its breath reeked from the smell of rotted meat. Burbon was determined. "Never corner your prey, ugly. That's when I'm the most dangerous." The gobtroll snarled, sizing up his small opponent.

Burbon dropped to the cave floor, crawling between its legs. As he passed under, he smashed the end of his sword's handle down on the gobtroll's foot. It jumped up in pain and knocked its head on a stalactite before falling unconscious to the ground. Burbon stood up. "These gobtrolls are ugly *and* stupid."

As quickly as the ambush started, it was over. The remaining creatures eyed their diminishing numbers and beat a hasty retreat to the back of the caves. Taro saw an escaping gobtroll carrying a bag.

"Get the one with the sack!" she yelled.

Stonewall grabbed the gobtroll by the ankle and dangled him upside down. Several items tumbled to the ground, including the sack.

"I believe you have something of ours." The gobtroll fainted at Stonewall's words. Stonewall dropped him unceremoniously to the floor. The other gobtrolls scurried away.

"And don't come back either," Burbon kicked one in the rear as it ran away. "Cowardly lot."

"Be thankful that there weren't more of them," responded Stonewall.

Burbon reached into the sack and pulled out several more items. The last was the amulet.

"Ah hah, my treasure!" Burbon cried.

Taro grabbed the amulet from Burbon.

"Not so fast. This belongs to me."

"You're sadly mistaken, my dear. I purchased it fair and square."

Taro gripped the amulet tighter.

"This has been in my family for generations. A thief took it from us, and I will not let another thief try to claim it now!"

The tug of war ended as Taro tore the gem out of its mount. Both she and Burbon crashed to the ground. She dropped the gem as it exploded into a flash of light causes her to step back. The voice of the Seer emanated from the stone shimmering with colors. His voice reverberated throughout the cave.

"*I am the Seer. You have obtained an object of great power. This stone is part of a larger orb that will give its holder unlimited power. You must use this stone to complete a larger piece before it is too late. If evil forces obtain this, our world will go dark for a thousand years.*" Taro was puzzled by the arrival of the Seer and unaware of his connection to Burbon and Stonewall. Before she could ask, Burbon interrupted.

"What nonsense is this? I've had enough! I'm going back to sell these trinkets," he pointed to the contents of the bag, "at my store. I'm not here to save the world!"

"You no longer have a choice. Already evil forces are alerted to your presence and will stop at nothing to capture you...or worse. They will never stop searching. You have no choice but to journey for the remaining stones.

"Journey, what journey?" Burbon stared at the amulet stone. "You're a fraud! I don't believe anything you've uttered. We beaten those gobtrolls, who else is there to fight?"

The rays of light from the amulet stretched out from the stone into a vision of the village. The image shimmered and changed to Burbon's store being smashed by gobtrolls. Their weapons destroyed everything in the store. A hammer crushed a glass statue as the image abruptly disappeared.

"That's my store!" yelled Burbon. Before he can question why this was happening, the vision quickly altered. Taro blinked as the image changed to a majestic forest where her family lived. The image was a rooftop home with elves clutching their throats, attacked by an unknown force. Their faces twisted and several fell to the ground in agony.

"My family! What is happening to them?" demanded Taro ready to smash the stone as if it were responsible.

"A near future if you do not reunite the stones. There is nothing that you can do for them if you return home now." The image changed again to form a town meeting hall with notices placed across wooden planks. A picture of Stonewall's face on a scroll appeared with a bounty on his head. Burbon stared at Stonewall as if considering collecting the reward.

"Stonewall. You can no longer sell your mercenary services. The hunter has become the hunted," the Seer spoke.

Stonewall measured his words carefully. "Are these things happening now?" he asked.

"Now and in the days to come. These events will transpire as a result of today's events." Stonewall decided to ask a more personal question.

"What of my father? Can you tell me what happened to him?" He was transfixed by the stone as if ready to learn a great secret. He believed that he would finally learn the truth.

"I can show you nothing except to tell you that he still lives." Stonewall's shoulders lifted as if a great weight has been removed. Burbon was about to have a fit.

"How do I know if any of this is true? How do I know this isn't some trick to get us to do what you want?"

Stonewall spoke before the Seer could answer. "Why would the Seer lie? I believe him. We are in grave danger."

"No offense, warrior. You can believe in these things, but not me. I've had enough of this nonsense. I'm heading home," Burbon scooped up the sack. The Seer spoke with such force that Burbon was forced to cover his ears.

"This is your last warning. Go to the Fields of Solis and find the wizard, Oberron. He will direct you on your Quest. Leave immediately or this cave will become your tomb..."

The light dissipated and the gem returned to normal. Taro picked up both the stone while Burbon stamped his feet.

"I don't believe the vision of my store being ripped apart. I have a business to run, money to make...!"

"Do you ever care about anyone but yourself?" Taro snarled. "Why don't we settle the ownership of the amulet here and now?" Burbon threw his sack to the ground ready to battle her. Voices and the clank of armor rumbled in the distance, interrupting her threat.

"Enough," spoke Stonewall, standing between them. "We have other problems."

During the Seer's conversation, the gobtrolls have returned with reinforcements. Behind them in the shadows, several larger creatures appeared known as Rocs. They are stronger than gobtrolls and need no armor to cover their rock skin. One roc smiled through its broken teeth. The trio stepped backward as their enemy approached. Burbon made a brilliant observation.

"I think we're in trouble!"

Stonewall felt the hard rock wall behind him. Angry faces of their enemy stared back at him from the shadows of the cave. Stonewall drew his sword.

"It is time to fight!" he growled.

Taro felt a metal ring against her back. She turned and saw it lodged on the wall.

"Stonewall, Burbon, lean back against the wall with all of your might!" Burbon spied the metal ring.

"Could be a trap?" he asked.

"Or a passageway! At this point, I will take the chance!" she yelled. All three braced themselves against the wall pushing hard as their enemies advanced. Suddenly, their force caused the wall behind them to split in half and they fell into a secret passageway. Stonewall stood up in first and jammed a nearby rusted shield behind the doorway. It was lodged tightly behind the passageway door and prevented entry by the gobtrolls.

"Thank you," he said to Taro.

"It was luck. These caves are full of secret passages where thieves would hide their goods. It was fortunate that ring led us to this passageway. If it was a trap, we might not have survived!"

A loud bang against the wall caused Burbon to jump. "We've not going to survive staying around here for too long. That wall is not going to hold them."

Stonewall looked down the passageway. "There is light ahead. Run before they break through!" A heavy axe chipped away at the wall as the voices of the gobtrolls grew louder.

They dashed through spider webs and past rotten cave beams. Burbon ran too fast and slid outside to a ledge high above the ground.

"Whoa!" he tried to regain his balance. Taro stood beside him and leaned over the ledge. The ground dropped hundreds of feet below to a jagged rock bottom. She tossed a pebble that turned to dust on the ground below. Nothing could survive that fall.

"We can't go forward, and we can't go back. Where do we go?" she questioned. During their silence, they heard the gobtrolls breaking through the wall. Stonewall stepped from the cave and plunged his broadsword into the rock wall below the ledge. It gave them a handhold to climb.

"We go down!" he commanded.

"Don't forget me." Burbon jumped on Stonewall's back.

Taro drew a bolt from her quiver. She placed a rope at the end and shot the arrow from her crossbow to the bottom of the cliff.

"See you at the bottom," as she sailed past the men. They climbed down the cliff and surveyed the forest beneath them. There were a series of ledges and outcroppings and they used them to slowly climb down. After a few minutes, they reached the bottom.

"Where do we go from here?" asked Taro.

"The Seer said to go to the Fields of Solis. We must travel west," answered Stonewall.

"What are the Fields of Solis?" Burbon climbed down from Stonewall's back.

"It is where warriors go when they die in battle. It is told that the Fields are connected to the afterlife."

"Enjoy the walk, I'm not going anywhere," Burbon sat down on a large rock looking dejected.

"If you stay here, you'll be captured before the end of the day," Taro added.

"Why should you care?" he looked at her.

"I don't," she answered honestly.

"Then leave me alone! Your stupid amulet has cost me everything! I may never be able to return home."

"Your greed cost your livelihood. You can hardly blame me for that," Taro yelled back.

"I'm returning to the village. What if the Seer is wrong?" Burbon questioned.

"We all have lost a great deal, but we will lose our lives if we just bicker," replied Stonewall. "Come with us to meet the wizard Oberron, it is a day's travel. He can tell you if the Seer's visions are true."

"But I'm not a fighter. I'm not able to deal with this as well as you two." Burbon whined.

"You fought honorably and have earned our respect."

"Really?" He looked at Stonewall.

"Yes!" Stonewall turned to Taro to confirm but she remained silent.

"I suppose I have." Burbon smile as his stomach growled. "I'm famished. Does anybody have anything to eat?"

Stonewall replied. "With appetite comes hope."

"It will take more than hope to fill your belly. The question is, can a little trader survive in the wild? I'll be surprised if you can live one day outside of your comfortable home," Taro remarked.

Burbon stood up to his full size, ready for the challenge. "You don't know anything about me!"

"I know your kind," she replied.

"You know nothing about my people. We can live in the forest for months at a time, living off tree bark and sap. We are fearless hunters, able to catch any prey. I am Burbon of the Wilde Clan, afraid of nothing and no one." Burbon hopped to another rock and almost stepped on a garter snake, sunning itself on the rocks.

Ah!" Burbon screamed as the snake slithered through the grass. Burbon jumped into Stonewall's arms. "Snake, snake!" he yelled in fear. Both Taro and Stonewall laughed heartily.

"The fearless fighter, Burbon the chicken," jeered Taro.

"Let go of me!" He jumped down. "I just hate snakes, that's all. Unless you want the gobtrolls to catch up with us, we better get out of here now!"

4

The Bridge

Far away from Burbon and his companions, shadows danced on a castle wall from the torchlight. A brown mouse travelled along the top of a damp wall. Crumbs from a forgotten meal lay scattered along its edge. The mouse scurried towards it, but a scream in the distance distracted it momentarily. It shook its whiskers before continuing its journey. A wooden spear leaned across the top of the wall, blocking its path. The mouse shrunk its body and carefully dipped below the razor-sharp blade. Its whiskers narrowly missed the blade as it scrambled around the obstacle. The mouse stopped, seeing several breadcrumbs in its path. It ate the first of the tasty morsels.

A flapping sound grew louder in the distance, but the mouse was focused on its prize. It moved forward and ate two, then three pieces, before seeing the largest of the leftover food. It licked its paws in anticipation before running towards the piece. Its saliva dripped out of the corner of its mouth before the mouse bit into the spoiled food. It was delicious. Its mind focused on the joy of the food filling its empty stomach. It was almost the last thing it ever ate.

A winged beast swooped down to grab the mouse with its claws, its prey unaware that its life hung in the balance. The beast screeched with anger at the last second as its dark rider pulled on its neck and forced it to swerve away from its prize. The mouse scurried into a wall, safe to eat another day.

No Sunder, you will not feast on this animal. We have other prey to hunt. The animal heard and obeyed the silent command of its rider. Sunder was a mature griffin—half eagle from the head to the midsection and half lion to its tail with a sprinkle of dragon claws. It was not a creature to be trifled with. The castle slowly disappeared beneath them as rider and beast melted into the murky darkness. Their true prize lied ahead.

Taro stared at her reflection in the amulet stone. Her face looked older, wearier than when she left her home. Her thoughts were broken by the sound of a snapped twig. Burbon appeared sheepish.

"I see stealth isn't one of your strengths," she commented.

They had left the craggy outcroppings of the cliff and walked in the cool greenery of the forest.

"I'm sorry, but there is nothing around us. Wherever we are, we have lost the gobtrolls."

"For the moment, but this may not be the best direction to travel," she replied.

"Then you can certainly go on your own," Stonewall answered back to her.

"I hope one of you knows where we're going?" Burbon asked.

All three stopped as they heard a strange wailing in the distance.

"What is that?" inquired Stonewall.

"How about we not find out," Burbon answered.

Stonewall was serious. "Quiet, we should investigate."

"Sure, let's investigate the strange noise. Probably some creature waiting to trap us for its supper," replied Burbon. The howling increased as Stonewall searched behind a tree. He spied a wolf cub caught by a small snare.

"Let me help you." The cub cowered unsure of Stonewall's intentions.

"We don't have time for this," commented Taro. Stonewall glared at her.

"Make time." Stonewall bended closer to the cub. "Burbon come here and distract the cub so I can free him," motioned Stonewall.

"Distract him? How? I don't talk wolf! Maybe the elf knows..."

"We don't talk to animals. We hunt wolves and their kind."

"Well's it's lucky that the warrior has a soft spot for this little one," Burbon saw the amulet peeking out of Taro's pouch. "You know if you need any help carrying your belongings. . ." Before she could respond, Stonewall interrupted.

"Thank you both. Your talking distracted our little friend." The wolf cub was licking his leg where the snare had held tight. He wagged his tail and licked Stonewall's face. Its affection was short-lived as Stonewall heard a low rumbling sound in the distance. The wolf cub ran in the opposite direction of the sound.

"What are all of these strange sounds? What do we do, flee or fight?" asked Burbon

"Climb a tree," Taro commanded." You're the smallest and can tell us what's coming."

Burbon nodded his head in agreement and jumped onto a boulder. He reached for a low hanging branch and climbed onto a mighty spruce. He scrambled up thick dark branches to reach the top. He squinted his eyes to see a cloud of dust in the distance.

"What is it?" asked Stonewall.

"It's hard to make out. Wait! It's coming into view. It's a white mass with hundreds of heads! Come up and take a look," he beckoned. They climbed the trees to avoid the stampede. The sound of their hooves was deafening. Taro scanned the mass of bodies.

"It's a herd of sheep, you fool!" she yelled at Burbon. The sheep approached and bleated like frightened cattle. "They must be scared by something, maybe the gobtrolls." She turned back to Burbon and noticed something slithering in the branches.

"Burbon, slow down. Don't go down any further," she warned.

"Why? I want to see the sheep." Burbon stepped down and put his foot directly on the snake's back. The combination of fear and the snake's slimy skin caused him to lose his balance.

"TREE SNAKE! Why didn't you tell me?" He fell off his branch and hit other branches on his way down. But instead of landing on hard ground, he fell onto the backs of the moving sheep.

"I'm deep in sheep. Help me!" Burbon hung onto the back of a sheep for dear life, afraid to fall off and be trampled. Taro positioned a bolt from her quiver.

"Don't kill the sheep!" commanded Stonewall.

"Give me more credit than that, warrior." Taro aimed at a tree trunk and loosened the bolt, imbedding itself in front of Burbon's moving sheep.

"Burbon, grab the bolt!" Burbon crawled across the back of the sheep to reach out to the oncoming bolt. The sheep turned its head back at its unwelcome guest.

"Nice sheep!" Burbon yelled above the racket. Already agitated, the sheep snapped its teeth at Burbon's right hand, causing him to let go.

"Stonewall, help! This sheep is trying to eat me," Burbon cried.

"To your right," Stonewall commanded. Burbon spun around, his left hand letting go of the uncooperative sheep. Before he fell, his right arm grasped the bolt in the tree. He hung on for dear life waiting for the herd to pass by. The sheep jostled him and several times he nearly fell under their hooves. Finally, his arm tired and he fell to the ground. A few remaining sheep past by him as he dusted himself off. Taro ran toward him.

"Are you all right?"

"My bruises have bruises," he commented, trying to stand. He stumbled on his wobbly legs and fell back to the ground. Stonewall's massive hands pulled Burbon to his feet.

"We need to keep going. Whatever scared the sheep is probably coming this way," Stonewall pointed towards a route heading west through the forest hills.

They followed a trail rising up into the foothills. The trees were twisted and knotty, poor timber for milling. The forest was thick and overgrown with little light reaching the forest floor. Occasionally, something scurried across their path, then disappeared into the brush. The heat was oppressive, their sweat caused itching under their clothes. They cursed and hacked the branches to the top of the hill.

Stonewall broke the silence by turning to Taro. "I need to know more about the amulet stone. Did your family have any idea of its power?" Stonewall's question was greeted by Taro's silence. "Please, we must trust each other."

"I'm with Stonewall," chimed Burbon. Taro stopped and spoke to them.

"It's difficult to talk about. My father had believed our clan to be special. Every member of my family has been able to do simple magic. Growing a plentiful harvest, creating moisture out of the air, finding minerals in the ground - simple magic that benefits many. My father believed it came from exposure to the amulet. It was passed down from father to child for countless generations."

"What is your power?" Burbon became excited.

"When the time comes, I will show you. It took considerable practice and only through study with my father have I learned how to focus my magic. Most powers develop as you grow older. I fear without my father's teachings, I will never reach my full potential." Stonewall put his hand on her shoulder.

"I will escort you home personally when this is done," he stated.

"If we survive," Burbon whispered. Two hard stares returned his comment. He ignored them as the trees opened up to a magnificent sight. "What's that?"

A giant gorge appeared before them; Burbon walked to the edge. The cliffs were sheer with few handholds for climbing. It was difficult to see the ground below, a mist shrouded it from view. Burbon peered ahead to a rope bridge that crossed the gorge. Around the bridge were ruins of buildings and heaps of debris. There were piles of bones and pieces of armor sticking out of the mess. A shiver rushed through Burbon's body. *Was this a final destination or a crossing point?*

A rustling behind them caused all three to turn. A creature even larger than Stonewall stepped out of the bushes. It was man shaped but as hairy as an ape, with a deformed eye and gashes across its chest from fighting. He let out a low, menacing growl, causing the trio to draw their weapons. The face of the creature was half shrouded by shadow and drool dripped down from his sharp fangs.

"You must pay a toll to cross my bridge," it rasped. It carried a club bloodied from battle.

"Name your price or taste my steel!" Stonewall snarled and pulled his sword, ready to strike. The creature smiled, amused by this show of strength.

"To cross my bridge, one of you must fight me."

Taro looked at the others. "I say the three of us kill this monster and then cross the bridge."

"You can try," it sneered, "but if more than one of you attacks me, I will destroy the bridge."

Stonewall stepped forward. "I will fight you!"

"Maybe," it answered, "But I choose who I will fight."

Burbon stared at Taro and Stonewall. "Could we cross somewhere else and avoid this threat?"

"There is nowhere else to cross for leagues and we'll be caught if we go back down this hill," Taro answered.

"I have money, maybe I can pay him off," Burbon walked closer to the beast and placed a small bag of coins in his hand. "I am willing to pay for our safe passage." The creature swiped at the bag, sending it over the edge and into the chasm below.

"I have no use for trinkets!" it spit near Burbon's feet. Burbon slunk back to Taro and Stonewall.

"That went well, anybody got any better ideas?"

"Enough talk, I have chosen you," the creature pointed its dirty finger at Taro. "I want to fight the woman."

"Taro, let me ..." Stonewall tried to stand in front of her.

"No, warrior, I will show this misshapen beast that it has made a fatal mistake." Taro turned towards it. "I accept your challenge," and she brings her crossbow to her forehead.

"No weapons," it rasped. "You must defeat me hand to hand." It dropped its club and came towards her. Taro handed her crossbow and quiver to Stonewall.

"Watch my back!" Taro ran towards the beast. He held out his arms to crush her. She evaded him easily, jumped onto his back and straddled her legs around his throat. She squeezed with all of her strength and the effects were immediate.

"No," he wailed, "You must fight me, I cannot breathe." His face turned purple and his arms flailed trying to reach her. In desperation, the creature grabbed a handful of dirt and threw at Taro's face. She closed her eyes and the soil fell harmlessly away. He stumbled a few steps and then fell onto his knees, fighting for breath. His hands reached for his club in a last act of desperation.

"Taro," Burbon yelled, "Look out!" The beast swung the club at his own head to hurt Taro. She leapt off of his back and he smashed himself with his own weapon. He slumped unconscious to the ground. Taro brushed her hands clean and walked towards Stonewall and Burbon.

"Sorry that took so long. Let's cross the bridge." She reached for her quiver of bolts and crossbow. Stonewall and Burbon stared at each other.

"I'm not making fun of her again," Burbon stated with a newfound respect.

She pointed to the bridge. "Burbon, do you want to go first?"

Burbon held out his arm in a chivalrous manner. "You earned that right."

The rope creaked as Taro crossed the bridge. Burbon followed behind her. The bridge swung under their weight.

"I hate heights," he commented.

"There is not a lot you do like, trader."

"I like lots of things, but hanging over a gorge and falling to my death is not high on my list."

"Stop moving around so much you two," Stonewall yelled from behind. The bridge ropes strained under the added weight of Stonewall.

"Maybe you should wait to cross," Burbon yelled back to Stonewall. He considered Burbon's request and stepped back. He noticed the beast standing by the knot of ropes at the edge of the bridge. Blood was dripping from the side of its head and its eyes were seething with anger.

"The woman didn't fight fairly. For that you will all die!" He slashed the knots in a single swipe. As Burbon and Taro turned around, the bridge collapsed under their weight. They descended quickly until only their screams were heard as they tumbled into the gorge.

5

The Wizard Oberron

One end of the bridge had fallen while the far side strained at its mounting. They hung onto the remains of the bridge after slamming into the rock face. Burbon clutched his chest with his free hand as he regained his breath.

"For all the coin in the world, I would not go through that again." Stonewall was at the bottom of the rope, planks broke under his weight causing him to drop a few feet.

"Hold on!" Taro yelled down to Stonewall. She tied a rope around a bolt and shot it into the cliff face. She dropped the end of the rope past her for Stonewall to reach. He wrapped the rope around his hand.

"I'll hold onto the rope, you two climb down on top of me!"

Burbon and Taro scaled down the rope bridge to Stonewall.

"I don't know how much longer I can hold on." Burbon clung to Stonewall's massive shoulders.

"We can't stay here," Taro stated. The knot above them unraveled and they dropped another foot.

"Brace yourself, it's going to break!" Stonewall yelled. The rope bridge snapped and the three fell, hurtling down. Stonewall tumbled ten feet until the slack from Taro's rope was taken up, almost dislocating his shoulder.

"The rope is made to stand five hundred stone, it will hold us," Taro reassured.

"The rope doesn't worry me; it's the arrowhead. Look!" Burbon pointed up.

They look at the cliff where the arrowhead is twisting under their weight and working its way out of the rock face.

"What are going to do?" asked Burbon.

"Prepare to swim," replied Stonewall as the arrowhead pulled itself out of the cliff.

The three of them fall again, tumbling through the air until they plunged into a river. Burbon felt the icy water surround him, stealing his consciousness away. His lungs cried for air as the pressure increased in his chest. He kicked with his feet, driving himself to the surface. The current was fierce, and he thrashed wildly as he was dragged downstream. He swam to a large rock and crawled onto it to warm himself in the afternoon sun. He was completely out of breath but watched Taro climb on a nearby boulder.

"I'm c-c-c-cold," he shivered.

"It's a mountain spring you f-f-f-foool, what do you expect?" Taro's body shook from the cold.

"I expect something gg-g-g-oood to happen to us for once. I'm so tired now I couldn't fight if my life depended on it." Stonewall splashed out of the water and walked ashore seemingly unaffected by the cold. He removed his tunic and laid it out the sun to dry. The three of them laid on the boulders for several minutes, warmed by the reflected heat. Stonewall raised his head, sensing that they were not alone. He pointed upstream to a bluff of trees.

"We have company." A large female wolf bounded on top of the boulders, leaping from stone to stone. She snarled at them, her fangs a show of force. Burbon raised his head off the boulder.

"She's not going to find me an easy meal," Burbon responded. He struggled to draw his sword but found it difficult with his body racked with shivering. Taro drew a bolt from her quiver, but it was difficult to aim, the cold affecting her thin body.

"Wait!" Stonewall commanded. As the wolf drew closer, a familiar wolf cub appeared by her side. The cub jumped off several rocks before running up to Stonewall and licked his face.

"Well I'll be, that's the one you saved," Burbon recognized the cub from the trap. The female wolf's attitude changed immediately, and her body posture softened. The cub leapt from rock to rock, excited to be reunited with his rescuer. The female wolf cocked her head as if hearing a sound beyond the traveler's hearing. She barked at her cub, calling him to return to her. The cub scampered and both wolves looked back, as if to signal the travelers to follow them.

"It would appear that we have a guide," remarked Stonewall.

"But I can hardly move," croaked Burbon.

"We need to get away from this place. Either that beast or the gobtrolls will be sure to follow," Taro shuffled her bolt back into her quiver. With renewed energy, Burbon shook the water off his body.

"What are we waiting for?"

Into the early evening, the trio finally left the forest and crossed into the open plains. The land became flat and Burbon found it hard to estimate distance. A lone fire formed a beacon against the midnight sky. Flames licked the air from a fire on a small bluff, with gnarled trees surrounding its edges. A gust of wind blew a tumbleweed with dried snake-like tendrils of grass past Stonewall's path. As they strode closer, Burbon saw a wooden rack with furs dangling from its height. In the center of the bluff, a wigwam had with smoke rising from its center. Their guide stopped before the camp and peered to the entrance of the wigwam. Stonewall smiled.

"This is the destination we seek."

Stonewall entered the wigwam while the others followed. Through the flap, the interior was much larger than its outside appearance. The warmth of the fire overwhelmed them. A pot bubbled over a fire with an unknown meal. The flames flickered creating wild shadows on the interior wall. At the back of the wigwam, a dimly lit figure sat with his back to the travelers.

"Please sit down, I have been expecting you," the figure spoke. They exchanged glances and sat down. No one spoke until Burbon broke the silence.

"I've been chased, beaten, and dropped and now my stomach is growling up a storm. Why are we here?" The figure turned his head, but the shadows hid his face. He considered Burbon's words.

"Questions, I'm sure you have many. But first, feed the stomach and then the mind. Help yourselves to the bowls." He stepped from the shadows. He was very old and shuffled closer to the fire. Burbon needed no further encouragement and reached for the wooden spoon in the pot. He savored the smell before scooping food for each into wooden bowls. The old man sat down.

"I am Oberron, the wizard. The Seer has sent you to seek me out, and by fate's design you have arrived. I know not of your travel here, but I can tell you of your journey to come. You are three unique beings brought together to unite a stone of great power. Pieces of it are scattered throughout our world and only by bringing the pieces together can its power be restored."

Burbon looked over the fire to Oberron while speaking between spoonsful. "Wizard, no offence to my comrades, but we three are far from unique. I am a simple merchant; she is an elf archer and he is a mercenary for hire. I think you have mistaken us for other people."

"You are wrong, although it may take time to discover your truly special abilities," responded the wizard. Taro removed the amulet from her pouch.

"And is this one of the pieces?" She held the stone out for the wizard to see.

"Yes. Its power is more valuable than any of our lives." Oberron coughed while limping towards the back of the wigwam.

"What do we have to do with it?" asked Burbon, between gulps of his stew. His face was so deep into his bowl that his nose is hidden. The wizard turned around.

"You have given up much, yet you must give up so much more. There is a map which describes the locations of the three remaining stones. It was created when the stones where separated. These stones were spread across the world and will require a long and dangerous journey to retrieve them. Forces are working against you, especially those of a prince named Darkmoor - an evil man who is hunting you down as we speak."

"I have heard that name before, from soldiers in the north. They describe him as having many resources. What will he do with these stones?" Stonewall asked. Oberron walked back towards them and began his tale.

"Many moons ago, there was a poor farmer who worked long days on unforgiving terrain to plant his crops. He toiled for many years until one morning as he was tilling his soil; he unearthed a strange orb. As he brushed the dirt from the object, it started to glow and radiate heat. But as soon as it started, it stopped and went cold. The farmer was uncertain whether it was his imagination or not, but he decided to keep the orb until he could study it further. Days passed and he soon forgot about the orb, but as harvest time approached, his crop grew faster and larger than ever before. He remembered the orb and found it glowing again. The farmer realized that it was the power of the orb that has provided him with his bountiful harvest."

"He had to make an important decision, to hoard or to share the orb's power. The farmer was a selfless man and soon visited his neighbors, bringing them plentiful harvests as well. The farmer shared the orb's power with all those around. Soon the farmer became the mayor of his town and still he shared the orb's power with the merchants until their businesses prospered beyond belief. The man who was mayor soon became a great King who ruled a just and prosperous Kingdom. His people loved him for sharing his gift's power and the Kingdom grew under his rule."

"Unfortunately, there were those in the Kingdom who thought the power would be better in the hands of the few than the many. The King's eldest son did not share his father's need to spread the orb's power amongst his people. His son was lazy, he never learned from his father's work ethic, always living a much softer life. He planned a different rule and as the oldest of four children, he knew he would be the logical choice. The King realized that his son might not share the same values as him and decided upon his death that all four children would jointly rule."

"When the King died, the Kingdom mourned for many days until the four siblings commenced their ceremony as rulers of the Kingdom. Unfortunately, the oldest son disagreed with his father and named himself the sole ruler. The children fought over the orb until it fell from their hands and smashed onto the floor. The beautiful orb broke into four jagged pieces. Before the children could examine the pieces, an apparition appeared. It explained that the orb was planted by the gods to bring nourishment to the land. Now their greed had broken its power and only good could reunite them again. The apparition chanted a mantra, which explained how the stones could be joined again."

Once evil has divided the orb
Only the power of good can unite the broken pieces
To the bold and brave
Beware of deceit on the journey
Only strong shepherds will be your guide
Strength will provide protection
Magic will provide direction
Wealth will set them free
Prevent pure evil from claiming the power
If a piece is false, the holder will be punished

"The apparition disappeared and the four siblings each grabbed a piece of the orb. Unsure of its message the three younger children fled the Kingdom while the oldest son declared a bounty on their heads."

"I'm not good at riddles, what does all of this mean?" interrupted Burbon.

"I do not know," the wizard answered. "Perhaps you will discover its meaning after reuniting the pieces."

"What happened to the stones?" asked Stonewall.

"The children spread across the land in the hope of bringing wealth for themselves. The oldest son drove himself mad when he could not create the bountiful trade of his father and eventually his Kingdom went dark. Only the scared and the weak remained. The stones still had power, but the pieces were much weaker than the whole. Greed took them from family to family until they disappeared from sight." Oberron stood up putting his weight on his cane.

"Until now," answers Stonewall.

"Until now. A century has almost passed since the orb was found and Darkmoor must have discovered their truth."

"Why would a creature like Darkmoor want power that creates good?" asked Taro.

"The stones are a conduit for whoever possesses them; they can do great good or great evil."

"Where do we start?" Burbon put down his bowl. All three trained their eyes onto the wizard.

"You must travel a great distance to the Castle of Rendigar. There you will find the living map of the three remaining stones."

"A living map? How does that work?" questioned Burbon.

"A living map is organic and changes its terrain depending on the location of the object it has been guided to watch. It will reveal the exact location of the object, even if it is moving," replied Taro.

"Now that could make me some pretty coin at my store."

"It's always about money with you, trader," Taro exclaimed.

"Stop your petty bickering! Our world hangs on your abilities to retrieve these stones." Oberron expanded in size and they gave him their full attention. Instead of a withered old man, he appeared much more powerful.

"How will we get there, wizard? The Castle of Rendigar is long journey almost impassable by foot?" inquired Stonewall.

"You will be accompanied by…" Suddenly a strange look crossed Oberron's face. "They are already here."

"Who's here?" questioned Taro. She rushed outside to see three riders approaching with horses on tethers. Burbon, Stonewall, and Oberron accompanied Taro outside. As the riders' dismount, Burbon asked, "Who are they?"

"They are the Riders, creatures of the undead," Oberron responded. A figure stepped into the moonlight and its ravaged decaying flesh hung off of its body. Its face was covered with scars of past battles and its armor was ancient made of an extinct metal. It twisted its head menacingly at Taro. She removed a bolt from her quiver.

"Enough!" commanded Oberron. "The riders are not your enemy. Despite their appearance, they are here to take you to your destination." Oberron waved his hands and conjured an image of a castle high in the mountains. "You must journey to the Castle of Rendigar. It was a cradle of civilization, but now it's a burial place that most have long forgotten. There you will battle the elements and retrieve the living map. When you place your stone on the map, it will align and show you the locations of the remaining stones. You must leave now as the Riders will only travel by the light of the moon."

Burbon looked at a decayed soldier and his horse.

"I hope this one doesn't fall apart on me," as he placed his foot onto the stirrups. He sat on the saddle and stared into the eyes of the Rider. The experience was not pleasant.

Stonewall asked, "Wizard, do these creatures talk or hear?"

"No, warrior. The Riders are transports of fallen warriors to their final resting-place. They will not converse with you. You are their first living passengers. As long as you ride with them, no living beings will see you. They are helping you because of my aid. After they complete their task, you wouldn't want to meet them again."

"Why? Burbon questioned.

"You would be dead."

Burbon straightened up in his saddle, "Understood."

"Goodbye and good luck. Beware of the Castle of Rendigar. It will hold many challenges for you. May you complete your journey safely." Oberron stepped backwards until he was swallowed up by the darkness of the wigwam. Taro and Stonewall joined their riders.

The Rider's dark horse whinnied and trotted ahead. Burbon squinted toward the horizon as the land flew by at amazing speed. He swore that the horse's feet were not touching the ground.

Time sped by as the morning suns replaced the darkness. They raced past farmers and animals in pastures, yet none noticed their passing. As the landscape changed, the sky turned overcast. The plains rose to foothills. In the distance, a huge castle appeared, surrounded by jagged rock that reached to the sky. The rock, tall and looming, defended the castle from any attack. The castle rested in the middle of a valley with one main road to its entrance. The horses slowed their gallop and time reverted to normal again. In a few moments, the riders reined their horses to stop at the clearing before the castle path. The three of them dismounted as the Riders sat motionless.

"That journey was surreal, almost like a vision dream," commented Stonewall.

"A bad dream. It felt strange passing by unnoticed," Burbon said.

"I enjoyed the quiet, it gave me time to meditate," Taro replied.

Stonewall stepped in front of the Riders. "We thank you. I look forward to meeting you again when I meet the great reward." He bowed his head and put his palm to his fist to say goodbye. The Riders left as quietly as they came. Burbon nudged Taro.

"Do you think we meet them again when we die?"

"You don't have to worry," Burbon looked relieved, "they only accept valiant fighters," Taro stepped away.

The trio marched to the castle and surveyed the road in front of them, looking for possible traps. Burbon watched the turrets, reaching high into the sky. On the stone ridges sat several stone gargoyles glowering down on them. A motion caught Burbon's eye as he looked back at the gargoyle. *I could've sworn that thing blinked its eyes. I must be fatigued from the ride.* They crossed a drawbridge over a moat that swirled beneath it. Strange shaped shifted in the water and it was difficult to see into its murky depths. Burbon felt nervous and placed his ear down to the drawbridge to listen for noises.

"You think anything lives in there?"

"Why don't you stick your hand in the water and see if anything bites it off," answered Taro. Burbon ran to the other side of the drawbridge. The three of them stood before a huge impenetrable door. Two ornate doorknockers stared down at the trader. Burbon grabbed the handle attempting to open it, but it doesn't move.

"It's locked. I don't think even Stonewall will be able to open it. What do you want to do?"

A loud screech issued from the door and Burbon to jumped back. The doorknocker changed, its metal forming into a strange face. Its features were grotesque, like a jester with a large caricatured mouth. The face in the door spoke.

"Who goes there?" it shrieked as it tilted its head waiting for a reply.

"Who are you?" Burbon regained his composure.

"I am Xanos, the demon of the door. To enter, you must answer my riddle."

Burbon held his head in his hands. "I wish I had stayed in my village." Stonewall ignored Burbon.

"What is your riddle, demon? And how many chances do we get to answer it?"

"A demon's code is clear. One chance for each of the travelers. If you can answer my riddle correctly, I will let you enter. Guess incorrectly and no entry," Xanos smile was wide, it relished its power. Taro looked at her comrades.

"There must be another way in." Xanos frowned at Taro's suggestion.

"The castle is magically sealed. I'm the only way in, the only way out." Xanos gave another smug look. Stonewall pointed up.

"Taro, shoot one of your bolts at the left tower," he directed in the distance. She lined up her crossbow and loosened the bolt. A green shield flashed, causing the bolt to ricochet off the castle. It was swallowed up by the moat.

"Maybe he's right," Burbon commented.

"Perhaps, but demons are notorious for their trickery," replied Stonewall. He removed his broadsword and swung it with full force at the door. Inches before connecting, it bounced harmless off, forcing Stonewall to stumble from the recoil.

"Let's listen to the riddle," motioned Burbon. Xano's eyes bulged and rotated, switching positions. The demon was excited to begin.

"The rules are simple. I will ask a riddle. You will have three questions to ask and three answers to give."

"Don't try to trick us, demon," spoke Taro. The demon mocked an innocent look.

"Archer, that is exactly what I will do. This is your riddle. It is impossible for anyone to survive longer than one week without water. Every year, several travelers spend ten days crossing a desert without drinking water or bringing any along. They travel a different route each time. How do they survive? You have to answer before that ray of sun moves to the next stone." The demon's eye looked to a nearby rock on the castle wall.

"That's impossible without water! I don't know. Was there..." Burbon started.

"Stop, be careful. The demon is trying to get us to waste one of our questions. We should discuss this," gestured Stonewall. The three of them stepped away from the door.

"How do we know that this demon will honor his decision if he loses?" asked Burbon.

"Demons are very misleading but love the challenge of a solvable riddle. His code will force him to allow us entry if we guess correctly," answered Stonewall.

"Could these travelers be magic? Could they create water from the air?" asked Taro.

"That would make the riddle unfair. Demons love to cheat but the riddle they pose must have a fair solution," Stonewall answered.

"Is it ten days of normal time or some other type of day?" Burbon wondered.

"Maybe someone else was bringing water to them," commented Stonewall. Xanos interrupted.

"What's your first question?"

"The demon is rushing us, hoping we will make a mistake," Burbon interjected.

"No matter," said Stonewall. "Taro, ask your question."

"Very well, are the travelers magic or is water being brought to them?"

"That is two questions," Xanos replies. "The answer is no to both."

"Are the days of normal length? Or is it up north where the daylight is longer?" blurted Burbon.

"Days are always the same length no matter where you travel," answered Xanos.

"Hey, you didn't answer my question!" Burbon yelled.

"You didn't ask the right question," laughed Xanos. "Now you only have 3 chances to guess the solution."

"There's something we're missing," Stonewall paced on the drawbridge.

"Each one of us can give an answer," said Taro. "My guess is that the travelers stop at an oasis on each trip to drink from their springs.

"Wrong!" the demon responded. "The route changes each year and only a fool would head into the desert with a belief they would find an oasis. Second guess."

Burbon thought he has the answer. "The plant life," he exclaimed. "The travelers grind the plants they find for moisture to survive."

"Wrong! The moisture from plants would not provide enough water to survive. You have one last guess." Taro and Burbon turned to Stonewall.

"You mentioned the traders cross a desert. A desert supports little or no vegetation, like the tundra up north. But in traveling the tundra, you don't need water; you can melt the snow." Stonewall looked straight at Xanos. "The travelers are crossing the northlands." Xanos eyes popped and his face went red. He had lost.

"Correct," he grunted. "You are fortunate that I gave such an easy riddle." The massive doors split apart as the doorknocker made a final face. "Beware of the heat, it can kill you," the demon cackled as his face faded away.

"Great, another riddle," commented Burbon passing through the door. They walked into the castle and enter a great hall. As they stepped inside, the massive door swings shut behind them. Burbon looked back at the door.

"Hope we don't have to answer a riddle to leave."

"If we do, we'll let Stonewall give the answer." Taro answered with new respect for him.

Down a long corridor were knights' armor posed as statues along both walls. Huge granite tiles jutted out along the floor. Flaming torches lined the walls illuminated the hallway as if their approach was expected.

"Be careful as you walk," noted Taro.

As they moved forward down the corridor, Burbon stepped on a granite stone. The stone depressed slightly, spewing fire from a hole in the floor which sprayed Taro's back.

"Taro, you're on fire!" Burbon yelled.

Stonewall ripped a banner off of the wall and covered Taro. Burbon beat the flames on her back. Taro's muffled voice cried under rug.

"I think the flames are out." She got up and brushed herself off. Burbon slapped her back.

"Sorry. I thought I saw a spark."

Stonewall motioned them to the floor. "We must tread carefully; certain stones on the floor send out gouts of flame. Walk near the cracks in the floor and we should be able to avoid them,"

Burbon observed how narrow the cracks are between tiles. "This is going to be difficult."

They slowly zigzagged across the floor to avoid depressing a stone. Stonewall misstepped and a flame spewed from an armored knight. The flame narrowly missed Burbon.

"Hey, cut it out."

He jumped away from the flame, hitting another rock that blows fire at Taro again.

"Watch where you're walking!" she yelled.

She miscued and tripped on the wrong stone. This fire singed Burbon's mustache. They gave up being careful and ran to the end of the hall. Jets of flame shoot behind them. Huffing and puffing, they reached a door.

"That demon was right." Burbon collapsed.

"At least we're through." Stonewall opened the door, as Burbon slipped by him. Burbon stopped in midstep as he saw what awaited.

"What's wrong, what do you see?" asked Stonewall.

"Ever hear the term, out the frying pan into the—"

"Fire!" Taro yelled as a large blast of fiery lava flew straight at her head.

6

Besting the Elements

Taro ducked as a flaming rock smashed against the wall behind her. The flamed ignite a tapestry hanging from the ceiling, which quickly spread throughout the chamber.

"We won't be going back that way," Burbon decided as the fire rushed to the demon's door. The heat was scorching as lava gushed on the ground below them. Rocks marked a pathway crossing the flames. On the far end, a gargoyle set in rock watched over the flame. A bead of sweat dripped down Burbon's forehead. He turned around as fire blew past him. "Yikes!!" Burbon touched his forehead and looked at Stonewall, "Do I still have my eyebrows?" Stonewall ignored him.

"Come on! Follow this path and we'll meet the elements head on," commanded Stonewall.

He ventured forward as flames spewed out from the gargoyle's mouth. A fireball raced towards Stonewall. He blocked it with his sword and deflected it in another direction.

Burbon passed Stonewall and began crossing the rock pathway. He tripped and almost fell off the path into the lava.

"Concentrate on where you're going," yelled Taro. Burbon watched as another gout of flame spews from the statue's mouth.

"Whoa!" He ducked; the flame barely missed him. "Good thing that statue can't aim." He immediately regretted his words. Seconds later, stone chips shook loose from the fire gargoyle's head and fell into the lava. The gargoyle turned its fiery head and its right eye blinked open to stare directly at Burbon. All three stopped dead in their tracks.

"Watch what you say," directed Stonewall.

The gargoyle shook its rock wing, revealing a fiery form underneath. Flame spit from its mouth as it roared. It flew above to make their crossing more treacherous. The gargoyle sprayed fire down at them. The flame impacted on Burbon's rock. He jumped up as it hit and landed on the hot rock.

"Ouch, ouch!" He danced up and down like a hot potato. Taro cocked a bolt on her crossbow.

"Eat this!" She unloaded the bolt at the creature. It swerves out its flight as the bolt hit the rocks. Taro considered her options. "I need you two to distract it. Think you can handle that, trader?" Burbon nodded and stepped forward.

"Hey Fire breath! Why don't you fly down and get me? Look, I'm lying down on this rock just waiting for you to burn me into a crisp. What are you waiting for?" The gargoyle dipped lower aiming its mouth at Burbon's body. It pulled its head back and sent a mammoth flame at Burbon's head. Fear caused him to lie frozen to the rock. The flames rushed at him as Stonewall's sword deflected them away. Taro second bolt landed in the heart of the distracted gargoyle and it burst into a blue flame before vaporizing.

"Why did you just lie there?" Stonewall asked, lifting Burbon up.

"I thought Taro was going to get him before he shot the flame."

"What was on that bolt?" Stonewall questioned.

"Just a little bit of magnesium," she stated nonchalantly as she walked by him.

As they walked down the corridor away from the flames, the hiss of the flames dissipated. Soon the heat of the previous cavern was gone as well. Burbon ran his hands along the walls. They were uneven, with huge boulders at regular intervals acting as beams for the roof. Branches began to protrude through the rocks allowing outside light to shine in. Burbon's shadow stretched ahead of his feet.

For a short time, they walked in silence. The rock walls of the castle slowly become greener with vegetation and moist with moss with small bugs flying in the cracks. Droplets of water dripped from the ceiling to the floor forming shallow puddles on the floor. Stonewall's boots tracked a short trail behind him. Burbon felt a large drop of water fall onto his cheek.

Stonewall stopped at a fork in the corridor. Burbon looked right while Taro peered left.

"Which passageway?" asked Stonewall.

"What if we split up and take both ways," suggested Taro. Burbon turned his head slightly; hearing a low roar in the distance.

"I'm not keen on separating," Stonewall shook his head. Burbon looked up the left hallway.

"I think our decision has been made for us."

"What do you mean?" Taro was puzzled. The roar became louder.

"Look!" Burbon pointed. Down the left corridor was a wave of water crashing towards them. "Tidal wave!"

They ran down the right corridor as the water threatened to overtake them. They passed a series of armored statues. Stonewall grabbed a large shield from one of the statues. He laid it down in front of them.

"Quick, everybody jump on," he commanded.

They climbed on the shield as the water rushed to them. The water pushed the shield ahead of the wave. It floated to the top of the wave. Burbon couldn't grip the edge of the shield and struggled to hold on. The water pushed him, and he lost his balance, falling out of the shield.

"Burbon!" Taro yelled. His body sank into the water. Seconds later, his arm reached out to grasp the shield. Debris floated by and his right hand gripped onto a wide piece of wood. He dragged himself out of the water and straddled the plank to maintain his balance. The walls hurtled by as the water pushed them through the passageway. Burbon used his body and leaned to the right to steer the plank.

"Hold tight, little man. Taro will throw a rope to you," Stonewall turned to Taro. She aimed a bolt in her crossbow with a thin rope tied to the end.

"Thwack!" It imbedded itself in the opposite end of the plank.

"She would shoot to the opposite end," he complained. He pushed towards the rope while trying not to fall off the board. He grabbed the rope and a swell of water threw him into the air. He landed like a cat back on the board while holding the rope. Burbon was amazed and pushed his newfound agility to the maximum. He weaved back and forth, mastering the current to surf the water. He noticed an incoming overhang of the ceiling. "Stonewall – duck!!!"

Without even looking, Stonewall bent his massive frame and missed colliding with the overhang.

"Thanks," Stonewall nodded. Burbon continued to surf the wave.

"This test of the elements isn't so bad." Burbon yelled to his friends. Behind him a head pulled itself from the depths of the water. Its features were identical to the fire gargoyle except this creature was made of water. The gargoyle rose from the current and aimed its mouth at the shield. It shot a hard spray of water that almost knocked Taro off. Stonewall grabbed her back to the center.

"Hold on!" Burbon said to them and rode the water to distract the gargoyle. He sprayed the gargoyle by stomping on the end of the plank. The water had no effect, simply dripping down the gargoyle's body. But Burbon had succeeded in focusing the creature's attention on him. Its mouth became a weapon and fired directly into Burbon's path. The surge of water caused Burbon to lose his balance and he fell forward onto the plank. He straddled the board with both leg and held tightly. Flowing through the rough water, Burbon got an idea.

The gargoyle pursued, trying to shoot Burbon with its spray. Burbon slowed his plank's speed so that the gargoyle flew between him and the shield. The gargoyle had its back to the next overhang.

"Water breath, try and hit me," Burbon taunted.

The gargoyle filled its cheeks to twice their size, priming itself to hit

Burbon with a hard shot of water. Its eyes surged with realization as it followed Burbon's gaze to the upcoming beam.

"Spoosh!" the gargoyle exploded into water droplets as it hit the overhang.

"Sucker!" Burbon screamed as he centered himself on his plank. Soon the current subsided and the three of them rode out the torrent of water.

The water petered out and both plank and shield rested on the corridor floor. Burbon stepped off of the plank as Stonewall picked up the large shield and puts the interior strap around his forearm.

"Keeping a souvenir?" asked Burbon.

"It may be useful again," he replied. Taro walked several steps ahead and then held up her hand.

"Quiet, both of you. What's that?" she motioned. A droning sound whirled in the passageway ahead.

"The last time we heard a noise, an avalanche of water almost washed us away," Burbon mentioned.

"It doesn't sound water," stated Taro.

Stonewall walked down the hallway toward the noise. "Let's hope we are going the right direction." Burbon ran, his little legs pumping to keep up with Stonewall's easy strides.

"I know that noise. It sounds like..."

"Wind!" as a gush of air knocked Taro back two steps. The hallway opened to a large cavern; its walls seem unlike the passageways of the castle. These walls were worn smooth, eroded by the constant wind. Burbon looked around, the cavern was in a circular tower with beams of light from outside. In front of them, a narrow bridge arched across the cavern. Burbon peered down from the bridge to view a seemingly bottomless pit. Wind gushed both above and below them. At the opposite end of the cavern was a rock door.

"I take it that our destination is on the other side of that door," Burbon pointed. "We can do this. It's just a walkway with some wind." The currents swirled above them. A vortex spun larger and larger. From its center, a familiar shape formed out of the air currents.

"Don't these creatures ever give up," Burbon said with a depressing slouch.

The wind gargoyle opened its mouth and aimed a blast at Taro. The blast made her slip and she lost her balance. Her right leg hovered off the bridge and she almost toppled off the walkway. Stonewall hauled her back.

"Quick, get behind me!" Stonewall pulled his shield in front of them to cover their advance. The face of creature with fangs was embossed into the shield. "Will it protect us from their blast?" as Burbon hunkered behind it.

"Only one way to find out," answered Taro.

The gargoyle aimed at Stonewall, sending a wave of wind directly at the shield. Stonewall deflected the force back at the gargoyle causing it to vanish.

"All right, Stonewall," Burbon cheered.

Almost on cue, another gargoyle formed out of the wind.

"Stay behind me and I will guide you to the door," Stonewall directed. Slowly they stepped toward the far end with the shield in front of them. The gargoyle flew around them trying to attack from behind. It fired at Stonewall's back knowing he couldn't turn the heavy shield around in time. Instead Stonewall used his sword to split the blast away from them.

"You are doing well, warrior," commented Taro.

The gargoyle looked down, frustrated from its lack of success. It decided to aim at a new target. Its mouth expanded and it aimed its force at the bridge to knock them off. Several gusts hit the walkway, each shockwave knocking Burbon closer to the edge. On the third hit, Burbon fell off the edge into the oblivion below. Before the emptiness could swallow him, Stonewall's hand grabbed him by his vest and he threw him forward onto the bridge. The gargoyle was off balance and fired a blast at Burbon. The wind force missed and was reflected on the rock wall bouncing back to its sender. The gargoyle vanished as Burbon rushed to the door.

"What a wind bag," Burbon commented as the Taro and Stonewall reached the door. A larger gargoyle formed out of the air above them. They slammed the door shut behind them. The blast from the gargoyle caused the door to shutter. Burbon doubled over, putting his hands on his knees to catch his breath. "I'm sensing a theme," he remarked as they checked their weapons to make sure all items were accounted for. "Do you think we've gotten through the worst of it?" Burbon asked Stonewall.

"No," he replied and marched down the passageway away from the wind. The castle was a huge maze and they travelled for a while as the sunlight changed. The were forced to turn back several times as they came to dead ends. At one point, Burbon thought Stonewall was going to lose his temper and punch his way through the wall. *If we don't find a way soon, I'm going to hope for another gargoyle to fight.*

His thoughts were interrupted by something unexpected. Not a noise, not an attack, but a strange odor caused them to stop. Taro knelt to sniff the air.

"What is that smell?" she asked.

"Flowers!" Burbon exclaimed as he rushed forward.

As they turned a corner, they saw a beautiful indoor garden with trees and fragrant flowers. Stonewall bent down to smell an orchid, wary of a trap.

"This is beautiful," Stonewall scanned the surroundings. Lush foliage encircled them, and sunshine flooded down from the cracks in the ceiling on the vegetation. Vibrant red flowers circled the rock walls lined with vines. A bird flew between trees and sailed out through an opening in the roof. Burbon walked up to Stonewall.

"Too bad we couldn't have found this opening at the start; we could have avoided those tests."

"Don't let the surroundings fool you," Stonewall warned. "There is a ceremony in my homeland where boys at the age of manhood must walk through the forest. Men hide and try to capture the boy before his time runs out at sunset. They camouflage as brush or hide in the ground, whatever tactic they can to scare the boy away from his destination."

"And did anyone scare you?" Taro asked.

"Yes, one of my classmates dressed up as a rock. I sat down sit on this rock and he leapt on my back. I screamed and ran through the forest.

My classmate was laughing so loud that he never saw the branch that knocked him out. I couldn't leave him there and had to carry him with me. I almost didn't make it out of the woods by dusk. To this day, I have never trusted a rock." He poked a nearby rock with his sword.

"Maybe these flowers are going to attack us," Burbon picked a flower and mimicked it lunging for his throat by rolling on the ground. His antics were ignored by Taro and Stonewall. Behind him a hand rose from the soil, like a body from a grave. An earthen gargoyle pulled itself out of the ground and stood over Burbon's rolling form. Burbon failed to sense it until its shadow crossed over him.

"Help!" Burbon yelled.

Stonewall and Taro raced towards him. Burbon backed up from this new menace until hitting something hard from behind. He turned and stared at the kneecap of another gargoyle. The earth gargoyle was a giant, eclipsing Stonewall in size and mass. At its feet, a third smaller gargoyle pulled itself from the ground. Stonewall charged and drew his sword. "Leave the biggest one for me," he yelled

"If you insist," replied Burbon and ducked between the legs of the third gargoyle. Stonewall blocked a fist from the largest gargoyle, knocking him into the dirt.

Taro loosened a bolt at her opponent. The bolt sailed through the gargoyle's body and imbedded on a tree behind it. The hole in the gargoyle quickly reformed. "This isn't going to be easy," she said to Burbon.

Burbon ran from his opponent. The gargoyle was identical to its previous element incarnations except this body was made of rock-hard earth. It had no wings to fly and instead walked with purpose. Burbon stumbled backwards and fell over a rock. He splashed into a small stream and looked up into the eye of the gargoyle as it sent its fist at Burbon's face.

Taro jumped on a rock to avoid her pursuer. The gargoyle advanced at a steady pace, knowing its prey had nowhere to go. It swung its fist and hit the rock underneath, missing Taro's feet. Its fist breaks apart from the force sending dirt into the air. The gargoyle examined its damaged arm. It shoved its arm into the ground as the dirt reformed another fist.

How do we defeat this creature she thought?

Stonewall rushed toward his target. The huge earth gargoyle shook the ground with thunderous steps. As they rushed each other, the giant swung his massive fist at Stonewall. The warrior ducked and slashed his broadsword across the gargoyle's leg. The blade sunk deep cutting both legs in one slice. The gargoyle fell forward, the rest of its body unable to hold its weight. It slammed into the ground as Stonewall rose to behead the creature. Before he placed the killing blow, new feet grow out the ground as the gargoyle regains its fighting stance.

How can this thing be beaten, Stonewall wonders?

The gargoyle's fist pounded into the stream, barely missing Burbon's head. Burbon spun and swallowed a mouthful of water. He watched the gargoyle stand tentatively over the stream. Burbon watched as droplets of mud flow down its arm and onto the water's surface.

"Stonewall! Taro! Get down here!" he yelled.

"Fight your own battles, trader!" Taro replied as she evaded her pursuer. Stonewall's large hand grabbed around her waist and pulled her towards the stream.

"Come on, Burbon needs our help!" Stonewall answered. They dashed towards the stream. They passed a tree so fast that they don't see Taro's gargoyle until it was too late. Instead of slowing down, Stonewall sent it sailing into the gargoyle by the stream. The two collided and fell into the water. Burbon jumped on their bodies turning them into mud before they could reform their bodies. The current washed the two gargoyles away.

"Two down and one big one to go!" yelled Burbon. The giant gargoyle lumbered out of the foliage but walked cautiously to avoid the water. It turned to Taro; its mouth expanded to swallow her whole. She backed against a rock, cornered by the gargoyle. It was ready for a meal.

Suddenly it stopped, its eyes opened wide. It turned its head; Stonewall held his sword over his shoulder. The gargoyle's head tumbled into the stream below. The body walked a few steps before falling into the stream. Burbon took his knife and stabbed the earthen body repeatedly until it broke up in the water. "Overgrown sandbox!"

Suddenly something shiny in the distance attracted his attention. "Look over there!"

A glow emanated from a wooden platform and they ran towards it. On top of it, lay a large chest with its contents exposed. Burbon rubbed his hands in anticipation.

"Treasure!"

"Don't be a fool Burbon, there is something here more valuable than precious metals," Taro reached down to grasp a small map. It lurched away before Taro could grab it. She scooped it with her other hand and smoothed it out. The map relaxed to her touch. Taro scanned it over, but the paper was blank. Taro removed the amulet from her pouch and placed it on the parchment. The map folded itself around the stone and it lay still. Taro coaxed open the paper so she could read its content. She gazed in wonder. "The Living Map!" she exclaimed. "This is our world with the locations of the remaining stones." Three symbols were drawn on the map, a bolt for Taro, a sword for Stonewall and gold coin for Burbon.

"Let me see." Burbon approached but the map folded up.

"I don't think it likes you," Taro replied.

"Who cares, let me gather what's truly valuable here." Burbon stuffed jewels into his pouch.

"Stonewall, where must we go?" Taro asked. He looked closely, reading the locations of the other stones while other moving objects danced on the page.

"It will take some time deciphering, but I think the second stone is located in the land of Valdawn, many leagues from here. We must travel through the swampland of Nagermire. The There will be many dangers. Are you both still committed to our quest?" Taro nodded as Burbon dropped a gem on the floor. He looked up at their stares.

"I have no store to go back to, remember?" He tied the string on his pouch as gems threatened to flow out. "One question - can we go out a different way than we came in?"

7

Swamps of Nagermire

The Castle of Rendigar shuddered from the blast. A winged beast flew straight towards a turret and shattered the rock into rubble. Whatever magical force field withstood Taro's bolt was no match for the fury of Sunder. His talons were razor sharp. Nothing living could withstand his crushing grasp.

Enough! Your frustration annoys me. The three travelers have left with their prize, this castle is not our enemy. Darkmoor's psychic link pierced through Sunder's mind. The animal knew better than to ignore his master's command.

Where would you have me go? Sunder barely contained his anger at not being able to destroy the castle.

Circle wider until we pick up their trail. I can still smell their stink.

As you command. Sunder rose into the clouds for greater altitude.

The gemstone consumed Darkmoor's thoughts. Suddenly, he saw an animal dashing through the bushes below reminding him of a moment from his youth.

The horses and riders galloped through the meadow intent on their prey. His father had been riding them hard through the forest for several days on their annual hunt. As King of their land, he felt it necessary to teach him the rites of manhood. So far, their prey was being difficult to kill.

"You hold your spear too low, boy, hold it higher like a man," the King commanded.

"Yes, father." The boy held the heavy spear in his left hand. The King stared at his only son with disdain.

"You hold it like a woman. Sometimes I think you're more like your mother. What kind of heir have I sired?" his father questioned.

"I'm trying. There, I almost have it," the boy pleaded. The bushes rustled ahead of them. Their game was near.

"I will show you how a man hunts." The King advanced on the bushes. He pushed the branches aside to reveal a stag with many wounds. It looked up with proud eyes ready to accept its death. The King's mouth snarled as if rejecting this animal's plea for a quick death. He turned his horse away from the animal. The boy's horse galloped up to him.

"Father, why don't you slay this animal. Its time is done!" The boy asked as his father scowled.

"I'm the King. I decide when a life is to end or if deserves to suffer more. Look at this animal; it can barely move, and its blood is thick in the air. Evening is not far away. Let the scavengers of the forest prolong its agony." Cold hard eyes stared back from the stag. "Come boy, we are returning to the castle."

The boy hesitated and his eyes meet the eyes of the stag. In the seconds they looked at each other, the boy felt its pain and the request to end its life. He was frozen to the spot and slowly lifted his spear. His arm shook but his mind was willing to deal a killing blow. The stag bowed his head. Suddenly the boy felt the sharp cut of metal on his neck. His father's spear.

"Kill this beast, and I will gut you and leave you for the wolves," his father commanded. A tear welled up his eye as the stag turned away. The boy faced his father.

"Yes, father," as he lowered his spear and climbed on his horse. The sorrow in the stag's eyes would forever be tattooed onto Darkmoor's brain.

Now father, I decide when someone dies.

Sunder screamed.

What is it? Darkmoor cursed.

I have found their trail. They are walking through the Swamps of Nagermire. It will be difficult to follow them.

Difficult but not impossible. Find them! Sunder flew into the murky depths of the swamps.

Stonewall's boots squished in the muck. Reeds and cattails swayed in his wake. The smell was vile; gases bubbled up through the brine water and burst, exposing their odor to the surface. The air was so thick with fog it is hard to tell the time of day.

"Are we there yet?" Burbon complained.

"Must you ask that question every five minutes?" Taro sighed in exasperation

"You said this was the quickest route to travel. You didn't say this was the foulest route to travel!" Burbon exclaimed.

"The swamps are full of surprises. Spend your time walking rather than smelling the air," commented Stonewall.

"When will we hit this oasis you described so we can camp for the night?"

"Soon. When the tree line appears, we are close to our goal," replied Stonewall. A sound echoed in the distance.

"What's that?" stuttered Burbon. A gust of wind blew, drowning out any further sound. Suddenly Burbon jumped. "I felt it! Something slithered by my leg."

Stonewall drew his broadsword. "Quiet! Let me listen." All three of them stopped, waiting for an attack that never came. Burbon was the first to speak up.

"Maybe we should keep moving?"

"Unless the creature feels by vibrations as we move through the water," offered Taro. Burbon reacted by freezing like a statue, even his lips barely moved.

"Maybe, Taro, you should move to flush it out," he squeaked. Stonewall moved first.

"There is nothing here. Let's move on." He took two steps and the water exploded behind him. It was large like a python snake but

Stonewall realized the attacker was a slandoran. A slandoran was an amphibious snake; its mouth had three rings of enormous teeth ready to maw its prey. It streaked through the air, aiming for Stonewall's chest. Stonewall moved at the last second and swung his sword through the air, slicing the head of the slandoran inches before it made contact. Its death was instantaneous. Burbon tentatively stepped closer to the trophy head of the slandoran. He brought out his dagger to take a souvenir tooth.

"I bet I could fetch a fair price for this," as he worked his knife out of his sheath. The head lurched towards him, its teeth chopping. Burbon fell backwards into the water holding his arms straight out from his body. His mouth moved but he was unable to form words.

"I've heard that the head of a slandoran can survive several minutes after its cut from its body," commented Taro. Burbon looked as if he had emptied his bladder.

"Wh-why didn't you tell me that? That thing almost bit me."

"The teeth aren't the worst part. The venom speeds up your heart causing it to beat faster and faster until it explodes." Taro marched past Burbon onto a dry part of the swamp. Burbon turned to Stonewall.

"She's just joking. Right?" he asked. Stonewall shook his head and moved on. Burbon hurried to catch up with them.

Hours later, a spark floated in the air and swirled above the treetops before burning itself out. Flames licked high around the campfire, illuminating a cloudy sky with a few twinkles of starlight. Taro filed down tree branches to make more bolt shafts. Painstakingly, she sharpened each branch into a perfectly balanced bolt that would fly flawlessly to its target. Several rejected branches lay at her feet or smoldered in the fire. Burbon gnawed on pheasant bones, chewing every last piece of the meat. He tossed his bones on the fire, the grease igniting in the flame. Stonewall pulled letters out of his pouch and went through his personal objects. Burbon noticed Stonewall's intent gaze on his belongings.

"What are you looking at," inquired Burbon. Stonewall looked up with a smile on his face.

"These are presents from my father as I was growing up. My mother died when I was young, so my father made a special effort." Burbon saw a small medal - 1st in fishing for father and son. A ribbon from a marksmanship contest. A small carving that looked rubbed smooth from handling. It was in the shape of a massive man beside an equally strong but younger version of Stonewall. It wasn't hard for Burbon to see the love that existed between the two.

"You have no idea what happened to him?"

"None at all. I spent several years serving in the military. I was thrilled to return to my farm and spend time with him. He was overjoyed that we would work together in his blacksmith shop, as father and son. One night, we had an evening planned at our tavern where many of our friends were coming to celebrate my homecoming. My father went home earlier that day as I finished an order in our shop for the army. I returned late, dirty and tired from a day's work. I opened our cabin door to be greeted by the emptiness of our home. I searched every room expecting him to jump out at me; hiding like he used to do when I was a child. All that remained was a cup of tea on the table." Taro stopped her whittling and looked at Stonewall.

"Was there any sign of a struggle? Anything that was out of place?" she inquired.

"None. For days I examined our cabin. There was nothing missing, no tracks away from our home. If the cup of tea had not been there, I would have thought that he had been away for hours or had never reached home.

"What did you do after you couldn't find him?" asked Burbon.

"I scoured the town, talking to everyone. All loved my father. He made no enemies; there was no reason for anyone to hurt him. Finally, after many weeks I gave up trying to find answers there. I boarded up our home and began searching for him across the land. Taking work where I had to, always hoping that I will find some clue to his disappearance." Stonewall folded a paper sheath around the objects and placed them back into his pouch. Burbon shook his head.

"That's quite a tale my friend. I was one of ten siblings, so I didn't have the bond with my father that you had. But he taught me a few things about the art of the deal. I wouldn't be the trader I am today if he hadn't shown me how to stretch my money."

"With ten children, I'm not surprised," Taro commented.

"Why don't you share a little about your family?" Burbon asked.

"My family is none of your concern," Taro whittled on her branch. The large warrior stood and placed his hand gently on Taro's shoulder.

"Nay, fine archer. It is time to hear your history. The three of us have come far and we have many moons to go. It is time you shared with us. Our very lives may depend it." Stonewall peered kindly at Taro. As she looked up, her anger turned into tears and she dropped her knife. Both Stonewall and Burbon sat closer to listen to her tale.

"I come from a proud lineage of elfin trackers; our land is plentiful with game. Yet we hunted only what we needed and used everything we killed. The animal's meat coursed through our body adding to our strength. The bones are our weapons, their hides are our clothes. Our culture revered the animals and the forest, and we maintained the chain of life. But over the last decade the balance of life has changed. The game is less plentiful, and our hunters have had to go outside our lands to survive. Our people have always been a solitary race. We have never ventured beyond our borders except in rare occasions. Then the clashes occurred.

"I have heard about your battles with the goths. They have been ugly and bloody," commented Stonewall.

"And with no clear winner. Especially a land as rich as ours," Taro continued.

"What about your family? How do they fit into this?" Burbon questioned.

"My father and his father's father and his father before that were the greatest trackers of our people. As a female elf, I had to work twice as hard to gain the favor of my father over my brothers. I traveled farther and faster than any to prove time after time that I was the greatest tracker of the family."

"I bet your brothers loved you for that," Burbon added sarcastically. Taro stared back at him.

"They loved me more than you can know," she said with all seriousness. "It was my father's respect that I had to earn. After one hunt, I tracked a young griffin in the woods of Gillandor, east of our home.

"They are vicious beasts, even young," added Stonewall.

"Aye. I had led the entire family to its home, my brothers marveled at my skills to detect it. It laid in its nest, gnawing on a huge bone unaware of our presence in a nearby tree. When my father pointed his arrow at the griffin, the beast raised its head and looked me directly in the eyes. It shouldn't have been able to see me; my camouflage was complete.

But something stirred in me. Despite the many days' travel and hard work to find this beast, I suddenly knew one thing. I knew it should not die. Call it a gift of sight, I knew this griffin had greater things to do in its life and I should not end it. I placed my hand on my father's. Without speaking a word, he knew what was in my heart. The griffin flew into the sky.

My brothers teased me for weeks for letting it go but something changed between father and me. Back at home; he took me aside to his study where only the adults entered. From a jar, he pulled out the amulet with my stone and laced it on my neck.

"Dear daughter," my father began in his slow but wise voice, "you have proven time after time your amazing tracking abilities, but until today you have never exhibited this new ability."

"And what is that, father?" my naive brain asked.

"The ability to see beyond our time, our lives, and to see the fates of others."

"But father, it just seemed that by killing that griffin, we would be doing more harm to ourselves. It has a higher purpose."

"And how do you know? Perhaps you felt sympathy for the animal?"

"No, father, this was different. I have led you and my brothers on many hunts and never felt any remorse towards our game. In the hunt, the prey must always lose."

"Time will tell if your judgment is correct. You must learn to harness the power within you." He gently touched the amulet hanging around her neck. "This will augment and channel your force. Wear it always and you will learn your abilities."

"But how father, how will I learn? How do you know?" My dad stroked his beard as if recalling a great memory.

"Your great grandfather had such an ability and foretold that another of our lineage would also carry this power. I believe you are that one. I will teach you what I know. The rest, you will have to discover on your own."

A log crackled as it tumbled from the fire, breaking the hold of the story.

"What powers have you discovered since then?" inquired Stonewall.

"How about turning these stones into silver," Burbon brought a handful of pebbles.

"Money! Is that the only thing you think of?" Taro knocked the rocks out of his hands. "Did you consider how I started the fire tonight that cooked our meal? Neither one of you could have done it rubbing sticks together in this wet bog." Taro gestured by placing two bolt shafts together.

"Prove it!" taunted Burbon. Taro raised her hands into the air.

"Somectra vascula!" she yelled. The pile of wood next to them ignited into a fiery explosion.

"What do you think, trader?" Taro's brow furrowed; the little man had disappeared. "Where did that little chicken go?" A pair of eyes blinked behind a bush.

"I believe," Burbon yelled. "I believe! Promise me you won't do that to me."

Stonewall asked Taro. "Why didn't you use this power during our battle with the gargoyles?"

"Magic demands intense concentration. In battle, it is hard to focus and not be injured while trying to conjure a spell. It is draining physically. I can conjure the fire once but to do two or more times in a row would be beyond my strength."

"Got any water spells handy?" asked Burbon. A large foot kicked the wood and beat the second fire out.

"Sorcery is not needed to put fires out," stamped Stonewall. "Your heart and spirit are strong elf, but beware. Magic can corrupt the purest of souls."

"My magic is limited; fire is the only thing I can conjure, although with more exposure to the amulet, my abilities may grow. Perhaps it will help us on our journey."

"Speaking of our journey, how far before we reach the next stone?" Taro reached into her pouch and removed the map. Burbon grabbed it from her. The map didn't pull away from Burbon as it did in the castle

"See! It likes me now." He looked down but was puzzled. "Oh no, there's nothing on it, the living map is blank."

"You fool, look at how it is breathing. The poor thing is sleeping," Taro pointed out. Burbon placed his head down to hear it murmuring in its sleep.

"Wake up, little map, I want to know where we're going." He pinched the paper in an effort to rouse it awake. It stirred slowly and then peered at Burbon. Then it shrieked uncontrollably and pulled itself towards Taro.

"What the hell is wrong with that thing?" Burbon was exasperated.

"Enough! Rest. We will have a full day of travel tomorrow." Stonewall pulled out his bedding and lay down. Burbon sulked to his bed.

"Stupid map," he muttered. The three settled into a deep slumber. The fire embers burned and smoldered in the darkness. A twig broke in the distance and a silent curse filled the air. Yellow eyes flashed in the dark and disappeared into the night.

8

Dinner of Three

The morning light brought little relief as the fog of the swamp shrouded the suns. The three were silent; the weather affected their mood and spirit. Burbon rolled up his bedding while the others secured their belongings. Taro placed her new bolts in her quiver and locked her crossbow to her back. Stonewall was disturbed by the movement of the mist.

"We need to get moving. Now," he commanded.

"All right, we're coming. Hold your sword. Another moment is not going to kill us," Burbon whined. Stonewall's silence disturbed Taro.

"Is something wrong, warrior? Did you see something?" she asked.

"The swamp feels unsettled. The sooner we travel through it, the better I will feel." He walked into the thick mist. Burbon bundled his belongings as he kept pace with Stonewall's big steps.

"The swamp feels unsettled? The swamp's felt unsettled ever since the slandoran tried to bite my head off."

For the next while, the splash of their boots was the only sound heard in the fog. Gnarled tree roots grew along the water's edge. Spiky beetles flew through the air, feeding on nearby animals. One beetle floated above Burbon's head again and again, hoping to land on his neck. Burbon swished the beetle away with his dagger. The beetle landed on a tree and Burbon readied his dagger to split the beetle. The beetle scratched its back while Burbon stabbed the tree. In a flash, he sliced the beetle in two, causing it to burst into black spores.

"No one tries to bite Burbon without paying the ultimate price. It will never bother me again." He froze, as he smelt the air. The black spores had a pungent smell that made Burbon almost retch his breakfast. "What is the awful smell?"

"Stink beetle. You just chopped one in half. It's a signal to other beetles. They usually release the smell to tell other beetles that food is nearby," answered Stonewall.

"More of them are going to show up?" Burbon looked sick.

"Leave it to you, Burbon. If you have two choices you always will pick the worst one," added Taro.

"Why don't you use your magic and burn the smell away," he mocked.

"Magic takes energy. I'd have nothing left if I had to clean up everyone of your mistakes," she answered. Burbon was about to respond when he slam\ed into Stonewall's back. Burbon fell backwards into a mud puddle.

"Why don't you keep moving, Stonewall? Walking into you is like walking into a...a..."

"Stonewall," Taro added.

"Yeah," he responded. Stonewall raised his hand to silence their talk.

"What's wrong?"

"We are not alone." Stonewall stared straight into the mist.

"Is it another slandoran?" worried Burbon. He saw movement at the end of the swamp's edge.

"It's worse," responded Taro as small shapes emerged from the mist.

Their heads were bald with hideous tattoos extending from their faces to their bare chests. The tattoos were ritual, documenting everything they kill...and eat. They carry primitive weapons sharpened with deadly accuracy. Burbon looked down to study their faces—they had one main feature that stopped him from considering them a threat.

"They're pygmies! I can squish them under my boot." Burbon's assessment of their stature was accurate. It would take five of them standing on their shoulders to match his small height.

"Don't let their size fool you. Their tribe is called the Vorians and they are fierce fighters. Their hunting parties search for slandoran prey or other large creatures to take back to their village." Stonewall watched their gathering mass. "Today we are their game."

"You mean," Burbon gulped.

"They're cannibals, little man," answered Taro. "They'll eat anything. Even you." From the fog, a miniature spear flew into the tree behind them.

"Do we fight?" asked Burbon as a dozen more emerged from the fog.

"No, they travel in huge parties of hundreds. We run." As Stonewall pushed into the fog, a small metal weapon with spiked balls spun like a top in the air smashing into a tree by Taro.

"Now!" she yelled. Burbon saw the face of one of the Vorians. His grin revealed a nasty row of razor teeth. Burbon required no further encouragement. The three rushed into the fog bank. Their feet smashed into the mud, their footprints filling with water. Close behind, they heard a strange guttural language as the Vorians screamed commands at each other. Burbon caught up with Taro as she was bounding over a small boulder.

"Can we outrun them?" he yelled.

"I think so, because of their size they shouldn't be able to run as fast as we can. I hope your short legs are up for the challenge."

"I can travel a great amount of distance with the proper motivation," Burbon answered.

Burbon caught movement from his left as a spiked branch tumbled from above. Burbon pushed Taro to her right. The tree crushed the ground inches from their landing spot. They looked up to see Stonewall's outstretched hand.

"Be careful, they have laid out traps to slow us down."

"That trap would have done more than slow us down," Burbon replied.

"We must find higher ground!" Stonewall commanded. The three veered out of the low-lying swamp onto a small rise. The view was heart stopping. From all angles there was a mass of arms and legs as tiny Vorians chased their quarry. They had been herded from all sides like cattle. Burbon realized there was no escape.

"I hope I give them indigestion," he gulped.

"They'll not get a piece of me so easily," Stonewall barked. The tide of little bodies rushed towards him and he slashed his mighty broadsword to cut a swath out of the masses. Their bodies and weapons went flying in all directions. Taro pulled out one of her flare bolts and aimed at the forefront of the incoming mass. She loosened the bolt and it ignited the ground. A group of natives went screaming into retreat.

By a nearby large rock, the Vorians pushed a small catapult into position. In its scoop, was a spore like mass with painful needles sprouting out its edges. Burbon stared at the machine.

"Do something," yelled Taro as she pulled back another bolt to fire at an incoming mass. Burbon looked around his feet and spied a flat rock. He picked it up and aimed, squeezing one of his eyes shut. He hurled it through the swamp. Once, twice, three times, the rock skipped over the water until smashing the little catapult to pieces.

"Good shot, Burbon," complimented Stonewall as he kicked a swarm of Vorians into the air.

"I was always good at games at the fair," he replied as a metal chain flew through the air and wrapped around his feet. He teetered and then fell face first into the swamp.

"Help me! I'm drowning!" he gurgled as his head stuck out of the ankle-deep water. He watched two groups of Vorians slinging thread-like ropes behind them. Before he could move, they threw their ropes around his torso, pinning him deeper into the water. The little savages jumped from rock to rock intent on tying up their prey. Burbon struggled to stand while his hands were useless as the rope tightened and lashed his arms to his body. Burbon turned into the face of a Vorian who was intent on making the trader his catch. He stood on Burbon's boot with his spear as if he had conquered a new land. Burbon kicked his foot outward, sending the small native headfirst into the water. The Vorian jumped up and spit out water. He pulled his spear and with unexpected speed leapt toward Burbon. He landed a second time on the same foot and before Burbon could swat him away, he rammed his spear into Burbon's big toe.

"Ahhh!" Burbon screamed and lost his balance, landing on his back in the swamp.

Taro grabbed another bolt from her quiver and aimed at an oncoming mass. Before she could launch it, the shaft exploded into shards from a jagged rock. She turned as a living mass of bodies jumped on her back. They threw ropes around her torso to bind her. She was lost underneath a sea of arms and legs.

Stonewall rose above their onslaught. He swung his mighty sword over and over, knocking dozens off their feet and into the swamp. They climbed over each other like ants; standing on each other, pushing their weight against Stonewall's strength. The warrior swung dozens of times, but they returned over and over like a swarm. His swung slower as his body became tired. His sword finally was too heavy to swing and dropped from his hand. He punched into the mass but could not connect with any force. His blows were like hitting wet hay.

"By my father's strength," he yelled, fighting them to the last. Their weight finally became too much and he fell on his back, crushing many of his attackers. Before he could get up, the tiny natives circled with their ropes.

All three travelers were bound from head to toe. The natives' little hands carried the three like ants robbing a picnic, carrying their meal to their final destination. As Burbon was carried, he watched a rock in the path. As they walked over it, the impact with the rock mercifully knocked him out.

Burbon woke up suddenly, not knowing if it has been seconds or hours since he lost consciousness. He saw a huge fire burning in the darkness. He moved his head to his right to see Taro bound as securely as him. He lifted his chin and noticed Stonewall lying on the ground with his hands and legs bound together. But as he stared straight ahead, the next sight sent chills straight to his bones. Around him hundreds of eyes stare out of the darkness, their mouths salivating. The sound of their gnashing teeth filled the air.

Behind the mass of natives, a small village was with tiny huts made of twigs and mud. Racks of poles were laid out for drying meat. Spears leaned blade down against thatched walls. Clotheslines covered with animal skins ran between the huts. He stopped looking at the scenery, he was there for their dinner.

A drum thumped in the background and the natives formed a circle. They thumped their feet into the dirt in a strange ritual matching the rhythm of the drum. It beat louder and the natives circled faster. Burbon stared at the procession. Suddenly the drum stopped. All eyes faced to the left of them. Burbon strained his head against the ropes to see who the focus of their attention was. A larger native wearing a wooden mask walked into the circle as the natives stepped aside, allowing him to enter. Burbon whispered to Stonewall, the ropes biting into his neck.

"Is this guy some sort of witch doctor?" he asked.

"Almost. He is the village's necromancer. He will have some magic abilities. He decides who should be sacrificed to the gods and who should be eaten by the tribe," Stonewall answered.

"Delightful choice," responded Burbon.

The necromancer yelled to quiet the crowd. Then he turned his attention to the captives. He strolled over to Stonewall and looked up. Way up. He raised his hands to the sky and faced the villagers.

"O mancavor nata!" he chanted. The villagers screamed back, "O mancavor nata!" The necromancer drew a strange symbol in the ground before Stonewall.

"You're too big to waste as a sacrifice, Stonewall. I bet they just made you the main course," Burbon commented.

"Not while there is a breath left in my body," he snarled while straining to create slack in the ropes. The necromancer stepped in front of Burbon. He turned his head side to side as if sizing up the little trader. The necromancer faced the crowd and yelled, "O mancavor brota!" The villagers returned the words, "O mancavor brota!"

"If I'm a meal," said Stonewall, "then you're the appetizer."

"I hope you choke on my bones," Burbon swore at the necromancer.

Taro groggily woke up. "What?" she started.

"You might want to sleep through this next part," suggested Burbon.

The necromancer paced around Taro unsure of what to make of her elfish features. She snarled to startle him, but his eyes remain fixed on her face. Finally, he nodded and turned to the villagers.

"O Caulor vonoata! O caulor Vonoata!" He repeated over and over again. The natives screamed the words back in unison. "O Caulor vonoata! O caulor Vonoata!" they chanted in a feverish pitch.

"I have a bad feeling that Taro is the sacrifice," Burbon moaned. He tried with newfound energy to break his bonds. Both he and Stonewall struggled without success. The bonds were too tight.

The necromancer grinned at Taro and flashed an evil smile with rotting teeth. He raised his spear into the air, ready to plunge it into her heart. Her eyes smoldered and a strange fire flowed across her pupils. The anger of her helplessness overwhelmed her. The necromancer yelled one last time.

"Ma secruptes van oscans!" and jerked his weapon downwards. It was the last action he ever made. His body was engulfed in a flame bursting from Taro's eyes. The blaze soared at the necromancer, incinerating his body and the ropes that binded her. His ashes littered the ground, the only evidence that anything had stood before her.

"Remind me not to get her angry," exclaimed Burbon his eyes wide with shock. Taro fell to ground weak from her exertion.

"Watch how the villagers are reacting," directed Stonewall. Burbon surveyed the crowd; he couldn't imagine a worse fate than being eaten. All around them, the little people stared in amazement at Taro. They turned their heads to each other to understand what had happened. Their eyes showed a darkness that chilled Burbon's soul. *What vengeance could these little natives plan next?* Slowly one by one, they stepped forward with unknown intent. Suddenly, they all knelt before Taro with their hands outstretching on the ground before her. Taro worked herself free of her last remaining bonds. As she stood, the villagers chanted "Ali Mandran! Ali Mandran!"

"Way to go, Taro! Because of your fire spell, we've gone from the main course to the guest of honor." Taro reviewed Burbon's ropes.

"You're not out of the cooking pot yet, trader," she jeered. Burbon looked nervously at Stonewall.

"She's joking right?" he asked. Taro cut Stonewall's and Burbon's bonds. Burbon watched the still kneeling congregation.

"What are you going to with these guys, march them over a cliff?"

"There is no need, they pose us no threat now," stated Stonewall.

"Do you always have to do the noble thing, Stonewall? Is there no malice within that large frame?" asked Taro.

"I only kill that which tries to kill me. You now hold their fates in your hands."

"Why don't you decide what you'd like these little people to do?" she asked Burbon. He looked nervously to the pots and meat racks in the background.

"This may sound strange, but surviving being eaten has really increased my appetite. Do you think they would cook us a meal?"

9

The Making of a Trader

The next morning as the suns reach the middle of day, Taro crossed the last swamp waters and crossed into the wastelands. The small Vorians stopped at the border as if hitting an invisible wall. They stared at Taro with pained faces as if they would lose their idol. Slowly they turned one by one and disappeared into the swamp mist. The last native grinned back with razor teeth as he vanished into the fog.

"I hope we have seen the last of them. They make my skin crawl," Burbon shuttered.

"You weren't too scared to eat their supplies," said Taro.

"What do you expect," Burbon waved his arms. "Their portions were so tiny it took platefuls to get full. A trader has to eat, doesn't he?"

"You made a pig of yourself. You ate so much slandoran meat that I expect you to slither the rest of the way," commented Taro.

"Slandoran! One ugly beast, but one sweet meal. If I ever return from this, I have to tell the tavern to bring some in." He licked his lips.

"Stop thinking with your stomach. We have a lot of ground to cover before dark," Stonewall advised.

"Tell us a story to pass the time, Burbon," said Taro.

"What do you want to know?"

"Tell us why you became a trader?" she asked.

"Where to begin?" as he stroked his mustache.

The pebbles scattered under the wheels of the horse drawn wagon. The horse stepped over a pothole while children ran across the street. They giggled as they rushed inside a candy store. As the dust settled, a young boy marched down the boardwalk. He combed his scraggly mustache, hoping some day it will grow in. He pulled out a wrinkled list with ten items written in black ochre, seven were crossed out. Three remain unchecked. Three needed items that will complete his list. He fingered a small pouch hanging from his belt with a number of soft and hard objects bouncing inside. His favorite teacher had assigned him and his class the list and he intended to finish it. He looked at the suns above. It was almost time to return to the school. If he was late, he won't win the contest.

He scanned the street—*where can I find the seventh item, a coin from a faraway region.* He scrambled through the currency in his pocket. The five coins were all unfortunately local. He sat on the edge of the boardwalk trying to plan a way to get a foreign coin. He was so deep in thought; he almost missed the stranger walk by. He looked up and saw the strange features of a mainlander—a rugged face with a bushy beard covered in dirt. Mainlanders lived in the mountains in hermit like cabins and only ventured into town periodically for supplies. *Maybe he'll have a foreign coin.*

The boy ran up to the mainlander and tugged on his cloak. "Sir, Sir. Do you carry any foreign coins?" The mainlander stopped and peered down at him.

"The beggars get younger every time I venture into town. My money is for my own use, now go away," he swept his hand to dismiss him away.

"Sir, Sir," the boy quipped not ready to give up. "I'm not asking for your money, I'm willing to trade for it." He reached into his pocket and pulls out his five coins. The mainlander was amused and bent down.

"None of these are worth very much," he pondered pushing the coins around in the boy's hand. "What are you looking for?" and he pulled a number of coins out of his pouch. The boy looked excitedly throughout the coins. *Local, local, local, there must be one foreign coin.* All ten coins were in local currency, he was disappointed.

"Thanks for letting me look," the boy replied and turned away.

"Wait!" said the mainlander. Would this be of interest?" And he pulled out a dirty iron coin from the shores of Brine.

"Yes!" the boy replied, his heart swelled.

"I'll trade this coin for your five coins," the mainlander asked.

The boy didn't hesitate in his response, "Two coins." The mainlander laughed.

"Two coins it is—you drive a hard bargain. You'll be a merchant someday." He handed him the coin and patted his head before marching down the boardwalk to the general store.

Number eight! The boy danced down the street. *Time had almost run out. Maybe I should return to the school?* He ran; his school was blocks away. If he didn't get there in time, his items would be disqualified. He ran around a side street to avoid a rider and his horse.

The boy stopped dead in his tracks. In an alleyway across the street, it sparkled under a dumpster. *Number nine.* Burbon navigated around two wagons, avoided a hungry dog, and narrowly missed a fresh steaming pile of manure. He could almost feel the object in his hands as it gleamed under the dumpster. He strided with purposefulness towards his prize.

He slammed into a huge body and fell on his backside. He looked up into the huge face of his classmate Turgune.

"Well what do we have here? Why are you in such a hurry, Bur?" Turgune asked.

Stonewall stopped and looked back at Burbon. "Bur?" he asked.

"Apparently some people find my personality abrasive and because of my size they called me..." Burbon started.

"Bur! Like the weed that sticks to your tunic?" laughed Taro. "A better name for you I have not heard!"

"Can I continue my story?"

"Please continue...Bur," chuckled Stonewall.

"None of your business, Turgune." Burbon lifted himself up. "You big fat lumpuss," Burbon whispered under his breath. Turgune was large. Very large. Dirty black disheveled hair covered his face, which was a good thing. His frame was massive, tipping the scales at three hundred pounds. But Turgune's mass was not muscle, but a blubbery, saggy weight. Under that weight was a bully looking for a victim.

"Bur, what's in the bag? Got some candy for me?" His chubby fingers reached towards Burbon's belt.

"Leave it alone, Turgune." Burbon backed away. Turgune grinned, showing off his blackened teeth.

"Bur, let me see what you have collected for the scavenger hunt at school?" There was no mistaking Turgune's menace. He intended to shake Burbon down and keep whatever fell out. Once Turgune grabbed you, there's was no escaping his grasp. Turgune lunged at Burbon who dashed between his legs. He ran towards the wooden dumpster with its gleaming prize. Object number nine—a rock sized piece of limestone. As Burbon admired his prize, a shadow darkened the ground beneath him.

"Let's have look Bur. Give it here." Turgune's massive frame filled the alleyway and he bent his knees, lowering his center of gravity. Burbon would not sneak through his legs a second time. Burbon used the only weapon he had.

"Let's talk about this, Turgune. I have to return to school to get these items back. But if you let me pass, I will be happy to give you some of them after the contest." Turgune scratched his thumb on his chin, contemplating the exchange. He looked at Burbon.

"But, Bur, what if I don't want to wait." Turgune wore a wicked smile. He knew Burbon was not in a bargaining position. Burbon looked at the alleyway. The buildings were made of rocks with mortar. Burbon ran his hand along the wall. None of the rocks stuck out far enough to get a climbing handhold. In the corner, a log door was closed. *A back door for the establishment to throw its garbage out.* Burbon stepped backward and grasped the handle on the door.

Damn, it's locked. Burbon's hand slipped off the door handle. He was cornered like an animal.

"Relax, Bur, just give me what's in the bag and I won't have to hurt you." Turgune waved his hand for Burbon to pass over his spoils.

You won't get my hard work that easy. He knocked vigorously on the door.

"Nobody's home," chided Turgune. Then the door opened. The cook walked fives steps with his steaming pot of animal fat and then stopped. He seems more surprised than the two boys and the three of them stood still, gaping at each other. Burbon was the first to break the hold. He kicked the pot out the cook's hand and into the face or Turgune.

"Have a bite, fatso!" Burbon yelled as the hot liquid flew onto Turgune's chest. The fat was mostly congealed but the hot bubbly mess drenched his clothes. Burbon ran into the building to avoid the wrath of Turgune and the cook.

"Get out of my tavern," the cook yelled from the alleyway. Burbon quickly ran through the kitchen and dashed into a smoke-filled room of sullen patrons. One looked up at the intrusion.

"Child, do you work here?" he asked.

"No," he answered, "and I have to make a delivery." He flew through the swinging door of the tavern and slammed into Turgune's gut. Burbon spun around and fell onto the dirty street.

"You're going to pay for this," Turgune pointed at his clothes and cocked his fist behind his head.

"Give my regards to the dirt. Bur!"

"Am I interrupting something, boys?" They both looked up to the oncoming carriage of Mr. Orno, their teacher. He was tall, gaunt yet regal in a blue suit. Burbon saw himself in the reflection in the teacher's glasses.

"Aren't you both supposed to be returning to school from the scavenger hunt?" Mr. Orno raised one eyebrow up for effect.

"We were just heading back, Mr. Orno." Turgune put Burbon in a headlock and guided him down the street towards the school. Turgune's tight grip prevented Burbon from speaking. Mr. Orno intervened.

"That's where I'm heading as well. Jump into the wagon and we'll go together." Turgune stopped in surprise and loosened his grip. Burbon made his escape, trotted towards the carriage and jumped into the back. Turgune remained rooted to the ground.

"I'll catch up later, sir, I have one more thing to pick up." Turgune ran off in the opposite direction of school. Mr. Orno lifted up the reins and tapped the horses to move forward. Burbon climbed up front and sat beside him.

"Having some bully problems, Burbon?" Mr. Orno asked while looking straight ahead.

"Yes, sir."

'Don't worry, son, everyone goes through it. Besides, you seem to be holding your own."

"Not everyone is as small as me, sir." Burbon looked up into Mr. Orno's glasses but could not see his reflection again. Mr. Orno changed the conversation.

"How did you make out with the scavenger hunt?"

"Almost perfect, sir, see my list." He handed the list to Mr. Orno who handed the reins to Burbon as he looked over the checklist.

"Nine out of ten is very good, Burbon. I dare say you will win this contest."

"Not if someone gets the tenth item. Where can someone find a Doric's cube?"

"Let me tell you a secret, every year the teachers put that item in and every year no one is able to find it."

"Give me a hint, I was able to gather the rest of the items. I bet I could find it".

"I bet you could, Burbon. You have the makings of a great collector or a trader. But the truth is that the Doric's cube doesn't exist. It's a myth for students to waste their time trying to find it."

"What does it do?" Burbon was interested.

"The cube is a wish maker, allowing the holder to create anything you want. Riches worth more than an entire King's treasury. But the wishes are never permanent, the cube's wealth never lasts. In one rotation of the moon, the objects revert back to the cube. Anyone who was paid with the wealth of the cube soon finds that it has disappeared." Burbon was hooked.

"Someday I will find it, Mr. Orno. I will find it and I will have more wealth than anyone in town." Orno took the reins and stopped the carriage.

"Better people than you have tried with much nobler of intentions. I doubt it will be found by someone motivated by greed." Burbon blushed.

"Sorry, teacher. If I did find it, I'm sure I would share its wealth with my father and friends."

Mr. Orno started the horses forward again.

"I wouldn't spend time chasing a myth, Burbon. And remember, sometimes the journey is more valuable than the prize." The horse and carriage arrived at the schoolyard.

"And I won the contest that year. And the next. But I never did find the Doric's cube. But as I grew older, I became a trader in the hopes of finding it and other precious items," Burbon completed his story as dry moss crunched under his feet. He surveyed the blackened land in front of them.

"Your whole motivation is greed? I could have surmised that without your story," Taro shook her head in disgust.

"No, no, no! Let me finish. I enjoy the prize; it is how I make my livelihood. But trading for something new, something that no one else has ever seen—that is my excitement, my adventure. That's what drives me. I love trading and the scavenger hunts taught me to determine what items are important and what price people will pay to have them."

"Maybe your talents will come in handy in the days ahead," conceded Taro.

"That almost sounds like an apology," laughed Burbon.

"Don't read too much into that, trader." The three continued their journey, their thoughts no longer distracted by Burbon's tale.

The day was long, and the travelers were wearied from their journey. In the distance, a tall pole stood alone in the barren landscape with a frayed rope hanging from a signpost. As the trio approach the post, they had difficulty reading the sign. It was written in a language unfamiliar to all three. A buzzard sitting on the pole, opened its wings and took flight into the sky.

"What kind of place have we entered?" Burbon asked. Taro scanned a small town in the distance as Burbon kicked a strange rock in the sand. He let out a surprised yelp as he realized the rock was a grotesque skull.

"The realm of Valdawn. The land of the dead," Stonewall replied.

10

The Town of the Living Dead

The living map shuddered in Taro's hands as a cool breeze blew from the north. The twin suns glowed red and purple on the horizon. Taro placed the map back in her tunic.

"We must pass through this town to reach the next gem's location," she pointed to the buildings.

"It's getting dark. We should make camp," Stonewall commented.

"In a ghost town? I'm tired but couldn't we push on a bit further," Burbon gulped.

"And waste this shelter? The wind is cold. The town will be our camp," Stonewall proceeded towards the nearest dwelling. They passed a sign, hanging on one chain that banged against a storefront wall. No lights emanated from the town, which slipped into darkness. Taro grabbed a piece of broken wood from the ground. She concentrated and ignited the wood, causing flames to sprout from the end.

"Can you do anything else besides make fire?" Burbon asked.

"Magic is fickle," her teeth gleamed in the darkness. "Some great wizards in the world are only good at preparing a few spells. Do you not know the rules of magic?" asked Taro.

"No, why don't you educate me?" Burbon responded sarcastically.

"Sorcery is a talent passed down through the ages, usually running through a family's lineage. Magic is ability just like archery and trading. It's a skill that you have a talent for, but you can't be good at everything." Taro acknowledged, "A sorcerer can't conjure hundreds of spells. If he or she is lucky, they can do several very well."

"Can you do any magic besides creating fire?" wondered Burbon.

Taro hesitated. "No, although I thought I could when I was young."

Stonewall interrupted and pointed ahead. "You two go to the house at the end of the street, I'm going to scout the area."

"I will scout as well. I will look for metal tips for my crossbow," commented Taro. Burbon stared to a mansion that stood on a slight rise overlooking the town.

"You want me to go to a spooky old house all by myself?" he stuttered.

"Yes," both Stonewall and Taro answered.

"Ok," he responded nonchalantly. "I need a fireplace so I can boil water for a bath."

"That's a good idea," answered Stonewall. "Don't use up all the hot water!"

"Don't leave me alone too long and you have a deal." Burbon marched down the street.

"I'll meet you at the house before the moons cross the horizon," Taro said. She walked over to an abandoned blacksmith's store. Stonewall went to the town jail looking for weapons.

I wonder why no one lives here, he thought.

The huge door to the mansion creaked open and Burbon stepped into a spider's web.

"Blast! Get this thing out of my eyes," he exclaimed. He tripped over a footstool and slammed into an antique couch. He inhaled a wall of dust.

"Cough, cough. I swear I've been here less than a minute and I prefer the little cannibals' village over this house." He spied an oil lamp sitting on a table. "About time I had some good luck." He turned the dial on the lamp and sparks ignited the wick. Its feeble light illuminated the sitting room. Antique chairs were placed in a cluster around the room. Flowery wallpaper covered three walls and dollies covered the tops of the tables. The couch's upholstery was covered in a garish purple mixed with green leaves. Ceramic vases and books lined the dusty shelves.

"I wouldn't be caught dead in a place like this," as he scanned the feminine decorations. He peered through to the kitchen and spied a water crank leading to a well. A board creaked from the landing above.

"I didn't mean that literally," he yelled to no one in particular. He walked across the room and trotted up the stairs. The first room on his right was a bedroom with a huge four-post bed and a fireplace in the far wall. A gold-rimmed mirror hung over the fireplace. He placed the lamp on an end table. "I don't care what those two say, I want this room." He used the flame from the lamp and ignited some dry moss and kindling in the fireplace. He blew on the flame. He added chopped wood from a bucket next to the fireplace before leaving the room.

Minutes later he returned with a bucket of water and placed it on a hook above the fire to boil. He found a large tub used for washing clothes and turned it into a bathtub. The water bubbled and he poured it into the tub. He disrobed while spying some bath rocks in a container by the door. "Why not," as he tossed a few of them into the water. The stones bubbled and dissolved to form a soapy mass.

Burbon slid one foot into the tub. "Ouch!" he exclaimed as the water scalded his foot and he jumped away. He grabbed the remainder of the bucket's well water and mixed its cool contents into the tub. He placed the bucket back on the floor and slid effortlessly into the tub. Immediately, his tired sore muscles found relief. He surveyed his tiny oasis. "I'm exhausted. Nothing will make me leave this tub."

The fire went out. Burbon was unfazed. "Stupid fire—must be a draft in the chimney." He closed his eyes and felt a gust of wind. He turned his head, straight into two bloodshot eyes.

"Ahhhhhhhh," the scream curdled through his throat as he leapt out of the tub. He stumbled towards the bed and grabbed the sheet on top. His teeth shivered but not from the cold. The room was empty. "What the heck?" Burbon's fear became confusion. "I know I saw something," as he gripped the sheet closer to keep warm. He stepped back to the tub and looked into the mirror. The face that stared back at him was shaggy.

"Yech, I need to shave." He pulled the sheet tighter. He looked closer in the mirror. Behind him, he saw movement. He turned but was greeted by the emptiness of the room. "Where is it?" And then the sheet moved in his hands. There was no wind to cause its movement—the sheet was alive!

"Ahhhhhhh," Burbon dropped the cloth and ran naked out of the bedroom door to the hallway. The sheet formed a luminescence mass that flew through the wall into the stairwell. Burbon ran straight into the waiting grasp of the creature. "Ohhhhhh," he fainted while tumbling down the stairs.

"Crack!" Stonewall stopped as the branches crumbled beneath his feet. He had searched the perimeter of the town and found no sign of activity. Every building was deserted, with the smell of decay throughout the air. Most buildings were intact. No damage, no broken windows, all valuables remained. It was a puzzle. *Where had the inhabitants gone?* No destruction. No bodies. No answers. He looked ahead at the one area he hadn't searched. The fence kept most visitors out the town cemetery.

A wrought iron fence surrounded the headstones. A statue of an angel stood in an archway over the entrance. As Stonewall walked beneath her, he noticed she knelt in prayer. He stepped towards a tombstone. The name Georgian Philips was engraved along its face. No date, no eulogy. He turned to another headstone with a different name and again no date was listed.

How odd. Most headstones were new with only a few weathered ones. In the center of the graveyard was a huge crypt with a stone gargoyle sneering down over the tombstones. Stonewall tapped the gargoyle's chin. The gargoyle's face stayed stationary. *Good thing Burbon isn't here.* Even with his night vision from walking in the dark, it was hard to make out any details besides a large coffin in the center of the crypt. The coffin was made of stone with a huge slab over the top. Stonewall stood still and heard total silence. No sounds echoed off these walls. Stonewall noticed the slab was not perfectly flush with the top. He leaned over the edge to examine it closely. He pushed the slab and it grudgingly moved several inches. He peers into its dark depths. Empty.

A bony finger tapped him on a shoulder.

"Looking for me?" a menacing voice asked.

Taro kicked a rusted can through the door of a grocer's shop. Empty shelves lined the walls, dust covered a few pieces of hardware and a glass candy jar. Taro examined the store and the knotted planks of the floor creaked under her weight. A strange collection of animal trophy heads covered the wall. *Maybe a conversation piece for the storekeeper with his customers?*

The owner must have been a hunter. She walked into a storage closet. The walls were ten feet tall and the shelves were empty. Except on the very top row, a couple of small metal objects rested. *Could be something useful for a bolt tip.* She looked around for something to stand on. In the corner were two baskets, probably used for gathering fruit. She grabbed and stacked them. She stood on top of the second basket which bent under her slender frame. Her fingers grasped the top shelf and she ran her hand along it until it she touched something metal. Her left hand wrapped around a metal hook and she dragged it towards the edge. Suddenly the door to the storeroom slammed shut, sending the room into a complete darkness.

Terrific. She teetered on the basket. *I'm about to fall with a sharp heavy metal object in my hand and I can't see a thing.* She tried to stand perfectly still, her heightened elfin eyes adjusting to darkness. The gleam of moonlight reflected under the door. A loud thud rung from the main store and her surprise almost knocked her to the floor. A shadow crossed by the edge of the door. *If that's Burbon,* as she jumped to the floor, placing the metal object in her pocket.

She kicked the door open ready to strangle Burbon's neck. No one was in the main room. The glass candy jar laid shattered on the floor. Taro looked around cautiously. The door from the outside swung open allowing the moonlight to cast shadows around the store.

"Wind," she muttered. She stepped over the glass. As she crossed to the door, one of the animals hanging from the wall grabbed her and pulled her through a hole in the wall.

Cold water splashed onto Burbon's face. He shook his head trying to recollect where he was. He propped his hands onto the stairs and looked into the face of a hideous white ghost.

"Ahhhhh!" He fainted a second time.

The water hit him again seconds later. He searched for the hideous face, shivering but not from the cold. He faced his tormentor.

"Stop fainting, I'm not going to hurt you," it yelled. Burbon looked into its misshapen face.

"That's easy for you to say. You're hideous!"

"Well you're no treat either. Besides this is my house you are trespassing in."

"Trespassing, but you're a..."

"A ghost! How very observant of you. That doesn't mean I can't own property. I was sleeping soundly until your splishing and splashing in the tub woke me." Burbon looked down at his nakedness and grabbed a cloth from a nearby end table to cover him.

"I think we got off on the wrong foot. My name is Burbon and I am a traveler coming through your fine town." The ghost spit on the floor and disappeared.

"Fine town! You obviously don't travel very much." Burbon studied the ghost as it glided down the stairwell and sat in a rocking chair. It wore a flowery semitransparent dress and had a face of a craggy old grandmother.

"Have a seat, Mr. Burbon, I will tell you about this great town of mine," she added sarcastically. Burbon sat at the opposite end of the couch adjacent to her.

"You don't have to sit so far from me, I won't bite," she frowned as her face morphed into a huge set of teeth and grinded a horrible bone breaking sound. Burbon jumped from the couch in fright.

"Relax," as she morphed back to her original form. "You living people have no sense of humor. Burbon's look of fear changed into dread but he moved no closer to the ghost. She continued with her story oblivious to Burbon's feelings.

"Many years ago, our town was a hub for travelers, a safe haven in a land of dangers. People stayed a day or two, bought supplies, rested, and moved on to the places they really wanted to go. That was until *he* arrived. The stagecoach arrived at dusk, the usual time. But its passenger was anything but usual. His tall frame barely made it through the doors. He looked like a spider exiting out of the stagecoach. He reached up to take a large metal trunk off the roof of the coach. He lifted it over his shoulder like it was air. The suns were setting making the light dim, but his eyes glowed like embers. Like death. He called himself Crom."

"This home was an Inn. I have lots of rooms. The moment he walked through my doors; I had a premonition that I should turn him away. Claim the inn was full. But money was scarce, and greed held my tongue. He had lots of money. It was a mistake that I regretted for the remainder of my life. And every second of my afterlife."

"Was he some kind of wizard? A mercenary?" asked Burbon. The ghost looked over at him, her lips expanded to twice their size and stretched towards Burbon.

"How can I tell this story if you insist on interrupting me?" she screamed. Burbon sunk into the couch.

"How rude of me. Please continue," he stammered. Her lips smacked back to her face.

"Despite his appearance, he was quite a charming man. And his abundance of money made him a hit with the townspeople. He paid for a full month and walked through town every day. He claimed he was a doctor, selling elixirs to prolong lives, to heal sores, to cure sickness. Yet it was a ruse for what he really intended. He was a soul taker."

"It was hard to notice what he was doing. A few people died at first, their bodies littered our cemetery. More looked pale or sickly, while others barely acknowledged your presence. I went into the bakery and Loungo the Baker treated me like he didn't even know me. I would learn later that he was already dead. His body hadn't figured that out yet. I went to see our law enforcer, Fat Toby, to tell him my fears. As soon as I walked into the jail, Crom faced me. He greeted me with a grin and raised his hat in mock politeness."

"Good day, madam, I look forward to supper with you tonight." I nodded in agreement wanting to get away from his presence as quickly as possible. As soon as I spoke to Toby, I knew I was too late. His eyes were fixed on me, but they were sightless. I can't remember what I said but I know Crom remembered every word because he recited it back to me at supper."

"I had no other guests at the time and the room included one meal a day, so I often sat and ate with my guests. I made a simple meal hoping to get the ordeal over with quickly. Crom was in no rush and prolonged the meal. Just as he was wiping his mouth, he shared with me the news."

"You have a beautiful home here, have you ever thought of selling it?" He enjoyed making idle chitchat.

"No, never. Is there anything else I can get you, Mr. Crom? I feel like retiring early tonight." I really did feel tired, so much that I accidentally dropped one of dishes to the floor. Crom bent down to pick up the pieces. I felt dizzy as if the world was spinning around.

"Here, let me help you," he said as he eased me to the couch. I felt detached as if I was watching my body from above.

"Would you like any more to drink?" he asked. And he pulled a strange vial out of his coat. My tongue was too heavy to speak but my mind was clear enough to know what he had done.

"Don't bother to answer, your body is no longer under your control." I found it harder and harder to concentrate on his words. But I did have one moment of clarity where I saw Crom for what he really was. A light emanated from his entire body and every bone glowed. All I could do was watch as my soul flowed out of my body and into his. He was a monster and everyone in this town has become his victim."

"Is he still here?" Burbon inquired.

"Yyyyyyooooowwlllll!" she screamed. A glass vase shattered in the kitchen from her scream. "Didn't I say I hated to be interrupted," she glared.

"I thought you were done!" He stood and backed away from the couch. "Can you at least tell me your name?"

"I have no solid form; my name is immaterial now! You must leave now before he finds you. You cannot fight him; you can only run. Go now, as fast as you can."

"I can't. I came with two others who are searching the town. I must go and warn them."

"No!" The ghost flew through Burbon to block his exit. He shivered as a dark cold chill shook his body. "They are lost to you. One of the other townspeople has surely found them by now. You are going to your death."

"They are my friends." Burbon was determined and ran upstairs to gather his belongings. On his return, the ghost was nowhere to be seen. His teeth chattered.

Get it together, Burbon. Gather Taro and Stonewall and get as far away from this cursed town as possible. He opened the large door and walked through the ghost as she hung upside down from the doorframe. Cold raced through his body.

"Stop doing that! You're going to stop my heart!" He noticed that she had a look of determination on her face.

"I was too late to save my town. I won't squander a second chance!"

Taro's arms were pinned beneath her. She felt hot breath at her neck. Her captor had her immobilized as if waiting for its next move. It would not get a chance. Taro worked her slender leg free and rammed it between the attacker's legs. He immediately loosened his grip. Taro spun around on the floor to face her assailant. His body was hairy with dirty matted fur with pincer like hands. He was shorter than Stonewall but just as wide. His face was skewed to the right as if an invisible hand was pulling it into that direction.

"What do you want from me?" she yelled.

"Your life," it replied with little feeling, "to trade for mine." Taro kicked his chest knocking him against the wall.

"You're going to have to work for it," Taro motioned the beast to approach. The moonlight glimmered off his teeth.

"It's nothing personal." His fist sent Taro through the hole in the wall into the main store. As she got up, the beast stuck its head through the wall.

He watched me the entire time I was in the store. How did I miss it? Nothing alive can fool me like that.

The beast slammed its foot to the floor as Taro avoided being crushed. She sprung up to her feet and into a fighting stance. He charged her, aiming his fist at her stomach. She evaded the blow, twisting to the side and stuck her foot out. She grabbed his oncoming fist and used his momentum to throw her attacker through the window into the street. Taro jumped out the broken window as he was picking the glass off its body. Taro marveled that none of the glass cut him.

"Can't you bleed?" as she punched him in the jaw. His head rebounded with little effect.

"I have no blood," as he cocked his fist back. Before he could land the blow, Burbon jumped on his shoulder.

"I don't know what you are, but hands off my friend!" as he gripped the monster's neck. The beast pulled Burbon off like a rag doll and prepared to slam him into the ground.

"We'll get two souls tonight!" he crowed.

"Enough! Crom will not get these souls," The ghost flew in front of the beast. "Let them go. Our lives are lost, don't endanger them as well. Crom will never honor his promise." Her words defeated the beast.

"I'm sorry," he declared and lowered Burbon to the ground.

"Good thing she came by. I wouldn't want to have hurt you," taunted Burbon to the creature.

"My reluctant hero," smiled Taro.

"Where's Stonewall? We have to get out of this town. Now!" commanded Burbon.

A huge bony hand cradled Stonewall's face and slammed him into a nearby tombstone. Stonewall's head rung from the impact.

"You picked the wrong town to visit, warrior. Didn't they teach you not to wander around graveyards at night?"

"Must have missed that lesson," as he knocked the skeleton back into the crypt. The skeleton's arm was jarred off. He picked it up and snapped back into its socket.

"Feel my power!" the skeleton yelled. Beneath Stonewall's feet, the ground stirred. Two hands grasped his boots, anchoring him to ground. He turned his body and was smashed back by the skeleton's bony fist.

"You have entered my domain, warrior. You are outnumbered."

"Then I will even the odds!" Stonewall grabbed his broadsword from his back and chopped both hands off at the wrists, freeing his feet. He advanced towards his attacker. "We'll see how you like the taste of my blade," and slashed right, taking the skeleton's arm at the elbow.

"You seem less threatening." Stonewall swung again taking both legs off at the pelvis. The skeleton stared up from a much shorter position. Stonewall twisted his blade behind his back and in a massive swing, took the skeleton's head off its shoulders. It landed on the top of the crypt. The skull head laughed hysterically while Stonewall watched in puzzlement.

"You are incapacitated, my flesh challenged foe. Do you want to share your joke with me?" The head laughed even louder at the question and gathered its senses to speak.

"You are worthy foe, warrior. But I'm afraid the joke is on you," the head spoke. Behind it, the severed arm crawled on the ground towards the skull. The trunk of the body rolled towards it. Both legs bent at the knee and marched towards the head like an inchworm. Before Stonewall could act, all bones went flying toward the head. In a whirlwind of motion, the bones rejoined to the skeleton's frame. He stood before Stonewall ready for a renewed attack.

"Warrior, you can't kill what's already dead!" It leapt at Stonewall knocking him down. The skeleton's teeth chattered towards Stonewall's face. "I'm going to eat you all up!"

Stonewall kicked it into a headstone sending pieces flying. Quickly, Stonewall took each arm and cut them into smaller pieces, and threw the remains away from the crypt. He chopped the legs and the rib cage in many pieces. The skull looked at him.

"How could you?" As an answer, Stonewall placed the skull on a flat gravestone and punted it off in the distance.

"Try to reform yourself now," growled Stonewall. He sheathed his blade. "I better find the others." As he walked to the cemetery entrance, he looked at the Stone Angel. "May your soul rest in peace," Stonewall walked into the waiting hands of his attacker. The skeleton smashed Stonewall back several paces with his bony first.

"Not very smart, warrior; it doesn't matter how small you make the pieces or how far part you throw them, I will always reform." The skeleton swung a rusty blade that nicked Stonewall's arm. Unable to defeat his foe, there was only one other avenue. He retreated. Stonewall dashed over to a tombstone near the entrance.

"I won't make it that easy," it gestured to the gravestones ahead of them. The ground exploded above a fresh grave. A half-decomposed woman pulled herself to her feet before Stonewall.

"Going my way, sailor?" she blocked his exit. Stonewall zigzagged around, not wanting to hit a woman, even a dead one. Two smaller skeletons appeared on either side of Stonewall. Both jumped from headstone to headstone, closing the gap within seconds. They leapt at him from either side as Stonewall fell to ground. Both skeletons slammed into each other, their bones flying everywhere. As Stonewall stood, the smell of rotting flesh overwhelmed him.

"I want to hold you nice and tight," the decomposed woman purred. Her grip was anything but ladylike. She squeezed an inhuman bear hug with a strength that did not match her size. *If her smell doesn't knock me out, I'll pass out from lack of air.* His lungs gasped and he fell backwards, slamming her body against a tombstone. Several of her ribs snapped from impact and she loosened her grip.

"Not nice for a first date," she yelled. Stonewall turned to face her. "I'm going to steal your heart," she cooed as her sharp fingernails clawed at his chest.

"Leave me," he cocked his left arm and aimed at her head, "alone!" His fist connected knocking her back to a nearby tombstone. Several skeletal bodies gathered at the gate of the cemetery, blocking his exit. Stonewall withdrew his broadsword and charged away from the entrance gate back towards the woman.

"I knew you'd come back to me," as she held her hands out to receive him. Stonewall ran and slammed his blade in the ground, using the momentum to propel him high into the air. He sailed over the woman and barely missed the tips of the fence posts surrounding the graveyard. He landed outside the cemetery and drew his sword back, ready to disembowel the first creature to attack. Many hands reached through the fence.

"Come back and play, warrior. I hunger for your flesh," the large skeleton beckoned through the fence. Unable to climb the wall, the others staggered through the cemetery.

Stonewall whirled around as a hand touched his back.

"Making friends?" asked Burbon. Stonewall's blade was inches from skewing him. "Was it something I said?" he quivered.

"No." Stonewall regained his composure. "Sorry, I thought you were someone dead." His shirt moved as though alive and he felt something wiggling. He pulled out a bony finger that tried to scratch his eye out. He tossed it back over the cemetery fence.

"We have no power outside of town," said the ghost as it flew overhead, "it is the source of our strength and the center of our weakness."

"Who are you?" commanded Stonewall, alert to another potential threat.

"A friend," said Burbon.

Taro stood behind them. "Apparently she and the things you met in the graveyard are some the town's former inhabitants."

"What are they and what do they want?" inquired Stonewall.

"There is no time for this," yelled the ghost. "All you have to understand is that there are worse horrors in this town than the graveyard. If you don't leave immediately, you will find out firsthand!"

"I need no further motivation," Stonewall replied.

"Follow me, I will show the quickest route out of town." The ghost flew ahead of them.

"Where did you meet her?" asked Stonewall.

"I'll tell you later," Burbon blushed recalling the bathtub. The buildings past behind them as they returned to the sign on the pole.

"Veer left around the circle of the town and it will take you through the rest of the barrens and into the mountains. Please go and do not return," she commanded.

Taro leapt to her right as a body dropped from the top of the pole. He landed and his movements were deliberate—the light of the moon illuminated the side of his face.

"I didn't know we had company. Let me welcome you to our charming town." The tall man's voice was shrill; he wore a black narrow hat and had eyes of fire. His teeth gleamed giving him the appearance of a venomous snake. Stonewall drew his sword and Taro readied her crossbow.

"You will find those ineffective against these townsfolk," smiled Crom. The shuffle of feet surrounded the travelers as the rest of the townspeople circled the small group.

"I'm so glad you three could join us," Crom said with macabre delight. He waved his arms to gain everyone's attention.

"Let's welcome our guests with a meal," he motioned them toward the ghost's house. He looked at Taro with interest. "I'm so hungry I could eat just about anything right now."

11

Supper of Souls

The inn was full of of townspeople in various stages of decay and torment wandering around the main level. Some sat in beautifully ornate chairs with high backs cushioned in green velvet. The dining area was in a large windowed room, which overlooked the darkness of the town. The ghost became solid to prepare food for the guests. The table had Stonewall, Taro, and Burbon seated with several townspeople standing behind them to prevent a hasty exit. At the head of the table, Crom sat while chewing on bones with obvious relish, feeding on the tension of his three guests. The townspeople watched the travelers like insects caught in a spider's web. Crom finished his bone and tossed it onto an empty plate.

"Please help yourself," he pointed to an unknown dish that was moving, "I hate to eat alone."

"I'll pass. I heard you like to add something to the food," sneered Burbon.

"Oh, really?" Crom was unconcerned and gazed towards the ghost in the kitchen. "I wonder who told you that?"

"What do you want with us?" snarled Taro, banging her fist on the table and knocking her wooden spoon to the floor. Crom was unfazed by her outburst and looked at Stonewall instead.

"Women! They want all the answers. Always asking a million

questions. Enough to drive a man to drink don't you think, warrior?" He toasted Stonewall whose face was a mask of fury.

"Answer her question or I will crush the life out of your body," Stonewall cracked his massive knuckles and for a spilt second Crom's face showed a glimmer of fear. He quickly regained his composure and pointed to several townspeople to press down on Stonewall's shoulders to prevent him from leaping across the table.

Crom signaled the ghost to come into the room. She floated over the table carrying a silver tray covered by a metal lid. She pulled off the lid to reveal a large globe. At first glance it seemed ordinary, but as the travelers stared closer, they noticed movement in the globe. To their horror, they realized that they are looking at the eyes of trapped souls. Their eyes blinked back in pleas of desperation. Crom tapped the globe to terrorize its residents further.

"You are a soul taker!" accused Burbon.

"Taker is such a dirty word. I prefer the term soul collector. And the three of you have the rare pleasure of observing my treasured collection!" answered Crom

Clap. Clap. Clap. Taro slapped her hands together in a slow rhythmic motion mocking Crom's performance.

"I've gone to a lot of trouble to bring you here tonight as our honored guests. You are about to embark on a journey that many have never taken," Crom continued. Taro looked into Crom eyes and lost herself for a split second.

She blinked and she was no longer in the inn. She turned around and saw the forest she grew up in as a child. A bird flew across the sky, its silhouette marking the ground. Taro raised her eyes and saw a small hawk perched in a tree. The wind blew through the woods carrying a sweet scent of pine. Taro felt the sounds and smells of the forest.

Where am I? One moment I'm sitting with a madman and the next I am home in my woods. Did I dream everything about Burbon and Stonewall? Or this the dream?

A crashing sound in a nearby thicket interrupted her thoughts. A golden stag burst through the trees and ran across the meadow to a small rise. Halfway across the meadow the stag stopped to stare back at Taro as if challenging her to a game of chase. It quickly galloped away.

I may as well follow this through. She pursued the stag as it bounded into a small cave opening. She focused on the opening as the darkness swallowed her in.

Stonewall's hatred was focused on Crom as he glared across the table. "I won't be added to your collection without a fight." Stonewall spit on Crom. It hit him on the cheek and dripped down his chin. Crom calmly wiped his face with a napkin.

"That's the beauty of my collection," he added. "There never is a fight." He stared back at Stonewall who returned his gaze. Their eyes meet in fiery combat. Stonewall blinked.

The Inn was gone. He sat at a rough wooden table in a small cabin. A steaming frothy cup laid across the table from him. *I'm home!* Several blacksmith tools were stacked in the corner by the door. On the table was a picture frame with a drawing of Stonewall's father holding his son in a headlock. A much younger Stonewall smirked under the tangle of long unkempt hair.

Stonewall was mesmerized by his father's eyes in the artist's sketch. Down the hall, a shadow passed, and a door slammed shut. Stonewall stood up from the table.

"Father," he inquired, but only silence answered. He stepped towards the bedroom door and placed his hand on the smooth brass handle. The handle turned and the door protested as he pushed. The door opened part way as Stonewall squeezed his large frame through. The darkness of the room swallowed up all of the light as he entered.

Crom walked behind Stonewall to the other end of the table. He looked at Burbon, but his face was blocked by the others standing around them.

Burbon tried to get his friend's attention but both Taro and Stonewall were oblivious to their surroundings as their eyes stared out into the distance.

What is the matter with those two? They look like they have already given up, thought Burbon.

"Despite what you may have heard, I can offer you more than you can imagine," stated Crom as he slowly moved around the table.

"And what would that be?" inquired the little trader.

"Why immortal life of course. Join me and you shall never die. Forever you may experience this world and its wonder."

"Immortal life?" Burbon yelled in anger while looking at the townspeople around him. "You call this immortality? I call this a living hell! No one here is happy; they are slaves to your desires. You've taken everything from them and you're selling this to me? I've traded many things in my life, but my soul is not for sale!" Burbon turned around to face Crom who peered deep into his eyes.

"It's really only a matter of how you see things," he smiled.

Burbon blinked and found himself back in his store. He walked over to his till, which is overfilling with currency. He held coins in his hands and let them drop back to the register.

How could I be home? The store's shelves were filled with new and interesting goods, some he had never seen before. He stepped down an aisle to the front of the store and scanned through the big glass window. The streets were swarming with patrons walking, running, and riding in various directions.

Never have I seen business so busy. It will be a good day for my store. He readied the store with last minute dusting. At the back of the shop, the storage room door swung open slightly. Burbon approached to close it but something sparkled in the darkness.

Eh, what's this? Another valuable to sell? Burbon cackled to himself. *This is too good to be true.* He walked towards the door and stepped into the darkness.

He stopped as the ghost flew out of the room.

"Do not enter, it is a trap for your soul! Crom gives us what we want most and when you accept it, you lose your soul in the bargain." She blocked entry into the room. Burbon could still feel the magnetic pull to the room.

"Where am I?" he implored the ghost.

"In your mind. Your body is still in the dining room at my inn. You must resist and I must go, Crom will suspect my meddling. I do not want to forfeit my existence, meager as it is."

"Tell me what to do?" he yelled at she became more transparent.

"Resist the temptation!" as she vanished into the wall.

Burbon's hand rested on the doorframe. A bluish sparkle in the room filled his imagination with the promise of wealth. The urge intensified. Burbon took his hand and slammed the door shut. Behind him the main door opened.

"Merchant, I have wares that I must part with. Please name your price!" The man was tall with fur skins wrapped around his arms and a leather hat. His skin was white, and his cheeks were sunken. He unwrapped a cloth satchel revealing twin red gems of immeasurable beauty.

"I must buy some horses from the blacksmith immediately. Quick, tell me if these are worth anything?"

Normally Burbon would treasure a moment of acquisition, but his instincts were repulsed by the deal. Something was wrong. The man was perturbed and handed the gems out to Burbon.

"Just hold them for a moment," he commanded. Burbon's hands came out in front of him, possessed by their own desires. The gems pulsed, beckoning him to forfeit his soul. The man smiled and dropped them from his hand towards Burbon's. With unexpected strength, Burbon yanked his hands away and the gems fell to the floor. The man was furious.

"Are you an idiot, merchant? Pick up those stones now!" His words were like magic and Burbon felt his body compelled to bend down. But for a second, the man's facial features resembled Crom and his eyes glowed like coals. The spell was broken.

"Take your gems and get out of my store. I'm not buying these!"

The man's body morphed as the store faded into the background. Burbon was no longer in his store, everything had vanished. He stared into the cold dark eyes of his tormentor. Crom looked as if he had lost his composure.

"How dare you resist me? I offer you the world."

The spirits in the globe looked out longingly. Burbon saw only one option. Before anyone could intervene, he leapt onto the table. The townspeople stared in amazement. Burbon's hands flew though the air, hitting the globe, sending it closer to the edge. Time slowed down; Burbon scanned around as townspeople moved in slow motion. Their bodies lurched to reach the globe before its inevitable conclusion. In the globe, the faces twisted and swirled glowing with anticipation that their prison would be shattered. The globe ran off the table and hung momentarily in the air before making its downward plunge. The globe crashed down onto the floor. It bounced and rolled unharmed to the edge of the wall.

"Is that the best you can do, little man?" cackled Crom. "Do you know how many people before you have tried the very same thing? They all thought that the globe was a fragile glass bauble to be shattered. Fool! Its power, my power, is greater than you can ever imagine. I have lived centuries and collected souls from across the land. Its magic cannot be disrupted by regular means. Only magic can defeat magic. Now look into my eyes, for this will be the last thing you see in the land of the living." Crom grabbed Burbon by his clothes and brought him closer to his face. Burbon was unable to resist.

Crack! Crom turned with Burbon in his grasp to see Taro standing over the globe. A large crack with a narrow hole shimmered in its surface. She held the amulet intact in her left hand.

"This amulet is magic!" she yelled. The room erupted into a whirlwind of motion. The globe screamed as spirits fought over each other to escape its confines.

"Cover the hole! Keep the globe away from those three!" Crom commanded. Taro sidestepped one townsperson but was tackled by another and the amulet went flying across the room. A spirit ripped itself free from the globe and flew through the house to return to its rightful master. Burbon escaped Crom was tackled by one of the townspeople. Burbon bounced backwards to land on the floor.

"Leave me be, I am trying to help you!" Burbon yelled looking into the creature's ugly face.

"I have no soul," it wailed. "I'm too weak to resist Crom's will," as his fist tried to connect with Burbon's frame.

Crunch! The floor splintered as the massive fist impacted the floor as Burbon rolled to his left.

"Ooooooooohhhhhh," another spirit soul gravitated out of the broken globe. It floated around the room and reconnected with a short villager in the back of the room. He immediately stopped pulling at Taro and pushed one of the other townspeople away. Taro leapt onto the table and kicked someone's jaw, sending him through the window.

"Ahhhhhhhhh," several villagers wailed as they clung to Stonewall's massive back. He scooped them off, one at a time.

"I am getting tired of being attacked," as he sent another body sailing into the china cabinet.

"Fools! They are only three, sit on them if you have to," Crom's face was contorted in a mask of rage. Another soul flew out the globe and sailed out of the house.

"Help!" Burbon yelled as three villagers pinned him to the floor.

Taro jumped off the table toward the dropped amulet. Before she could reach it, a large arm grabbed her body and forced her against the wall. She hooked her foot on the amulet to bring it closer. Her captor pushed her down to the floor. Unable to move, she grasped the amulet with her right hand and tossed it to Stonewall.

"You're the only one left," she yelled. Stonewall took the amulet and moved towards the crack in the globe. His advance was slowed by the townspeople who grabbed his arms and feet, trying to weigh him down. Their mass eventually became too much for Stonewall's strength and he fell to the floor, several feet short of the globe. Crom walked towards the amulet in Stonewall's outstretched hand.

"This pretty bauble is more than meets the eye," Crom commented. All three travelers watched as Crom bent on one knee to grasp the amulet. Suddenly the outside door slammed open, distracting Crom. A large bony hand reached through the door and the skeleton from the cemetery stepped through.

"How come I wasn't invited to supper?" His body was covered in a light blue glow. "By the divine, my soul has returned to me! Now you are going to pay!" he pointed at Crom who stepped back toward the couch.

"Don't just stand there! Get him!" Crom screamed. Several villagers jumped off Stonewall to attack the skeleton. The bony fighter swiped two of them with his right arm.

"No time for appetizers when I want the main course," he advanced on Crom. Stonewall used the distraction and shook the remaining townspeople off of his back. He took the amulet still in his hand and reached towards the globe.

"Do," started Taro.

"It," ended Burbon. Stonewall stood above the fallen globe and brought the amulet down with all of his might into the crack.

"WWWWWooooosshshhshshh," as souls escaped from the broken globe. Souls lost from centuries of torture wailed and flew around the room. They climbed over each other trying to find their hosts. One large creature's face became tranquil as his soul returned. His body relaxed and he released Taro from his hold. The villagers on top of Burbon had their souls return simultaneously and rolled off his body. The ghost's soul returned to her in mid-flight and she fell to the floor as she lost her other powers. Gradually all in the room had their souls returned.

Crom laid on the floor, his face withered and old. The released souls had aged his body, decades passed in seconds. He tried to stand and stumbled back to the floor. All the townspeople stood around and glared down with hatred. The skeleton raised his fist while Crom cringed. Stonewall stepped between the two to stop the killing blow.

"Why help this animal? He made us his slaves," the skeleton snarled.

"True," Stonewall responded. "He deserves the cold, dark hand of death. But are sure you want be the one to deliver it?" He looked around the room. "All of you are free, his control of you is over. Does anyone of you want your revenge? To become him?" No one moved until one townsperson stepped back to make a path for Crom to leave through the front door. Then another person stepped back. Then another. Crom had to walk the gauntlet of townspeople to leave through the house.

Their eyes blazed with hatred. Crom raised his head to meet their eyes. His power had vanished; their souls would no longer feed his evil. As he reached the door, he felt their eyes boring into the back of his head.

"Even without my globe, I will channel another magical object to steal their souls. I'm too weak now, I will need to feed soon to survive. After I find someone, I will return to make everyone pay!" His thoughts ended as a steel blade sliced his body in half. His top half landed on the floor draped over his lower torso. The skeleton's smile gleamed off of his sword.

"He'll never take another soul in my lifetime," he yelled. Stonewall stepped forward but Taro placed her hand on his chest gently to stop him.

"We can only imagine the pain they have endured. Let them have their closure." Stonewall nodded while Burbon helped the innkeeper.

"Thank you for warning me in my dream. I don't think I would have seen through his trickery." Burbon pulled her up from the floor. Despite her loss of flying, she still looked remarkably like a ghost.

"No one should have to share the pain we have endured," she said to Burbon. "I hope that time will heal our wounds."

"True, but at least your soul is yours again."

"Thank you for releasing us. We are all in your debt."

"Then I intend to cash in my debt now," replied Burbon.

"What do you want?" the woman asked.

"I want to know your name!" inquired Burbon.

"Dorthea," as they join the jubilant townspeople.

Crom's soul withered through the air high above the town. The wind threatened to wipe out his feeble spirit. He searched madly below for someone to satisfy his hunger. Animals were of no use to him; he was unable to inhabit their souls. Beyond the cemetery, he saw a vessel to inhabit. An old man with rotting skin limped outside of the town. Crom sensed he could push out the man's soul and insert his own. This would be his only chance to live. Crom's spirit flew down and oozed into the body. Despite Crom's weakness, he fought the poor man's soul and forced it out of his body. The old man's head looked back at the inn on the hill and his eyes blazed with fire.

"This is a pathetic husk but will suit my needs. All of them will pay, especially the three travelers. What they seek will be mine," as he limped beyond the outskirts of town.

12

Stonewall's Duty

As they climbed into the hills, the outline of the town faded into the horizon.

"How do you think they will manage?" He pointed back at the town.

"Now that their souls have been released, some will finally find peace. Those who survived are strong enough to rebuild their town," answered Stonewall.

"How far do we have to go?" Burbon motioned to the advancing foothills.

Taro took the living map out her pouch. The map stretched its four corners after being cramped up for so long. She pulled the map flat while it struggled as if it was being tickled. She pointed towards the north.

"Beyond the foothills, deep within those mountains, lies the second stone." She folded the map and placed it back into her pocket. The three walked in silence, mentally exhausted from their struggle with Crom. Stonewall gazed into the azure sky. The clouds raced by, journeying in the direction of their destination. One cloud stood out from the rest. Its edges were sharp and its form unmistakably like an anvil. A blacksmith's anvil.

Clang! Clang! The heavy hammer smashed the molten steel on the solid anvil. A large gloved hand pulled the hot steel back into the coal-fired oven. The blast furnace blazed with heat; the blacksmith wiped his goggled forehead with sweaty hands. His shop was lined with metal weapons, tools and farm implements hung on the walls. A workbench straddled two corners with an array of tools scattered over the tabletop. The blacksmith walked outside and dipped his face into a wet trough to cool off. He raised his head and looked into the face of a young boy with a remarkable resemblance. The boy squirted water into the blacksmith's face. He laughed and tried to run away but the massive arms of the blacksmith clamped onto to his back and reeled him in. The boy was caught like a fish in a net.

"Shouldn't you be in school, Stonewall?" The blacksmith looked stern but had a hint of humor to his voice.

"But, Dad! You said this afternoon, you needed my help with the furnace." The young Stonewall was concerned as if he misunderstood his father's orders. His dad smiled.

"I'm teasing you, son. I need your help with this big order. These iron rods have to be done for the Chancellor and the new barracks. I hate for you to miss school because of my business. It wasn't like this when your mom was alive." His father's face took on a distracted look as though he remembered happier times. Unfortunately for Stonewall, he was too young to remember her. Stonewall tugged at his father's sleeve not realizing his father's momentary grief.

"What do you want me to do first?" he asked. The blacksmith regains his composure. He looked behind the building to a small pile of coal.

"Grab a wheelbarrow and fill it with coal. I need that furnace white hot to shape the rods," he commanded. Stonewall ran with youthful enthusiasm.

"Mr. Rothguard! A moment of your time please." Stonewall's father turned to face a man on a tall dark steed. His garb was bright with lots of frills and his hands were ordained with rings. His face was middle aged and soft, someone used to the power of money, but not to the hard work that obtained it.

"Yes, Chancellor!" The blacksmith stood ramrod straight before the man on the horse.

"Mr. Rothguard, you do understand the importance of my men receiving all the steel rods by this evening?"

"Yes Chancellor, there will be no delays. I have some assistance to complete your order."

Crash! Stonewall's wheelbarrow moved too fast and rammed into a shelf of poles. Like a domino effect, it knocked every pole to the ground including the last one. It landed a few feet from the Chancellor and his horse.

"This is unacceptable! This buffoon is ruining my order!" The Chancellor was mortified.

"This buffoon is my son! We'll get your order done on time." The blacksmith swelled in size. "Send your men after they've eaten tonight. Everything will be ready." The Chancellor was startled by the blacksmith's impertinence.

"You make sure it is ready, blacksmith. Or it will be the last order you will ever receive!" He swung the moneybag, fastened to his rope belt and the coins clicked amongst each other. The Chancellor slapped the reins and dug his heels in his steed's flesh. The horse galloped away as the Chancellor sent a final icy stare towards Stonewall's father. Stonewall stood beside his father with his head held down.

"I'm sorry, father, for making a mess of things. Please forgive me." He looked up expecting his father's grim face. Instead he saw his father's humorous gaze.

"How many times have I told you to walk the wheelbarrow?" He patted Stonewall's head and walked towards the furnace. Stonewall tugged on his father's sleeve.

"You're not angry with me?" His father laughed.

"I'm furious with you!" he joked. "Now make sure you work twice as hard to get this order done on time!" he placed his goggles over his eyes.

"Dad, why don't you yell at me?" Stonewall asked. His father turned.

"Because, son, no matter what happens to us, no matter what goes wrong, we only have each other to turn to. I promised your mother before she died that I would always look after you." He glanced at the overturned pile of iron rods. "Even when you make mistakes."

"What about the Chancellor? Why do you let him yell at you?" The blacksmith flicked up the goggles and brought his head closer to his son.

"Last question, Stonewall. And then you and I must get to work. If you learn only one thing in life from me, remember these four words. Always do your duty. No matter how people treat you, no matter how tough it is to complete your task, always do your duty. Many people are cruel and lazy and will try to avoid responsibilities, but you should never shirk your duty. The Chancellor is not a good person. I don't trust him, I don't like him, and I don't respect him. But I must complete my duty. Good things come to those who keep their promises, son. Now," he grabbed an unshaped rod with his thick leather gloves, "keep your promise and get to work."

And work they did. For hours Stonewall assisted, running coal, bringing steel, every menial task possible while his father performed the more intricate work. They worked, they toiled, and they sweated. And they got every steel rod done in time. Barely. His father branded his insignia (the letters RG) into the last pole.

The sun had set when the soldiers came with their wagon in tow. They pulled the wagon up to the shop just as the blacksmith shaped the last rod on his anvil. He patted Stonewall on the back.

"Good work, son, I couldn't have done this without you." Stonewall smiled and pushed his hair out of his face. The captain of the soldiers stepped up to Stonewall's father with a steel rod in his hand.

"Excellent craftsmanship, blacksmith. We always can count on your work." He shook his hand and returned to the soldiers loading the steel rods. The blacksmith folded his arms in a contented gesture.

"Always do your duty, son, and good things will come to you."

The galloping of a horse and rider filled the evening air. The Chancellor rode forward and jumped off his horse by the wagon. He immediately grabbed a steel rod and examined it. He grabbed another. And another. He threw it into the wagon. He was frustrated, then he saw several of the steel rods that had fallen earlier in the day. He grabbed one, examined it and smiled.

"Captain, take this rod with you and make sure the King sees it. It is obvious to me that this blacksmith's order is inferior, and he will not be paid for such shoddy work."

"You must be mistaken, Chancellor, I have examined the order and the quality is superior as always," the captain replied. The Chancellor erupted in anger.

"Do not question my order. This rod has a gouge out at the top." He handed the rod to the captain that Stonewall had knocked down earlier. Stonewall ran forward only to be restrained by his father.

"That's not fair. That one got knocked over. The rest of them are fine. You tell him, Dad!" Stonewall looked up to his father.

"Don't argue with the Chancellor, son, I'm sure he will properly assess their worth once he checks the whole order," the blacksmith replied. The Chancellor smiled and caressed his money pouch.

"I wouldn't count on that! Captain, bring the rods to the barracks foundation, I'll inspect them there myself. And if I find any more defects, you won't get paid and you can forget any more orders from the King. Heeyyyaaaaaww!" he yelled, kicking his horse to attention. Stonewall was overcome with rage as the Chancellor galloped away.

"Dad! He's a thief! We worked hard to complete his order and now he is going to take it away and pay nothing!" Stonewall was unable to contain himself. He looked up and for one of the few times he could remember, he saw his father angry, but not at the Chancellor.

"Hold your tongue! You will not insult the Chancellor in front of all his men! What did I tell you earlier?" Stonewall was taken back and couldn't remember.

"I—I don't know," he cried.

"I told you to always do your duty. Do your work to the best of your ability and you can always hold your head high. People like the Chancellor will try to take advantage of you, but do the right thing and good will come to you. Now, come in for supper and tomorrow, cooler heads will prevail." The blacksmith stepped towards their house and walked through the kitchen door, leaving it ajar for Stonewall to follow. Stonewall watched as the Chancellor disappeared into the twilight and the soldiers followed with the wagon full of steel.

"I'll make sure that the Chancellor pays. You can count on that!" he muttered to himself.

He waited for several hours after bedtime and his father's snoring before he dared to venture out of the house. He slipped through his door without making a sound. Stonewall heard the distant cry of an owl. *Creak!* The floorboard squeaked under his weight, he stopped, waiting to hear the rhythmic snoring of his father. Moments later, he was rewarded with another snort from his father's room. He closed the outside door and put dried meat in his pocket left over from supper. He would need strength before heading to the soldiers' encampment. If the Chancellor wouldn't pay for his order, then he would have to get it himself. Not a stone more, not a stone less. The Chancellor was a selfish man and Stonewall knew that he would keep any leftover currency to line his pocket. He had a reputation for cheating tradesmen and pocketing the money, claiming he saved the King money by not paying full price for inferior products. His father was too trusting. Although it was risky, he'd make sure his father was paid.

Most soldiers would be sleeping deeply in the encampment. There had been no war for years and the few sentries on duty would likely be asleep at their post. He would sneak in and out and be away before anyone knew. He saw the fires illuminating the camp's interior. Only one guard stood at each end. There was plenty of darkness for a small boy to hide himself between them. A small moat surrounded the encampment with timber planks covering the muddy spring water. Halfway across the planks, a sentry stepped around the tent with a flaming torch. Stonewall slipped his feet off the plank and slid quietly into the freezing water. The sentry crossed slowly, measuring his steps. Stonewall's body shivered from the cold water and he clamped his mouth shut in an effort to stop his teeth from rattling.

In and out, he kept saying to himself, *and no one will notice.* Several moments passed and the sentry's steps faded away. Stonewall pulled his body slowly out of the moat and straddled the board to get his bearings. His clothes were soaked, and his hair dripped into his face. Past the center campfire was a tent with ornate posts with detailed canvas sheets. A flag with an emblem blew lightly in the wind.

That must be it. The Chancellor was a man of comfort as evidenced by his soft hands. I bet he sleeps on big fluffy pillows. Stonewall suppressed a giggle with mixed results. In the distance, the horizon brightened.

Oh no, the suns will be up soon, I must hurry, or I'll never get out undetected. He creeped through the main flaps of the tent, almost stepping on the tail of the Chancellor's dog. Stonewall's heart leapt into his throat and he contemplated running back the way he came. *Trying to outrun a dog would be a foolhardy task. There was only one other thing to do.* He pulled the leftover meat from his pocket and placed in his hand. It was dark but he hoped the animal had a keen sense of smell. The dog wore a frilly collar and had a manicured coat. It tilted its head at Stonewall and stepped forward taking the treat from his hand. Stonewall petted the dog with his wet hand and was rewarded with a lick of its tongue.

A lot friendlier than its owner. It barked a low chirp of approval. Stonewall looked at a table and noticed a small moneybag lay on top. *In and out before anyone is the wiser.* He took one step towards the pouch.

"Princess, what's the racket?" The Chancellor spoke from the corner of the tent. Stonewall immediately stepped into the wardrobe off to his right. The dog returned to its master.

"Good girl. Come see me." A moment of silence. "Why are you wet?" The Chancellor got up from his bed and crossed the tent interior. "I bet the captain forgot to lash my tent again. Princess, did you get into the moat? I will give that man a piece of my mind!" The Chancellor's hand reached into the wardrobe and took the robe next to Stonewall. Light shone in from the morning sun as the tent flaps were opened.

"Chancellor! The King requests your audience." A soldier yelled in.

"The King! Why is he here so early! Is something wrong?"

"I don't know, sir. He wants to talk to you before leaving on his hunting party in the northlands."

"I'll be right there!" The Chancellor was a whirlwind of motion slapping clothes on and dabbing powder to add color to his face. Stonewall watched the Chancellor race into the morning sun.

Great, the suns are up. How will I ever get out of this camp with the pouch? Stonewall wondered.

Looking flustered, the Chancellor walked hurriedly with his badly applied makeup and his robe dragged along the mud-encrusted ground. As he rounded the corner, he saw the King talking to the captain of the guards. The King was middle-aged with a weathered but kind face. When he turned to face the Chancellor, some of the kindness left his face.

"Good morning, Chancellor, sorry to wake you up so early," said the King.

"I was already up, our majesty. Did you come to see the barrack preparations?"

"Yes, I am leaving shortly, and I wanted to inspect the work." The King paused and looked around the campsite. "I have to admit, Chancellor, you are doing excellent work."

"Why thank you, your majesty, everything is going according to plan," he beamed.

"Everything?" the King asked as his eyes wavered between the captain and the Chancellor.

"Everything," replied the Chancellor not suspecting the trap. The King knelt down and picked one of the blacksmith's steel rods. He inspected it from head to toe.

"Excellent quality, your choice in craftsman is impeccable." The King admired the steel.

"I have yet to inspect all of them, your majesty," the Chancellor replied.

"I understand you have not paid for these materials," the King directed his gaze straight at the Chancellor's face.

"I found one defective bar. I'm concerned there could be more." He tried to sidestep the question.

"And how many others have you found, Chancellor?"

"Well I haven't checked them all yet, your majesty." The King shook his head.

"Both the captain and I inspected quite a number of the rods and they seem to be of the highest quality. Isn't that right, Captain?"

"Yes, your majesty," he replied, his face a mask of neutrality. The Chancellor was barely able to disguise his hatred of the man.

"But, my lord..." the Chancellor began. The King raised his hand.

"You're not disputing my judgment are you, Chancellor?"

"No, your majesty!"

"And everything is going according to your plan?" The King had a look of mirth as if he enjoyed verbally sparing with the Chancellor.

"Absolutely!"

"Good. Send a rider to pay the blacksmith immediately for his fine work." The King nodded at the captain who walked away. "Now, I need you to show me the rest of the work," the King beckoned to the Chancellor to show him the remainder of the camp. The Chancellor lifted his muddy robe off the ground and proceeded to the north end of the encampment with the King.

Stonewall grabbed the pouch and ran out of the tent into the rising sun. He crawled along the tent's perimeter looking over the encampment. Soldiers were slowly rising for the morning meal while others were trudging into tents to sleep a few hours from the night shift. If there was any chance of him escaping, now was the time during the confusion of the morning changeover. Stonewall ran towards the next tent and looked at the planks crossing the moat. It was empty, as most soldiers had gone to the mess hall.

It's now or never. Stonewall raced across the planks, his feet slapped the boards, which bended into the water from his weight.

Plonk! Plonk! Plonk! Stonewall's feet ran toward the bushes on the other side. His right foot slapped into the mud as a hand grabbed him from the other side. His other foot never touched the ground as an unseen rider on horseback lifted him into the air.

"I have caught a thief," a familiar voice replied. Stonewall turned in mid air as his hands slid onto the back of the horse. His father looked down at him and then at the money pouch that Stonewall grasped with his right hand. "I had a bad feeling when I found your bed empty this morning. But I couldn't have imagined that you would steal from the King, no matter what the reason." His father was disappointed.

"But father," Stonewall started.

"But nothing," the blacksmith finished. "I didn't raise a thief. I will march you into this camp where you will return this money and personally apologize to the Chancellor," his father commanded. A galloping horse from the encampment interrupted them.

"That won't be necessary, the payment is yours as expected," the captain replied, riding his horse from the camp. The blacksmith handed him the money pouch, the captain counted the eight stones and handed them back to Stonewall's father. He pocketed the empty money pouch.

"Thank you, Captain, I appreciate you talking to the King."

"He is always happy to oblige to his valued subjects, especially for your quality work."

Stonewall could no longer contain his shame and looked at his father.

"You knew you would be paid!"

"Of course, son, always do your duty and goodness will be returned to you." He looked at the captain. "Even if one must wait a day for it." The captain gazed at Stonewall.

"I won't charge the boy as long as I understand he will be punished."

"You can be assured that the long hours he put in yesterday are nothing compared to the workload he has ahead of him," Stonewall's father bowed his head to the captain as a courtesy for not punishing the boy under the law.

"We could use a strong lad like this around our armory once a week, cleaning and polishing our weapons. Who knows, we may even be able to make a fighter of him?" The captain ruffled Stonewall's hair.

"We'll see what he has time for," replied the blacksmith, realizing that the captain was not offering punishment, but an opportunity for Stonewall.

"Good day, captain, we will be in touch," the blacksmith saluted the captain and turned his horse back to their home.

"Let's go home, son, you have an exceptional amount of duties to perform."

The Chancellor cursed his misfortunate as he entered his tent.

Why did the King have to interfere in these matters? Couldn't he see how well I was managing affairs? As for the captain, I will not forget his interference. He took off his muddy robe and grabbed another from his wardrobe. He shrieked and threw it to the floor.

"Why is this robe sopping wet?"

Stonewall smiled at the anvil shaped cloud passing through the sky.

"Do you see something in the sky, warrior?" posed Taro. Stonewall glanced toward her.

"Did you ever see a shape in the clouds that reminds you of a memory?" Burbon poked his head between the two.

"Are you kidding, I see gemstones all the time. Look," he pointed to one long narrow cloud, "there goes one now!"

"Is your mind ever on anything besides money?" asked Taro. Burbon pondered her question.

"Sometimes I see food," he replied. Taro shook her head. "What do you see then?" Burbon questioned. She gazed skyward and saw a number of small clouds clumped together.

"Tracks," she answered. "Tracks of a wild Griffith."

The three crossed over a rise, near the end of the foothills. Before them stood a great expanse of mountains so high that their peaks were hidden in the clouds. The mountains were covered in rich colors - silver and quartz gleamed in the twin suns' rays. As they travelled closer, jagged rock pieces laid clumped at the bottom of mountain, broken off from years of weathering. An eroded stone walkway led to a huge cave entrance. Even in the bright sunshine, the entrance was dark and cold, but was the only route to the center of the mountain. The Mineral Mountains; beautiful to behold, deadly to enter. Taro pulled out the living map and examined its page.

"What we seek is deep within this mountain."

"It can't be any worse than what we faced," Burbon responded. Stonewall stared at him with reproachful disapproval. "What? What did I say?" he said.

"What dangers lurk within this place? I am not familiar with this region?" Taro asked Stonewall.

"I have never traveled here before, archer, but I have heard stories as a child. There are tales about a beast that lies at the belly of the Mineral Mountains. A beast whose hide cannot be injured by our weapons. A beast that has lived for centuries guarding its lair."

"Stop the travelogue and tell us what lives here!" wondered Burbon.

"No one has survived to describe it totally, but because of its hide and size it is known as the Iron Dragon!"

13

Pursuing the Iron Dragon

The old man stumbled in the brush; his careless actions startled a pheasant. It squawked at him and flew into the tree canopy above. His right leg was red from infection and threatened to fail him. He pounded the ground in frustration.

This body is rotting underneath me. Why haven't I found another suitable replacement? Surely there are beings that live within a day's travel of that cursed town. He was losing his confidence and concerned for his survival. Crom limped into a clearing illuminated by the moonlight. He looked up momentarily mesmerized by the red glow. Because of his inattention, he stepped into the trap.

The chalk pentagon was drawn in black, barely visible to the eye. When created by a magic user, its power holds all those that step inside. Caught by a boundary as solid as stone, Crom was trapped.

"What sorcery is this?" wailed Crom. The answer chilled him to the bone.

Why would an old man stumble around the forest in the darkness, unless running to something? Crom's brain burned from the voice and he turned to see the armored body of Darkmoor braced against a nearby tree. Darkmoor's breath hung in the evening air even though the night was mild. His eyes were hidden under his helmet.

Or perhaps you are running away from someone? Sunder sat quietly behind Darkmoor observing them both. A rat ran through the brush and Sunder dipped his head down to swallow it. Darkmoor looked at Sunder. *Be quiet*, he commanded. The savagery of the order surprised Sunder. Darkmoor turned his attention back to the old man. Crom filled with panic and excitement simultaneously.

I will stall him as long as I can. Just look into my eyes and your soul will become mine. One glance and I can leave this wretched body forever. He composed himself for his performance.

"Please don't hurt me, I am an old woodsman who has lost his way." Crom dropped to his knees to grovel for his release. Darkmoor stared at him as he traced the outside border of the pentagram.

Your body is old, yet your essence is ancient. There is more to you than meets the eye, old man. Tell me the truth and I will consider releasing you. The mental message was taxing and Crom tried to meet his gaze but Darkmoor paced back to Sunder. *I am searching for certain travelers, perhaps you have met them.*

"Describe them, my lord. I'll tell you if they crossed my path," answered Crom.

Description? Darkmoor stopped and turned back to Crom. *This is what they look like.* Before Crom could make eye contact his brain was overwhelmed by the images of Stonewall, Taro, and Burbon. His mind reeled and he had an uncontrollable urge to talk.

"Yes, I have met these travelers, in a nearby town. They could still be there." The images taxed Crom's mind and he shuddered from exhaustion.

Just look at me one time, Crom wished. Darkmoor turned his head directly toward him as if he obeyed the old man thoughts. *A little closer and you will be mine.*

You revealed much, old man, in your vision of my quarries. You revealed that you are more than you appear, but less than you believe yourself to be. Let me give what you desire. Darkmoor faced Crom and looked into his glee filled eyes. Within seconds, the glee turned to a hot flame of panic. Crom's eyes were locked with Darkmoor's and he was unable to pull away.

"No!" Crom yelled as his essence flowed through his eyes into the air. Darkmoor breathed and his frozen breath extinguished the essence. Crom's body withered to ash and fell to the ground, unable to support its own weight. Darkmoor's boots crushed the remaining ash into the ground.

Soul taker, you should never try to take something that doesn't exist. He turned to Sunder. *I know where they are headed.*

"Iron Dragon! That's a myth, Stonewall!" Burbon bounced up and down at the cave's mouth. "A myth told to scare young children around the campfire late at night." Burbon dramatized the myth. "Its hide is made of iron, impenetrable by any weapon. Its fire is so hot that it turns metal to liquid and flesh to ash. Tell me you're joking?"

"Myths can have some truth, little trader, and what better place for an Iron Dragon to evolve than the Mineral Mountains. Be calm, the cave inside the mountains is huge. Hopefully we will find the gem without ever meeting the dragon."

"With our luck, that seems unlikely," chided Taro.

"Nevertheless, I see few other options." Stonewall picked up a piece of wood. "Would you do the honors?" Taro gazed at the wood and it ignited into flame. Burbon ran ahead and grabbed a piece of wood as well.

"Can I have one too?"

"This is draining," as she lit the second branch.

"Maybe so," Burbon answered, "but I'm not going into that cave without being able to see."

"In that case, lead the way," motioned Stonewall. Burbon shook his fist realizing that his own enthusiasm has trapped him.

"Okay, but if I see that dragon, it's every man," Burbon looked at Taro, "and woman for themselves." He stepped into the entrance, the torch melting a spider's web hanging from the ceiling. The tunnel was exceptionally wide. He peered back at Taro. "That map of yours doesn't tell you how far we have to go..." a rock tumbled in the darkness, "...or if any big angry dragons are in our path?" Taro felt the rough edges of the living map as it struggled against her smoothing motion."

"Perhaps a league or two inside the mountain. And no, it doesn't show me if anything is in our path," she answered.

They followed the tunnel in silence; it was clear of any debris. If previous travelers had stopped here, their evidence has long disappeared. Dazzling minerals shined from the cave walls, their reflections causing the light in the cave to bounce in all directions.

After some time, a light glow emanated from the end of the tunnel. A popping sound echoed off the walls dispelling the silence. As they rounded the corner, they saw a platform cut into the rock. In the center sat a simmering black cauldron with a gruesome green liquid. They surrounded the cauldron, looking into its depths. Burbon reached for a large spoon beside it.

"I better keep stirring until its cook returns," Burbon offered and moved the liquid around.

"Wait!" yelled Taro. Burbon stopped stirring. The pot continued to boil.

"What's wrong?" he asked.

"I remember a story about such cauldrons. Let me think," as she stepped away from it.

"What?" as a green tentacle reached out from the cauldron pulling Burbon into its depths.

"Burbon!" Stonewall yelled as the trader crashed headfirst into the cauldron. The steaming liquid gushed onto the stone floor. Neither the tentacle nor Burbon were revealed as the liquid evaporated. Both Taro and Stonewall were puzzled by the disappearance. He hauled the cauldron over his head and smashed it into the ground.

"Where is he?" he bellowed.

Burbon felt the tentacle crush the air out of his lungs. He fought through the liquid trying to rise above its surface. The sides of the cauldron no longer existed as if he has been immersed in a lake. The tentacle jerked tighter, causing air bubbles to burst out of his mouth. His head felt like it's was going to explode when he pulled his dagger out of its sheath. He cut the tentacle and dark blood flowed out mixing with the green liquid. The tentacle suddenly released its grip and Burbon swum upward.

Why haven't I reached the surface, as his world grew dark. His arms hit air and he dragged himself to a rock ledge. He looked up and saw huge veins of quartz and gold in the walls of the ceiling. Beyond him stood a pile of gold coins.

Have I died and gone to heaven? Burbon thought.

Stonewall's fingers pushed through the green liquid coating the cave floor.

"What just happened?" He paced, trying to calm down his fear.

"It was a portal," responded Taro. "A magical trap set to lure creatures to another realm. It transports them to a lair where they can be...consumed."

"I've not heard of such traps," answered Stonewall. "But in a mountain as immense as this, dozens of traps could be set leading to the dragon's lair."

"Meaning that Burbon may have some time before he is eaten."

"Perhaps."

"What do we do?"

"Pull out the living map," Stonewall commanded. Taro rustled through her pouch.

"Why? It doesn't show where the dragon is?"

"No, but it might show where Burbon is. Our images appeared when we retrieved the map. The map may be tuning itself to our essences. Its repulsion to Burbon may make him even more evident."

"Or less. Let's look." She unfolded the map and her finger scoured the boundaries. One item flashed brightly from the parchment.

"There's the gem but I don't see anything else?"

"What about the coin shape right underneath it?" asked Taro.

"Yes, you're right. It's faint and appears to be moving."

"That's Burbon. We need to head out in this direction." Stonewall pointed. The two of them ran down an adjacent passageway.

"I have a feeling we are going to face the dragon after all," Taro commented.

The gems sparkled in Burbon's hand. Their cut was exquisite, well worth bargaining for at a trader's market. Next to them lay a golden staff with a bulbous figurehead; a bust of a king long dead. Behind Burbon was a huge pile of gold coins towering above while other gems beckoned at his feet. Burbon rushed from object to object, overwhelmed by their beauty and value. *How will I get these back to my shop?* His thoughts of wealth were interrupted by the sound of scurrying feet.

The gobtroll's breath came out in fast gulps of air, its body at the point of exhaustion. It ran by Burbon without even acknowledging his presence.

"What the...!" the trader exclaimed and considered pursuit until diverted by an even louder sound.

"Ayyyyyowwwwaaaaaaaaaaaaaaaarrrr," the dragon roared as it flew down from a high stalactite. The beast was small (by dragon standards), the length of three wagon carts but its skin was the most beautiful that Burbon had ever seen. Its sinewy wings glistened, reflecting on the gold below. Its body was strong with rippling muscles, no extra girth lying on its bones. Its flesh was a soft, flexible iron. Small feathers hung off its ears to guide its flight toward the gobtroll. Its eyes watched the gobtroll with intelligence and with insatiable hunger.

Burbon backed away to hide in the shadow of a tower of coins. The dragon advanced closing the distance to his prey in seconds. The gobtroll stopped by a golden chariot and turned to face the dragon. In desperation, it threw its dagger into the face of the dragon aiming for its glimmering eye. The gobtroll watched in vain as the dagger bounced of the dragon's eye and fell to the ground. The dragon's iron hide was impervious to weapons; its eyes were hard as diamonds. The dragon roared again. Its flaming breath ignited the air scorching the poor gobtroll for a final time. The dragon swooped and grabbed the smoking corpse like a scavenger. It bellowed in victory and flew high to survey its precious treasury. Burbon was entranced by the dragon's beauty and took one step back to get a better view. He tripped on a pile of coins.

The sound of their fall caused the dragon to stop feeding and it cocked its head toward him. Burbon's heart leapt into his throat and he looked around for cover. Burbon spied a half empty chest of bounty lying open, inviting him in. He leapt inside and closed the chest, unconcerned if locked in. The dragon landed nearby but Burbon could not see it through the keyhole. There was a rattle of coins falling from the sweep of the dragon's tail. The dragon sniffed the air. Its keen sense pulled it toward the chest. Burbon looked out again, and a large red eye filled his view. The dragon blinked but does not act right away. It was a selfish beast and didn't want to damage its valuables with him in the chest. Instead, it circled several times a nearby pile of coins, making itself comfortable in its nest. Its eyes focused on the chest, waiting for its prey to exit.

I'm trapped. I'm trapped with all the money in the world and I'll never be able to spend it. He collapsed in his tomb while his mind contemplated his fate.

Taro and Stonewall ran with all the speed they could muster. They raced through the tunnel passageway towards Burbon and the second piece of the amulet.

"How much further do we have to go?" Stonewall asked Taro as she glanced at the map.

"Not far, but there is a big open area ahead that I can't describe," she answered. As she turned the corner, Taro stepped onto open air. Stonewall grabbed her arm and brought her back. Her foot knocked a rock into the chasm, and they listened for its impact. There was no sound, either the pit was bottomless or the distance so far that the echo was too muffled to hear. To their right, a long plank crossed the span, its other end shrouded in mist.

"Ladies first," motioned Stonewall. Taro smiled.

Her elfin ability enabled her to walk across the beam with ease. She looked back at Stonewall and his slower approach. He had to balance his massive frame on the narrow plank. "Tread carefully, warrior, my strength will not be able to pull you up."

"I'll keep that in mind," he nodded as he followed her into the mist. At the midway point, it was impossible to see either end. The air was filled with a clicking sound, like an animal rolling its tongue in its mouth. "Are we there yet, archer?" Stonewall asked.

"You sound like Burbon," she answered, "I can almost see the wall at the end of this plank." The board moaned beneath her feet signaling its surrender. The board breaks as the two reach the end, pieces tumbling down below.

"We won't be going back that way," said Stonewall as they turned and focused on the other side. Ahead lay a narrow path carved into the rock face. The path split in two, both heading in the same direction but separated by a wall of rock. Taro viewed her map.

"I can't tell if we need to go right or left. Our destination is directly beyond this hill. Both paths may take us to the same location. We'll have to guess."

"It is not a chance I want to risk Burbon's life with. You go right, I will go left. Be careful."

"You as well. Let's find Burbon in time." Taro's voice faded into the mist as she rounded the corner. Stonewall focused on his path which soon diverted into a tunnel. As he steps forward, he was greeted by darkness. The walls were moist, and water dripped onto Stonewall's torch threatening to douse his flame. *I don't have Taro if it goes out.*

His foot slid into a muddy puddle. On the right wall, streaks of iron ore ran through the rock like a spider's web. Suddenly, a skeleton in warrior garb appeared, pinned to the wall by a metal spear. Its mouth was wide open in a silent scream; its bones were long picked clean of any flesh.

I wonder if this poor creature ever saw its attacker. Stonewall removed the spear from the wall and bones tumbled to the ground. He inspected the rusty end. *No one has thrown this spear in a very long time.* He tapped the end of the spear on the stone floor. It slipped out of his hands and as he bent over to pick it up, death missed him by inches. A large axe slammed into the wall behind him. Stonewall reacted by drawing his broadsword, ready to battle the hidden opponent. He awaited the attacker's charge. Seconds passed, the silence in the tunnel echoed back to Stonewall. When the attack never materialized, he turns his attention to the axe. Imbedded in the wall, its blade was dull and worn, while the wooden handle was pitted with holes. *Who would throw such a poor weapon? What kind of strength could throw it into the wall?*

Stonewall peered into the murky darkness. *I could turn back, but the time lost would be costly to Burbon.* He gritted his teeth. *Whatever danger awaits me can taste my steel!* He stepped forward and was almost beheaded by a flying mace. Only the sound of the oncoming attack and Stonewall's speed prevented him from being skewered. The mace was deflected off his broadsword to the ground.

"Show your face coward!" Stonewall bellowed. "Let us battle one on one." Again, Stonewall waited and was greeted by the silence of the tunnel. The mace lay broken on the floor, it spikes riddled with brittle flakes. Stonewall dropped down on all fours and crawled along the floor.

"Whoosh!" An elaborate dagger flew through the air and stabbed itself deep into the wall. Stonewall inched ahead, his knees wet with moisture. Another spear sailed through the air, landing deep into the mineral vein. Stonewall smiled in recognition of the trap. The metal weapons were drawn to the iron veins like two magnets pulling toward each other. Weights in the floor must pull the weapons out and then the iron ore draws them across. *Who knows how long these weapons have lain in wait? I only have to crawl out of this mess.*

For a second Stonewall felt safe until he saw a series of holes in the floor.

He rolled over and felt a dart whistle past his torso. He turned over again before another rusty dart could pierce his back. *This is getting ridiculous.* He leapt up and broke into a full out run while dart flew into the air inches behind his feet. *If I run fast enough, I should be able to outrun this danger.*

He ran face first into an imbedded axe in the wall. His head hits the blade and he fell onto the floor. Stonewall lost consciousness for several seconds. *If any weapons come at me now, I'm dead.* Nothing impaled his body as he rose. He looked straight ahead at the end of the tunnel; the axe handle was the last of the weapons. His hand ran down the edge of the rusted weapon. *Why would someone set up such an elaborate trap?*

The pathway narrowed to an overhang below the cliff face. A waterfall splashed from above, a sheet of water between the wall and the underhang. Taro hugged the cliff wall and stared down into the abyss. *I wonder what lives down there*? Her foot slipped on wet stone and she almost lost her balance. *I don't want to find out that way.*

Her musings were interrupted by a flapping sound from the passageway ahead. Taro grabbed a root from the clay cliff to anchor herself. The flapping sound increased until the sound was deafening but Taro didn't dare cover her ears and lose her footing. Hundreds of red eyes loomed out of the darkness.

The dark mass flew by Taro, reeking of rotting fruit. They were oblivious to Taro and soared to the ceiling and up into the sky. *What torment do those beasts plan tonight?* She loosened her grip on the root to step forward. But the root has wound itself around her wrist. Taro pulled, but the root was too strong, holding her tight. She planted her foot and pushed against the cliff wall until the root snapped under the strain. Unfortunately, she pulled so hard that she lost her balance. In seconds, she tumbled off the edge and into the mist below.

Taro fell several feet until her descent was stopped, and she hung upside down in the air. Another root had ensnared her foot and saved her life. Two bolts fell out of her quiver and into the depths below. The root was now her lifeline, snapping it was not an option. She fought a wave of dizziness as the blood rushed to her head. She pulled one bolt out and cocked it in her crossbow. She fastened a rope to the end of the bolt. The root tightened its grip on her leg causing her to grimace in pain. Another root swirled from the canopy above and searched for Taro's right arm. *I better shoot this bolt now while I still can.* The bolt sailed a short distance and sunk into the wall. The second root whisked across Taro's shoulders as she pulled herself up.

Upon the cliff edge, she cut the root on her leg with a small knife. The other end shriveled and drew back into the soil. From the canopy above, several more roots reach down like hungry snakes after their prey. Taro hacked them with her knife. *Leave me alone you blood-sucking vines!* She sliced at several roots and a brown liquid flowed out. She ran along the cliff edge. The roots were everywhere, writhing in the vegetation. *They look angry, almost like they wanted me for their meal. I'm not going back that way.*

Taro searched ahead to a rock overhang above a huge cathedral like cavern. She heard the roar of the dragon long before she saw it. She peered over the rock ledge looking down at a huge treasure trove. The area was the size of an open field, the view overwhelming. Piles of coins littered the room, with silver shields, gem-encrusted trunks, and beautiful staffs dotting the gold mass. There was a huge hole in the ceiling of the cavern with orange moonlight shining down, illuminating the interior.

But for all of the riches, their beauty paled in comparison with the dragon. Taro gulped at its iron hide; its silent gaze fixed on a golden chest amidst the pile of treasure. Taro slipped behind a rock column to hide from the dragon's view. She opened the living map, squirming in her hand. The gem's location was in the center of the cavern almost beside the dragon. So was the barely distinguishable mark of Burbon. *At least he's found a place to hide. How am I going to deal with a dragon? If its hide as tough as iron, no bolt will puncture it. I'll need a distraction.* Taro pulled out a large arrowhead with a magnesium tip. The tip would ignite on contact. Hopefully it would be enough.

She cocked the bolt back and aimed at a large tower of coins at the back of the cavern. She released the crossbow and the bolt sailed through the air.

Kchoom! Silver coins flew around the cavern, ricocheting off several statues. The dragon's attention broke from the chest and it glided over to investigate. Taro leapt over the ledge and hopped over several piles of treasures before landing on the ground. She hustled over to the chest and knelt before the latch. She looked behind her to watch the dragon still searching for the commotion caused by the coins. She picked the lock and lifted the lid of the chest to see the terrified eyes of Burbon.

"Taro! You are a sight. How did you get by the dragon? It has been watching me forever," Burbon sighed with relief and stepped out of the treasure chest. He jumped around like an excited kid.

"Are you really happy to see me or has your fear turned you into a quivering idiot?"

"Neither, I have to pee really bad!"

"Never mind. The other piece of the amulet is here." She pulled open the living map, a schematic of the treasure cavern appeared with the amulet at the center.

The smell of smoke filled the air. Both Burbon and Taro turned around to face the gleaming red eye of the dragon.

"My distraction didn't last long," Taro backed up.

"Watch his breath, it's a killer!" Burbon went in the opposite direction. The dragon's eyes filled with anticipation of turning two more beings to ash. It stretched its body back to fill its lungs with fire. The air was filled with heat as the flame split between Burbon and Taro as they dived in opposite directions. Burbon tumbled into a pile of coins while Taro slammed into the base of a silver statue. The dragon crossed the scorched ground in seconds.

Burbon peeked out of the coins while a giant metal tail slapped at Taro. She fell underneath the tail's swing as it ripped the head off the statue. Taro tried to stand but the dragon was too fast. It cocked its head back to ignite the air around Taro's body. A gold cup hit it head causing it to swallow its fiery rage.

"Come and get me you overgrown lizard!" Burbon yelled. The dragon was furious for ingesting its own flame and its iron skin glows red. Burbon ran around corner into a dead end. *Nowhere to go and no help in sight*. He turned back and the dragon's eyes reflected pleasure in releasing its fiery death. Burbon raised his eyes in defiance, "I hope you choke on me!"

"Not if I can help it!" Stonewall leapt from the cavern's ledge and landed on the dragon's head. His weight caused the dragon's head to lift and its fire slammed harmlessly into the wall behind Burbon. Stonewall grabbed the steely plates below the dragon's head and held on for dear life. The dragon roared, unable to roast its prey, and flew up trying to drop its rider. Taro dragged Burbon away from the coin pile and they dashed through the treasure.

"The map has the second amulet at the center of this cavern. Stonewall only has a few moments before the dragon will shake him off!" yelled Taro.

"Great. Even if we find the amulet, there's no guarantee that we'll get out of here alive with it," gloomed Burbon.

"We'll cross that bridge." Taro grabs the map and saw the object of their quest. A small lagoon sat in the center of the cavern with lush green water gently lapping on the edges. Red gemstones glimmered in the pristine water. Stepping stones lined the way to the center of the lagoon - a tiny island of precious stones. At the center of the island, a staff was placed tight into the pile with a transparent stone resting on top. The second piece of the amulet!

"I'll grab the amulet, you watch my back," Burbon ran to the first stepping stone.

"Wait!" she yelled. Burbon didn't slow down until a bolt slammed into the water in front of him.

"Are you trying to kill me?" he screamed.

"Look!" As she pointed, the water in the lagoon moved as if alive and wrapped itself around her bolt. The water acted like two hands, crushing the bolt in seconds.

"Look before you leap, Burbon. You should have learned that from the cauldron."

"Okay, I owe you, again. Now how do you propose getting the amulet out of the lagoon?"

The dragon smashed its body on the roof of the cavern to knock Stonewall off. A rock broke off and fell down into the water. The splash knocked the staff with the amulet into the lagoon.

"No!" yelled Taro. The water crushed the staff in seconds, but the amulet eluded its grasp. The water tried to clamp the amulet in its grasp. Burbon grabbed a steel pole, lifted the amulet out of the water and into Taro's hands.

"Nice move," she replied, putting the amulet into her pouch while Burbon tossed the steel pole onto the coins. They moved as the dragon aimed its head at the lagoon, turning the water into steam. The dragon flew over their heads with Stonewall's arms still fully wrapped around its neck.

"Get out of here. Now!" he commanded. Taro and Burbon ran toward the far tunnel exit.

Stonewall tried to plunge his dagger into the scales of the dragon's neck. But even with his strength, the blade never broke the dragon's skin.

Think, Warrior, you can't use your own strength to best this creature. The dragon ignited a stalactite that fell and impaled a skeleton to the cavern floor. The dragon hit into the cavern wall and Stonewall slid further down the dragon's back to its wings. The wings fluttered with incredible strength, trying to swipe Stonewall's body off. Stonewall gripped the wings so hard he felt like his fingers would break. The dragon roared in frustration and smashed more of the roof down upon it.

"Stonewall, we made it!" Burbon yelled from the mouth of the tunnel. "Get off of that beast!"

"Easier said than done," Taro commented.

At least my friends are safe now, Stonewall watched them wave frantically from below. The dragon showed no signs of slowing down, in fact it appears to be tireless. Stonewall contemplated letting go and ending the battle. The dragon tried to look back at him, its eyes filled with rage. Its mouth poised to release its killing flame; its breath so hot that the air scorched the hair on his arms. In seconds, it will burn itself to rid Stonewall as its passenger. Stonewall leapt off as the dragon engulfed its own body. He felt the sensation of flying.

Seconds past as he fell to the ground. He collided with something hard and tumbled down to the cavern floor. He heard the sound of running feet.

"Stonewall are you all right! Say something?" Burbon was shaking Stonewall's head. Stonewall checked his body lying amongst the gold.

"I am sore but alive. How did I survive?" Stonewall replied.

"You hit a pile of coins and tumbled down. I think it broke the worst of your fall."

"Where's the dragon?"

Burbon pointed behind them. The dragon lay in a heap, its beautiful metal body scorched and twisted. The only weapon that could defeat it was its own deadly breath.

"Is it still alive?" Stonewall asked.

"I haven't poked it with a stick to find out, if that's what you mean."

"It's alive Stonewall, but in horrible pain. We must leave," replied Taro.

The three rushed toward the tunnel out of the treasure cavern. The dragon heard the sound and raised its wounded head. The three travelers ignored the dragon's movement and fled into the tunnel. The dragon sent one last burst of flame.

Burbon yelled in the darkness of the tunnel. "We got it, Stonewall! The second piece of the amulet! Taro, show him!" The tunnel's darkness made it hard to see the two pieces.

"Wait until we leave here, and I will show them both," Taro answered.

"Hey why is it getting brighter in here?" Burbon commented.

The three of them turned to the massive wall of flame rushing at them like a tidal wave.

"Run!" Taro yelled as her long legs bounded ahead of the two men. The flame traveled at breathtaking speed and ignited the air behind them. The tunnel took an abrupt turn and all three dived around the corner. The flame traveled past them and burned a hole through the rock to the outside world. Burbon peered out the hole created by the flame. He felt the fresh air and saw a trail leading to the other side of the mountain.

"Follow me," he yelled to Taro and Stonewall, "before we're burned alive!"

14

Weapons of Science

The darkness wrapped around him like a shroud, it clung to his body. The air was hot and stuffy, his lungs begged for fresh air. His eyes adjusted to the gloom over the hours (or was it days?) that had passed. His hands were cruelly lashed with irons and tied in front of him. Tears fell from his eyes and landed in the dirt below. He turned his head as he heard scratches in the walls.

Rats he thought. *Filthy stinking rats.* They smelled his flesh and burrowed deeper through the walls to reach him. The boy heard a low rumbling in the distance, like steel on stone as someone climbed the stairwell. As soon as the footsteps stopped, there was the sound of a metal latch being turned. His prison door opened and the light from the lantern momentarily blinded him. When he regained his vision, he looked straight into the eyes of his demented father.

"Get up, boy, come to me." His father's eyes gleamed with disgust in the murky light. The boy rose slowly and kept his distance, wary of his father's temper.

"Is it time, father? Can I leave this dungeon?" The boy looked up with hope in his heart. His father looked down and smiled.

"No, my son. You disobeyed me. You must learn the importance of following my orders."

"But I am so cold; can I not have a blanket?" His father showed no signs of caring.

"You're soft, boy. Some days I don't think you came from me. To live above fear, you must learn to endure pain. Only then can you truly be my son." His father brushed dark hair out of his son's eyes. The boy swallowed hard and tried to find the strength to please his father.

"As you wish, father." His father's face was a mask of mockery and disdain.

"As you wish," he mimicked. "Where is the fire in you, Boy, where is your strength? Don't you want to hit me? Don't you want to strike?" The boy sensed a trap but the strain on him was too much. He gave in to his anger. He swung both his tied arms in a semi circle and struck his father with all of his might. He had the same effect as insect against a large bear. His father laughed in approval.

"Finally, some fire in your belly. I approve. Now let me give you your reward." His son held out his hands to have his bonds removed. His father brought his wrist back and knocked his son so hard that he flipped over onto his back. "I'll be back for you soon, when you have toughened up a bit more." He swung the door wide open and looked back at his son. "Maybe there is hope for you yet." He slammed the door shut and pulled the outside latch in one swift motion.

The boy refused to cry. *Someday I will make my father pay for this - someday.* A rat came through a hole in the wall and took a leftover crumb from the boy's last meal. The boy raised his foot as the rat continued eating unaware of the imminent end to its short life. *I will show my father that I am strong.* The boy hesitated, lonely for comfort. He lowered his foot and sat, watching the rat. For many hours, the prison rat was the Darkmoor's only company.

There is smoke coming from the mountains," Sunder stated while flying high in the sky. Darkmoor thoughts were interrupted long enough to see black smoke rising from the ground far in the distance. *They may be closer than I thought.*

Fly to it! If the second stone of the amulet is below us, I will find it!

The three travelers climbed down from the mountain rock face into the meadow below. They could hear the dragon bellowing inside the mountain.

"We should be far enough away from the dragon now," said Taro.

"Why? What are you going to do?" asked Burbon.

"Watch."

Taro pulled the two stones out of her tunic and placed them on the ground. Their rough edges fit together like a jigsaw puzzle. The remaining ragged edges showed the two spots to be filled. Taro connected the two stones and they flashed a red hue as they merged. The three of them stepped back but with no additional results.

"That was thrilling, makes the search worth while for this hunk of rock..." as he said sarcastically while reaching for the stone. Suddenly an electrical force radiated from it, slamming Burbon into the air and he slid to the ground.

"That's not fair, the stone was waiting for me!" he exclaimed. A familiar voice emanates from the stone.

"*You have done well and faced many dangers together,*" it spoke.

"The Seer!" exclaimed Stonewall.

"*My return means you have successfully melded the first two stones. The third stone will require passage across a major barrier. You must hurry, you are closely pursued by Darkmoor.*"

"Where must we go?" asked Stonewall.

"*Follow the trail of tears through the desert. At the end of three days, you will meet Turbine. He will provide you with supplies to meet the challenges ahead for the third and fourth stone.*

"Turbine? What kind of name is that for a wizard?" wondered Burbon.

"*Not a wizard, an inventor. He will require a gift for your entrance.*"

"A gift," answered Burbon, "what does he want?"

"*That will be for you to decide?*" the Seer responded.

"Seer," Stonewall started, "we have begun this journey in good faith to save our world, but will the three of us survive to the end?" Taro and Burbon fixed their attention on the stones for his reply. "*History has not been written yet, my power can not tell you which possibility will become reality. You must concentrate on the retrieval of the stones. Now go, time is your enemy,"* the Seer cried. His voice cut off and the energy from the stones vanished.

"Time is your enemy?" The Seer has a real gift for understatement. Everywhere we go is an enemy," commented Burbon. "And what does he mean by trail of tears? Why does the Seer have to talk in riddles?" Burbon was frustrated and sat on the ground in protest.

"Because it is his way," answered Stonewall.

Behind them the mountain echoed as the dragon raged.

"The Seer is right about one thing. We need to leave," said Taro as she scooped up the stones. The three of them began their travel into the desert.

Hours later, the suns hung high over the barren desert. The few plants that survived in this arid climate were black. Burbon snapped off a branch of brittle deadwood from a gnarled tree.

"I don't know what's worst—the fire from the dragon or the heat of this blasted desert! My throat is so parched I can't even get any saliva. Taro can I have a drink of your water?"

"No! We each have a ration for the day, why did you drink all of yours at once?"

"I thought the great tracker would have found us some water," he chided. Stonewall stopped him.

"This is a desert, Burbon. There is no water in a desert."

"Unless you're up north. Right? Get it, up north?" His humor fell on deaf ears. "Look, I'm sorry. I'm thirsty! I'm a trader not a traveler!" Burbon was exasperated and he threw his canteen onto the ground. His water skin bounced harmless off a sand dune and into a gully. A small pool of water formed under it. Burbon ran toward it and reached down, noticing his treasure.

"Hah, I don't need either one of you. I can find my own water," he scooped up water into his canteen. Stonewall knelt beside him and touched the water with his fingers. Burbon squirted the water down his throat.

"Is it what I think it is?" Taro asked.

"What are you blind? It's water. If you don't want any, that's find by me." He scooped more water into his water skin.

"You may want to slow down, little one," Stonewall sniffed the water. Burbon noticed the concern in his eyes.

"Okay, what's wrong with this water?" he questioned.

"It's wild water," answered Taro. "At first you can't drink enough of it. You drink and drink until you feel so bloated that you can't move.

"Then hallucinations begin, you see monsters that chase you constantly, even in your dreams," added Stonewall.

"Finally, your body dehydrates so fast that your organs turn to dust that melt away in the wind," Taro whispered into Burbon's ear. He jumped back sending the water skin sailing.

"How much do you drink to cause all of this?" He was very scared.

"Just a few drops," Stonewall answered.

Burbon screamed, "I can't stop drinking it!"

Both Taro and Stonewall rolled on the ground from laughter. Burbon realized that he has been tricked.

"Ha ha. If I didn't know better, I would think that the two of you are in cahoots."

"You are so gullible, little Trader," Taro laughed. Stonewall went to investigate Burbon's tossed wineskin. Another pool has formed underneath it. He smiled.

"Little man, you have strange luck. Sometimes remarkably bad and other times very good. You have just found the trail of tears." Stonewall stepped on another dip in the sand and another small pool appears.

"What do you think causes the moisture?" Taro knelt before the pool.

"A divining process. Water hidden below the surface made to create a path," Stonewall answered.

"Like breadcrumbs to lead you," Taro finished. "This should take us to Turbine."

"Don't forget I found it!" Burbon interjected. Refreshed, he skipped along tapping puddle after puddle to form a trail. "Are you two coming?"

Late the next day, the desert terrain slowly came to an end. Small hills formed in the distance with grass and shrubs covering the landscape.

On top of a small rise, they noticed an oddly shaped home with many windmills spinning on its roof. The building was large with different additions at several levels. Each addition was unique, not fitting the previous section's design. The roof was made of a green tin with wooden railings along the edges. For a second, the three of them saw movement as a trap door closed on the roof and someone scurried into the building. The red suns were dipping below the horizon and the travelers did not look forward to another night in the open.

"Do you think this is where Turbine lives?" asked Burbon.

"The trail of tears ends here," answered Stonewall. He tapped the ground and no moisture appeared. The three of them strode towards the house. Taro was the fastest and arrived at the front door first. On the large wooden door hung metal cogs placed strategically to appear like the interior of a clock. Near the top of the door, a piece of metal covered a small wooden hole. Taro noticed a switch to the right of the door. She knocked on the center of the door. "I hope there is no demon in this door," she mused. The others joined her and wait several seconds for a response. All was quiet.

"Nobody home," commented Burbon.

"Maybe you're not knocking the right way," stated Stonewall as he flipped the switch. A series of cogs and wheels rotated, whirling and twirling to their final destination. They stopped and the metal latch opened to reveal two spectacled eyes.

"What can I do for you?" a gruff voice answered.

"Are you the one called Turbine? We have been sent by the Seer to meet you." The creature considered Stonewall's words.

"Did you bring me a tribute? An offering to pay for my services?" he responded.

The three of them looked of at each other and shrugged. Stonewall leaned towards the door.

"Let us in and we'll pledge our services to you!" He stared into the spectacles.

"Not good enough," the voice whined. Taro pulled out one of her bolts.

"We bring weapons, let us in and we can give one of them and show you the means to use it."

"Bah, you are wasting my time." The metal latch was closing but then stopped as the voice saw Burbon fumbling in his pockets. "You little man, what do you have, show me!"

"It's just something I picked up, I'm sure you wouldn't be interested," he lied and dug his hand deeper into his pocket. Taro reached and pulled his hand out of his pocket while Stonewall opened his hand. An obsidian gem flashed back at them, a trophy Burbon had taken from the dragon's nest.

"You have been holding out on us, little trader. Where did you find this treasure?" Stonewall held the gem high enough from Burbon, who tried unsuccessfully to swat it from his hand.

"I made the most of my time hiding in a chest before Taro rescued me from the dragon. Finders keepers, I say!"

"Hand it to me!" the voice behind the door commanded. Stonewall's hands went closer to the greedy fingers, but pulled away before they could grasp the jewel.

"If I give this to you, then you will let us in?"

"Yes, yes!" Desperation colored his voice, worried he wouldn't get the prize. Stonewall handed the gem and the door immediately creaked open. Burbon blinked as he realized Turbine was not what he expected.

He was squat and built like an egg. He was far too short to look out the latch on the door. His glasses had leather coverings on the edges to prevent the spray of noxious chemicals from entering his eyes. Turbine wore dirty coveralls stained a multitude of colors. He turned his back and headed over to his workbench.

Burbon peered around the strange room of Turbine's laboratory. Dozens of glass tubes hung in racks with various liquids bubbling and brewing. Metals of strange composition shone and gleamed - some hung on the wall - others covered the tables and even more littered the floor. Odd plants lined the walls with sweet smelling flowers. A bee flew in from the window and landed on a red orchid plant. Burbon stepped towards it to smell the flower.

"I wouldn't do that," said Turbine. Burbon was amazed as the flower grew larger and swallowed the bee with a quick gulp. Burbon almost tripped as he stepped backwards.

"The monad plant is extremely dangerous, eating a hundred times its weight each day," the large spectacles looked up at him. "You would lose a few fingers before you knew what happened to you."

Burbon noticed a ladder connected to the back of the door for Turbine to stand tall enough to look out of the latch. Another ladder moved on a pulley system circling the room. Burbon jumped onto the ladder and the momentum sent him towards the inventor.

"Listen, Turbine, or whatever you call yourself. You have my diamond, how about giving us your attention?" Turbine didn't answer and moved towards another ladder. Burbon shook his head. "This guy's got a one-track mind."

"Remind you of anyone?" Taro chided. Stonewall stepped forward and put his hand on the ladder.

"You will speak to us now," he commanded. Turbine ignored him and tugged his cord to advance his ladder to another destination in the room. Stonewall held the ladder in its spot.

"Excuse me," Turbine whined. "The three of you are holding up my test of the authenticity of this diamond. Until I can determine if it is real, I will do nothing to help you." Stonewall released the ladder abruptly, Turbine lost his balance and tumbled awkwardly to the floor. He jumped up excitedly.

"That was uncalled for! I will help you as soon I am done," he shouted. His stature was even smaller than Burbon's. Taro advanced to one of the tables.

"We can do this the easy way," she ran her finger down a beaker, "or we can do this the hard way." Taro snapped her finger against the tube. Turbine ran over in fright.

"Stay away from that, Elf. Your grotesque fingers could break the tube," Turbine leapt on a box and pushed himself between her and the apparatus.

"Real charmer," Burbon said to Stonewall who was not amused.

"Inventor," he bellowed, "we have come a long way and fought many dangers. Do not test our patience!" Turbine stopped fiddling with his experiments.

"Why are you here?" he asked.

"We are searching to collect four stones to form a powerful gem. A gem that could destroy our land if wielded by the wrong person. The Seer has sent us to seek you out. Can you help us?" requested Stonewall.

"I don't know this Seer, but many people recommend my work. I have many resources, what do you need of me and my laboratory?"

"I can't answer that," Taro replied as she unfolded the living map. "This map may help you to guide us toward the objects we seek." It squirmed under her touch and Turbine's eyes enlarged with delight.

"What wondrous science is this? He grabbed a sharp tool and came closer to the map to cut off a piece. The map defended itself the only way it knew how. It screeched. Its high pitch screams broke three beakers until Turbine backed up.

"Step away, inventor. This is not science but magic. You'll be not cutting any samples of it as long as I breathe," Taro grit her teeth. Turbine put his tool back on the desk.

"The map finally met someone it likes less than me," Burbon muttered.

"Very well, show me what this map describes," Turbine asked. The four of them surround the map to watch it detail the location of the third stone. In the lower right corner, the symbols of the three travelers stand in a structure not dissimilar to Turbine's lab.

"Amazing! An organic living map with objects that change position. Fascinating!" Turbine mused.

"What's this in the corner?" Burbon questioned.

"The sea town of Amir, the largest trading post in this region. You would be wise to avoid it. The city is full of thieves and beggars," Turbine responded.

"We have no choice, our prize resides here, off the coast," answered Stonewall. "We will need a boat and captain who will take us here." His large finger pointed to an island with unusual symbols swimming around its perimeter."

"We can follow this map. What can you offer us?" demanded Taro as she leaned down into Turbine's face.

"To assist your journey," he answered, "I can provide science." He walked over to a shelf.

"I'm no fan of magic," Burbon commented, "but it has its uses. The elf here can make a hell of a barbecue! Go ahead, show him," he gestured to Taro.

"I don't perform tricks," she bared her teeth.

"And neither do I," returned Turbine. "Magic is horribly unreliable. Sometimes it works, sometimes it fails. Science is more predictable and efficient."

"Let's see your efficiency," asked Stonewall. Turbine grasped a metal staff and tossed it at Stonewall who caught it with ease. "For a warrior, a weapon even more powerful than yourself."

"A staff, big deal! It doesn't even look like it's worth anything," Burbon eyed the length of it while Stonewall felt its lightness.

"Its worth is priceless. The staff is a channeling conduit, its ability is to channel any of nature's elements and harness the energy into raw power. It can take lightning from the sky, rays from the sun, or fire from the earth and magnify the power a thousand-fold.

"We could have used that to fight the dragon. Hey what's this?" Burbon fingered a gem of exquisite beauty. He was barely able to take his eyes off of it. He stared at his twisted reflection in the gem.

"That is not for you!" replied Turbine and took the gem out of Burbon's hands. He slammed it down on the counter and it reverted to a lump of coal.

"How did you do that?" asked Burbon.

"It is a holo rock—it becomes the object of a person's greatest desire. I have spent most of a lifetime trying to perfect its amplifiers. It is too important to give to you."

"Excuse me. I did give you the diamond. What do have for me?" Burbon wondered.

Turbine motioned him to another table and Burbon sidled closer.

The scientist pulled out a frothy vile green beaker. He put a cork in the top and handed it Burbon.

"Unless this is the world's greatest ale, I'm disappointed," remarked Burbon.

"Nothing as primitive as spirits. The potion is a finely refined product from decades of organic tampering. I call it the army maker!" The scientist proclaimed. Burbon giggled, nearly dropping the potion to the floor.

"You've been holed up in this lab for too long, Turbine. You're not making sense."

"Just the opposite. Because of your small stature, you need an equalizer to assist you in the battles ahead in case your comrades are indisposed. By spilling small droplets to the ground, mindless servants can be created to do your bidding. Mind you, they will have a finite life. Give your orders immediately or they will expire before they can complete your task." Burbon was curious was about to place a drop on the table.

"Not here! Do you want to damage the lab? Besides they are a valuable resource not meant to be used frivolously!" yelled Turbine.

"Okay, don't burst a blood vessel! I'll use this at the proper time." *If it really works*, thought Burbon. "What you got for our elf?"

Turbine walked over to a shelf drawer and grabbed several small objects. He opened his hand.

"Wow, that's amazing. Little shiny balls. What genius!" Burbon mimicked.

"Ignore his gift of sarcasm and explain to me what these do," said Taro.

"They are portal openers. Throw them at a solid object and they will create an opening that will allow you to pass through a solid wall into the room beyond. My chemicals can break down matter but only temporally. Pass through with haste."

"Handy if you're locked into a cell," mentioned Burbon.

"Unless it takes you to another locked cell," replied Stonewall. He strapped the staff next to his sword. "Thank you for your gifts I'm sure they will prove useful. But..."

"But what?" answered Turbine.

"But we require something very powerful. Strong enough to negate the power of the four stones." Taro and Burbon looked at Stonewall in surprise as Turbine considered the request.

"Hhmmm. Give me a few moments. I have something I can adapt to suit your needs." He disappeared through several curtains into a darkened chamber.

The three travelers walked around the room looking at several contraptions, but were wary of touching anything. Burbon looked at his potion.

"Do you think these items actually work? I have seen salesman that have promised less than him, and there were a lot of disappointed people afterwards," commented Burbon.

"I don't sense he is lying," said Taro.

"Good, I feel a lot better," replied Burbon sarcastically. Stonewall looked out the window at a machine with wings. It was large enough to carry several creatures. *Could that thing actually fly?*

"That is a prototype," Turbine walked back into the room and interrupting Stonewall thoughts. "I sold the working model to an ocean town of Varna many years ago. I believe it sits in a museum now." He carried something in his hands covered by a small cloth. "Please gather round," he motioned.

Turbine removed the cloth to reveal a wooden cube with a recessed clockwork of gears inside. The interior corners were worn down with a clamp in each corner to allow four objects to be held within the cube.

"This is the best solution science has to offer. Each piece of your stones must be separated and placed at the four corners. Only if all four pieces are placed at exactly the same time, can the power be neutralized. If successful, the machine will absorb all the energy," Turbine pointed at the gears. "All danger will be removed."

"If this object negates magic, it doesn't sound like science to me!" commented Burbon.

"Your small mind can't comprehend anything complicated. I don't have the time to explain its mechanics to you. Just know that it works," Turbine reprimanded. Burbon made a face behind his back.

"But the gems can also do great good. Why must we negate their power?" asked Taro.

"Because as long as they can be used for evil, eventually they will. Destroy them now and remove the temptation for future evil," Stonewall stated.

"I want to keep my stone," says Taro.

"This is not a negotiation," answers Stonewall. "What if they in the fall in the wrong hands? You have to have a plan B."

Burbon gingerly ran his fingers along the top of the cube. He flinched as he touched a sharp tip.

"Ow! I'm not carrying this crazy object." He stroked his chin. "Maybe I should create some underlings to carry it for us?" as he fingered the top of his potion.

"I'll carry it, Burbon," motioned Stonewall.

"I have fulfilled my obligation, now please leave. I have important experiments to perform," Turbine stated.

"Remind me to recommend your hospitality to others, Turbine," Burbon flashed four fingers. "Four stars." Turbine ushered them towards the door.

"Use your items wisely, once used, they can never be used again." As they were leaving, a metal stand for beakers caught Stonewall's eye. His eye was drawn to the insignia RG embossed in the metal.

"Where did get you this stand?" Stonewall yelled.

"It is a common metal stand, I ordered it many months ago now. I believe it came overseas. The region of Solvana." Turbine was surprised over Stonewall's zealousness.

"Stonewall, what's wrong?" Taro asked. Stonewall carefully removed the stand away from the beakers.

"This stand was made by my father! You can tell by his brand. Since the work is recent, he must still be alive."

"Hey, Turbine, let him keep the stand. It means a lot to him," asked Burbon.

"Very well, I have many more in storage."

"Thank you for help. May the gods smile on your work," Stonewall placed the metal stand in his pouch.

"The god's have nothing to do with my science."

Turbine closed the door as the three travelers exited. The latched eye hole stayed open as a goggled eye watched them leave.

Under the fading light, Stonewall scrutinized the stand as if hypnotized by the insignia. Burbon put his hand on his back.

"Don't worry, after we find the remaining stones, we'll find your father. This is a good sign."

"I am happy for you as well," commented Taro, "but we must remain focused on our task."

"You are right," Stonewall stored the stand in his pouch. Where does that map take us next?"

"We need to find a ship!" Taro replied.

15

The Hunt

The three travelers broke camp early in the morning, hoping to walk while it was still cool. They were reflective and walked slowly in silence. The morning past and the suns sapped some of their strength. Taro sipped her water to conserve it for their long walk to the ocean. She admired the landscape. Although lacking the lushness of her home, she noticed many signs that there was plenty of game to hunt. *If only we had time, I could find out what type of animals live here.* As Taro stepped down into a small depression, she saw the footprint of a wild animal. She bent down and smelt the area around the six-toed footprint. Staring at it, she was reminded of a hunt many years ago.

"Is the footprint fresh, Taro?"

"Yes, Father. The animal that made this was here recently." A hole in the rock showed the entrance to its den. Taro looked up into the deep blue eyes of her father. "Father?"

"Yes, my daughter?"

"I know I am still a child in your eyes, but I would like to track the animal to its home. Alone. I can sense that we are close." Her father's kindly eyes surveyed his daughter's face.

"Have you grown up so fast that you can learn nothing more from your father?"

"No, Father. It will be easier for one of us to follow the animal to its den. Both of us will likely spook it, ruining the hunt."

"That's a gentle way to say you don't want your father around for the final part of the hunt. The most important part. Do you know the dangers of cornering an animal alone?"

"I do, Father. I know and I will be careful. Please, Father?" she asked, wanting to prove she can hunt on her own.

"It seems like yesterday that I was cradling you in my arms. Now you track and hunt better than me. How many moons have passed! Go, my daughter, but be careful. If you feel uncomfortable, come back to me and we will go together."

"Thank you, father! I will make you proud."

She kissed him and passed through the rock cavern into a sinkhole. The smell of limestone burned her nostrils as her feet slipped into the muddy surface. Minerals dripped down from the stalactites into to the water. As she touched the side of the cave, something slimy ran across the back of her hand.

"Ugggh!" Taro shrieked and lost her balance. Her knee landed in the soggy ground. *Maybe I should return to father.* A chattering sound in the darkness attracted her attention. As she walked forward, a slight luminance flowed through the water. The cave was illuminated by the creature's glow. It swished through the water and passed by her leg before she gauged its form.

Glad it doesn't bite. Water came up to her ankles. A distant glow grew brighter as a school of albino shrimp swam past her. Hairy feelers hung out of their mouths.

"You are too ugly to eat." Taro looked down and slapped her foot into the water. The sound scared the school of shrimp off into the distance. Darkness resumed as they swam away. The roof of the cave lowered causing her to bend her tall frame. *I better not get stuck down here.*

As Taro turned around a corner, the ceiling rose and shafts of light slipped through small recesses above. The light illuminated the interior of the cave. Something hairy jumped down from a stalactite, Taro almost bumped into it. As she turned her head, a pair of miniature red eyes gleamed. Jagged teeth smiled back as the creature rushed towards the ceiling. It chattered, a combination of mocking laughter and wildness, then disappeared into a crevice.

Is everything horrible to look at in the dark or is it worse in the light? The most hideous sight in our world is the tax collector, her father would say. *They smile pleasantly at you with manicured hands and fine clothes, but their hearts are dark. Appreciate the hideous things in life - there are many beings in life that will never show their true intent.*

That creature was still ugly! She straddled herself around a stone and into a larger recess with more deposits of limestone. A stalagmite rose in the middle of an open rock cavern, centuries of sentiment forming a wet deposit of stone. A chattering sound echoed from the ceiling again. Two red eyes stared down at Taro.

"Leave me alone!" she yelled and tossed a stone at the creature. It bounced harmlessly off an adjoining rock and splashed into the water below. Taro reached down for another rock. When she looked up and cocked her hand back, dozens of red eyes look down from the rock outcropping. In shock, Taro dropped the stone back into the water.

The hairy insect led me to all of his companions; maybe I can walk slowly back the way I came. Taro took two steps back. The creatures sensed her retreat and reacted with one mind. Half of the bodies leapt across the ceiling toward the entrance, blocking her escape.

Only one way to go now.

Taro charged to the opposite end as the furry attackers dropped from the ceiling like paratroopers. Their razor-sharp teeth grazed the back of her tunic missing her flesh. She felt their hot breath as they formed a terrible mass intent on subduing her. She climbed up a boulder and then another, trying to outdistance her pursuers. The cave was thick with the smell of their stench. She rounded the corner and met a rock wall. *Dead end*. She turned and their black hairy bodies covered the surrounding ground. She pulled out a small knife.

"Be gone, you foul underground beasts!" The creatures crawled within inches of her face; their gnashing teeth echoed throughout the cave.

If only I hadn't been so insistent to go this alone, Taro thought before the inevitable.

Suddenly the nearest beast ignited into flames. Its screams halted the progress of the others as they stared in wonderment.

"Leave my daughter alone!" yelled her father as he loosened another flaming bolt into the mass. Until a moment ago, the creatures had acted like a single mind with a single purpose. Now they scattered, unable to comprehend the burning heat of the fire. One fiery creature jumped to another spreading the fire. Their hideous screams filled the cave. The rest ran in a mass exodus. The creatures were terrified of each other and avoided the water without realizing that inches away was the salvation to their pain.

"Father! You followed me!" Taro bounded down the rocks and rushed into his arms.

"Of course." She cradled her head in his chest. "You don't think I would leave my only daughter to track an animal into a strange lair. What kind of father would I be?"

"Thank you, Father!" He looked at her hand, which still tightly grasped her knife.

"I should teach you how to use a crossbow and bolt. Your father won't always be there to look after you."

"Can you make me as good a marksman as you?" Taro inquired.

"Better, my dear. Something tells me you are going to be even better."

"What's wrong, Taro? Is this footprint from something dangerous?" Stonewall looked down at her with concerned eyes. The same expression that her father looked at her with. She smiled.

"No, Stonewall, is it a common track of a harmless jackolope. It just reminded me of a past memory," Taro replied.

"Must have been a good one, from the smile on your face," mentioned Stonewall. Before she could answer, Burbon interrupted.

"The two of you should look at the next rise."

Taro and Stonewall walked over to Burbon. The plain ahead of them looked like a battleground, with dozens of cacti lying shriveled on the ground like a decimated army. Their stalks were brown, all nutrition removed from their bodies.

"This desert is dry, but how hot does it get when the cactus can't even survive?" Burbon asked.

"The cactus didn't die from the heat, they died from something else," Taro explained.

"What do you mean?" Burbon was puzzled.

"There is a creature that burrows into the stalk and lives like a parasite, draining the life-force of its host until it has sucked every drop of moisture. It moves from plant to plant gorging until it runs out of hosts. I have seen them render a whole field of crops into dust. They are called cactus killers."

Burbon bursts out laughing. "Ooooohhhhh," he gestures with his hands. "Am I supposed to be scared of some bug that sucks on plants? Let's move on." He took a few steps towards the cacti and then stopped. "What does this thing look like anyway?"

"They are small but can enter any orifice and suck that creature dry," replied Taro. Burbon turned around.

"Orifice! You mean like my ears?" Burbon covered his ears with both hands.

"Or eyes," Stonewall pointed his two fingers to Burbon's eyes. Burbon hands covered his eyes

"Or especially your mouth," Taro commented as Burbon put both hands over his mouth as his eyes grew big.

"You know, Burbon, there are worst entry points than your mouth or ears," mentioned Stonewall. Burbon jumped straight into the air.

"What are we going to do? Can we go around the cacti?" he danced around.

"We don't have time to go around. We have to get to the ocean," answered Taro.

"Let's pick the narrowest section and cross as quickly as we can," replied Stonewall.

The trio travelled a short distance and saw a section of live cactus in the far distance that were beyond the parasite's touch.

"This is the best place to cross. Remember Burbon, be quiet. The cactus killers are sensitive to vibrations. If they hear us, they will come out of the cactus," Stonewall advised.

"And drill themselves into our bodies, taking every drop of water," added Taro.

Burbon took an extra gulp of water from his canteen.

"That's it; give them an extra reason to come after you," Taro commented.

Burbon choked and spit out his water.

"Ssshhhhh" Taro and Stonewall put their fingers to their mouths.

The three of them surveyed the terrain and walked together through the dead cacti towards their goal. They tread quietly, as if stepping through a minefield, afraid of the consequences of one misstep. Stonewall stepped over a dried cactus stalk, its needle-like leaves, brittle and broken from the wind. Taro zigzagged around the plants, taking care to avoid it. Burbon walked the slowest, his sweaty body reeking of fear.

Burbon slipped and accidentally stepped on a dried stalk. He stopped; his face a mask of shock. He stared at Taro and Stonewall who motioned him to stop.

For a moment, no one moved. Burbon closed his mouth as if breathing will alert the creature to his presence. After thirty seconds past and nothing happened, Burbon relaxed. At that moment, a small worm slithered down the edge of the cactus stalk. It moved slowly and purposively, a slimly trail following its ugly white bloated body. Burbon coaxed his head at Stonewall. *Is this the cactus killer?* Stonewall put his finger to his mouth to tell Burbon to remain quiet.

Burbon stepped back and accidentally crushes another stalk. He froze and looked back at the worm. Its red eyes surveyed him with unexpected intelligence for something so small. It stared at Burbon for several seconds and then bent its head and continued munching on the dried leaves. Burbon couldn't contain himself any longer. He fell on to the ground, exploding into laughter.

"That's the cactus killer! A tiny little worm! You two really had me going. How is that little thing going to hurt me?" Burbon's eyes closed in his attack of laughter. When he opened his eyes, he saw a sight that stole his laughter. Next to the worm on the stalk sat another worm. And next to that worm sat another worm. And another. And another dozen. And another hundred. Burbon looked behind and hundreds of worms have lined up on nearby stalks. Their hungry eyes watching him like a predator watches its prey before striking. Burbon backed up as they crawled closer. Inch by inch.

"That's okay, you worms had me scared for a moment. But unless you can catch me, I don't have anything to worry about." He peered down at one of the worms, it compressed its body back, like an elastic band. At that moment, a worm flew through the air past his ear. The next one landed on the ground before him. Then the air was thick with their bodies, a gummy soft rain. One landed on Burbon's head that he swiped away. Another on his foot that he kicked off. He saw a platoon of worms flying towards his face. He felt a scream welling up inside of him. Before he could open his mouth, a set of strong arms lifted him off the ground. The three of them ran through the clouds of worms, brushing them off before they could crawl onto their faces. They passed the last dried cactus stalk, Taro and Stonewall fell face first into the desert ground, exhausted from their run.

Burbon danced like a man on fire. "I have a hole in my tunic; one of those worms is trying to crawl inside of me." He tore his clothes off in a mad panic, beating each item of clothes on nearby rocks. He screamed like a madman until he was down to his underwear. He was disrobing further when the actions of his companions halted him.

Stonewall was bent over with laughter. He lay on all fours, his fist pounding into the ground in uncontrollable spurts. Taro was rolling around on the ground like a tumbleweed and with each revolution her laughter threw her body into convolutions. Burbon didn't understand until the answer came to him like a bolt from the blue.

"Those worms were just worms, weren't they?" he asked as he flicks a worm off his arm towards Taro.

"Sorry, my little friend, Taro suggested the jest earlier to me, but I didn't think you would believe it. The look on your face...was priceless," replied Stonewall stifling a big belly laugh. Taro stopped rolling long enough for Burbon to see her tears. He threw his boot at her, which she easily avoided.

"Very amusing, archer," Burbon put his pants back on. "I'll get back at you. Both of you!" He pointed at Taro and Stonewall, his eyes big and serious. This sent both of his companions into another fit of laughter. He grabbed his remaining clothes and dressed as he walks. He misstepped putting his pants on and fell onto the desert sand, which caused the laughter behind him to increase once again.

"I'll get even," he uttered under his breathe. He reached the top of a sand dune and stopped in his tracks.

"You two better come here," he yelled. Both Taro and Stonewall looked at each other as their laughter diminished.

"If you're trying to fool us, you could be a bit less obvious," as Taro stood up.

"Relax. When I settle this score, it will be less obvious. Now come over here, both of you."

Taro and Stonewall stepped towards Burbon. As they approached the dune, they saw what caught his interest. In the distance, was the sea village of Amir. It was a walled town with huge merchant ships docked in its harbor. Flocks of seabirds circled above the city scavenging for fish. The faint scent of salt stung the air and the breeze felt cooler than before. They had reached their destination.

"Do you think we can find a trustworthy captain?" Taro asked Stonewall.

"It will be difficult. Most of them are cutthroat sailors who would rather slit your throat while you sleep," Stonewall answered. Burbon ignored the threat.

"So much for positive thinking. Let's head to town and get a drink. I'm parched!"

16

Captain Nox

The village of Amir was a dirty sea town. The people who lived here were not the types you would bring home to mother. Filthy faces with unkempt hair greeted the travelers as they walked down the crowded street. Several children chased behind them looking for coins. Burbon spied their toothless grins as Stonewall tossed some silver. They greedily took the coins and ran off to the nearest eatery.

"I guess there are no dentists in this town," Burbon murmured. The three travelled deeper into the town. Several soldiers on horses rode past them looking them over with interest. Burbon nervously sidestepped and pulled Stonewall's tunic.

"Are we there yet?"

A body flew out from the door of a building and landed at their feet.

"This is the place." Stonewall walked into the tavern with Taro and Burbon behind him. The place was dark and the air thick with pipe smoke. The room was noisy, groups of sailors stood drinking mugs of brew. The men leered at Taro and then turned around when Stonewall gave them a stern glare. Burbon hustled to the bar and immediately ordered a drink. He took a big swig and spun around with his back to the bartender.

"This is the life. I wonder if this town needs a trader?" Burbon leaned back.

"Don't get too comfortable, little man. We are here for a reason," prodded Taro.

"Yeah, to find a captain who won't rob us blind." The three sat in a booth in the back and surveyed the bar. For a while, they watched sailors come and go from the tavern. Burbon picked at his food.

"What is wrong with your meat mash?" asked Stonewall, finishing his meal.

"The spices are too strong, makes me think they are trying to hide the smell of rancid meat."

"The meals on the ocean will be worse. I suggest you finish it." Burbon made a face but continued eating his food. He peered around the tavern and wondered how long it would take before there was trouble. He didn't wait long.

A mug shattered and two sailors started a shoving match. A wooden stool broke over one's head and he sunk to the ground. The other sailor stood over his fallen comrade and kicked him in the ribs. He immediately fell as another foot swiped his other leg from underneath him. The two fighting sailors looked up at the new arrival. His garb was flamboyant, a bright red hat with a black feather sticking out of its brim. His clothes were made of silky material, a black sash circled his waist. His hands were rough, but his face was clean, unlike most of the residents of the bar.

"Stop your fighting you mangy holgogs! I need all of you healthy for tomorrow's voyage. Barkeep, a round of ale for this worthless group of sailors." Choruses of cheers filled the bar and the men were pulled up from the floor to shake hands over an ale. The stranger ordered a pitcher of ale for himself and turned to Taro.

"What brings an elf to this part of the world?" he asked. Mutton chop sideburns framed a smile on his face. The smile changed to a frown as Stonewall stood up.

"We are looking for a seaworthy boat to take us to this island," Stonewall pointed to their map. "Do you know a captain that will take us?" The man looked down on the map.

"The Island of Modan? Depends on what you have to offer." The man stared at Taro with welcoming eyes.

"Three sets of strong arms and backs should pay for our voyage," Burbon volunteered. The man was unimpressed with the offer.

"I have plenty of bodies to run my ship. They take orders without thought. I don't need more mouths to feed." He tried to leave but Stonewall coaxed him to sit down by pressing gently with his massive arm. A couple of sailors looked up from the bar. Stonewall grabbed Burbon's pouch and slammed it on the table allowing several gems to spill out. Burbon instinctively scooped the gems back into the pouch before eliciting the wrong kind of attention.

"These gems are not for sale," Burbon snarled. The man stopped Burbon's hand.

"Too bad. If you won't part with your wealth, I only see one other thing worth bargaining for," the man again leered at Taro. She bared her teeth to answer his question. He smiled. "Seems the gems are the only offer on the table. What's it going to be?" Burbon held the pouch of gems to his chest much like a child treasured his teddy bear.

"Hand them over, Burbon. Remember who saved your life from the dragon so you could acquire those riches," Taro reminded him. Burbon shoulders slouched and he tossed the bag across the table. The man cradled the pouch and put three large stones into his pocket and threw the pouch back to Burbon.

"Half now and half when you reach your destination. And the three of you better be willing to put your backs into this voyage. Do you understand?"

"Completely," replied Stonewall. "And you understand what will happen to you if cheat us out of our voyage, Captain...?"

"Nox! Captain Nox! Yes, I understand the meaning of a deal made. I am many things, a scoundrel, a drunk, a loudmouth, but I am a man of my word," Captain Nox stood up. "Be ready to sail at first light, if you're late, then you forfeit these gems," as he rolled one of the rocks between his fingers.

"Wait a minute, how will we find you?" Burbon asked with concern of being taken for his money.

"Look for the grandest sailing vessel in the harbor and you'll find me and my crew." Captain Nox tipped his hat and proceeded pass the sailors who raised their glasses to him. He disappeared through the doors into the murky darkness of the village. Taro looked over to Stonewall.

"Can we trust him?" she asked.

"He has the respect of his men and carries himself like a man of honor." He turned to Taro. "Mostly. We have to trust him, for now."

"Easy for you say, I'll be sleeping with one eye open on his ship." Burbon yawned. "I need some shut eye and a bath. I still feel like a worm is crawling in my tunic."

In the morning, the three journeyed down to the town's harbor. The shore was a beehive of activity as sailors and shoremen loaded ships full of supplies. The saltwater mixed with sewage from the town creating a grotesque odor. Many men wore wraps around their faces to stop the smell. They walked to the main dock where men lifted goods onto ships. Exotic fruits and cargos carried off to strange destinations. A few sailors casted a wary eye toward the travelers; these boats were mainly for goods, not for passengers.

"How do we know Captain Nox hasn't lied? He didn't even give us his ship's name. He could have left with my gems already," Burbon mused.

"Patience," answered Taro, "we haven't even searched half of the harbor yet."

"I am a good judge of character. Captain Nox is a man of his word," commented Stonewall.

"I hope you're right, Stonewall," Burbon mocked. "I have a feeling Captain Nox isn't even a captain."

"Don't be so negative," chided Stonewall.

"Not negative, just realistic," Burbon jumped onto a crate to gain stature over his two friends. "I don't trust our dear captain." He moved his arms in grand gestures and mimicked the captain's mannerism. Not getting any response from his audience, Burbon leapt down from the crate.

"How are we supposed to find this ship of his anyway?" Rounding the corner, they viewed a majestic sight. Sitting in the center of the harbor, a huge vessel lay anchored with several ships running back and forth to it with supplies. The ship was massive with four masts and dozens of sails. Sailors climbed the netting, busily making last minute adjustments. The stern of the ship is covered with teak and a one-piece rudder dips deep into the water. Unlike most hulls, on each side of the ship, winged shafts jutted into the water to connect to huge pontoons. The pontoons lift the ship out the water while allowing the ship to catch more wind.

But the front of the boat is what grabbed their attention. The hull formed a sharp, narrow edge to cut through the waves. Adorned on the top of the bow were two dragonheads beautifully carved out of mahogany with life-like features. Only the eyes portrayed the deadness of the carving, one head had more teeth than the other. The second head was more colorful painted, but both would place fear in the hearts of anyone who might see them on a foggy day.

"I think we have found our ship," answered Stonewall.

Captain Nox stood on shore giving orders to several of the crew who were gathering his last supplies. He saw the trio and beckoned them towards him.

"Welcome to my ship, *The Dragon's Feast*. You are just in time; we are about to push off."

"Would you have left without us?" questioned Burbon.

"If you had been late," he smiled back. "Please join me on the dory." Captain Nox yelled to a sailor in a strange guttural language. "Orden be goda."

"Modasa!" The first mate growled back and surveyed the three travelers. They were unsure of the reply.

"What language are you speaking? It's not a common tongue dialect?" Taro asked Nox as the dory pushed offshore.

"Most sailors speak a broken dialect of braganese, as they don't come from the village of Amir. The people here are lazy and make poor seamen. In the ports of call across the great expanse is where I recruit most of my men. As a result, I spend more time on that side of the ocean. Perhaps you would like to join me," Nox looked at Taro.

"The islands of Modan is our destination," Stonewall answered for Taro.

"Very well," Nox replied to Taro.

"How are we going to talk to anyone if we can't speak their language?" asked Burbon. Nox ordered the men at the oars.

"Traveras von diem!" The men looked at Burbon.

"Osclan dos ver drapmen," the men yelled back with laughter.

"I think they are laughing at your shortness," jibed Taro to Burbon.

"Great, this voyage just gets better and better," Burbon added sarcastically.

By the time the first of the two moons rose, *The Dragon's Feast* had sailed many leagues. The crew tacked the sails to catch the ocean's strongest winds. Stonewall sat at the bow of ship sharpening his broadsword.

"Can you get that sword much sharper, warrior?" Taro stepped up from below deck.

"These are strange days; one never knows when the next battle will strike. A dull blade is a sign of a weak opponent."

"Well said," replied Taro. "But I think you sharpen your blade more to take your mind off the metal stand." Stonewall nodded back to her.

"Ever since I found my father's handiwork at Turbine's lab, my mind has been consumed with how it got there. Is he still alive? Why hasn't he contacted me?" Stonewall slammed his hand into the deck.

"You taught that wooden plank a lesson!" Burbon swung down from the upper deck. "Am I interrupting?" He noticed the serious of tone between Stonewall and Taro.

"No," as Stonewall stood. "We're late for supper. Where have you been hiding?"

"Oh, I've been around," as he barreled in front of the two and ran on ahead. "Come on, I'm starving." He dashed down the stairs to the galley. Burbon rounded a corner and went through the main doors. The sight that greeted him was worth the wait. On the main serving table was a host of wonderful meats and fruits. The smell permeated the room with its sweet aroma. "I think I've died and gone to heaven," Burbon muttered.

"And here I didn't take you as a religious man," said Captain Nox, entering the room behind Burbon. He sat in the chair at the head of the table. Several crewmembers scrambled to get seats near a huge boar roast.

"What's with all the food? Is this our last meal?" Burbon asked. Taro and Stonewall entered and were momentarily in awe of the feast before them.

"Is there a special occasion?" Taro sat at the opposite end of the table from Captain Nox.

"The start of a new voyage. My men deserve only the best," he answered. The tables filled up quickly as other crewmembers seated themselves. Captain Nox stood up to address his crew. "It is customary for the captain to thank everyone for this bountiful feast. But tonight, I would ask one of our guests to have the honor." He looked at the end of the table. "Taro, does your god have a blessing for this meal?"

"The elves have many gods we thank for our meals. Unfortunately, no blessings are appropriate outside our elfin culture," Taro answered. Captain Nox looked elsewhere on the table.

"What about you, Stonewall? How many gods do your people worship?"

"My people worship one god, a god of battle and victory. We have no blessing for our meals and for a quick victory over our enemies."

"That leaves only Burbon, would you do us the honor?" gestured Captain Nox.

"Oh no, my people have no gods, our hard work is our only blessing. We worship nothing."

"That's not true, you worship one thing every day. Wealth is your god," said Taro.

"My crew can understand that," Captain Nox raised his hands and brought the room to silence.

"I can't do the blessing. No one here will understand me," Burbon complained.

"Then I will translate." He gestured to his crew. "Vanso me blessa sur la Burbon." All eyes faced towards Burbon. He nervously pulled on his collar.

"Ah," he stuttered as dozens of faces hung on his words.

"Tell us one of your laws of business—your bible," teased Taro. Burbon was puzzled and then cane up with a thought.

"The first rule of business," he started.

"La mucho wava du comerca" repeated Nox.

"Know your customer needs…"

"Versa ma lindo von necisto."

"Know your abilities to provide…"

"Nuedago la bilutuns sur cedo.

"And always over deliver on your promises."

"Et tangira ba de ado vanduso."

"But most important…."

"Sat do muso ….."

"Never do business on an empty stomach!"

"Vas luso comerca dur la detra boutache!"

The room was silent as the crewmembers were still listening to the toast. Then the room erupted with laughter and enthusiasm

"Van da gusa!" they cheer, "Van da gusa!" They clinked their mugs and passed the food around. Stonewall nudged Burbon.

"Good job, little man," he whispered.

The mood was jovial and the food plentiful and delicious. Nox's men celebrated with much gusto. The captain walked over to Burbon, pulled up a chair and turned it around.

"I understand you have found a way to communicate with my men," he stated.

"What do you mean?" Taro asked with interest from across the table.

"Burbon has been teaching my men a game of cards although I am unfamiliar with the rules of Red Dog." Burbon choked back a piece of food.

"I'm just showing them a friendly game. No harm done," he replied. Captain Nox moved closer.

"No harm to you, but I understand you made yourself a lot of money today." Taro and Stonewall stared at Burbon.

"Is this true?" Stonewall asked.

"Maybe," he answered sheepishly. "But I won it fair and square!"

"For your sake I hope so. My men are simple and don't make a lot of money. If I find out, you are cheating them..." Nox let the sentence hang for a moment. Burbon wanted to hear the rest.

"You'll what? What will you do?"

"You'll take a long walk off a short plank unless your friends care to defend you."

"It would serve him right," answered Stonewall.

"I'll take him up right now if you would like," offered Taro. Burbon sulked away but the others watched as he approached several crewmembers and placed coins in each hand.

"Well done," Stonewall commented to Nox.

"A captain's job is to watch over his crew." The first mate bounded into the dining hall.

"Captain ma asicenta van nelson!" He yelled with concern and several others listened to his comments. Nox and several crewmembers scrambled up to the deck to investigate the alarm. Taro and Stonewall followed close behind.

The evening was dense with fog, it had rolled in during their meal and now was as thick as pea soup. Taro could barely see more than a dozen feet in front of her. Captain Nox stood quietly by the ship's wheel and listened into the distance. Stonewall knelt but could only hear the lapping of the waves against the ship's hull. Taro's keen ears heard it first.

"Maaaaaaowoooooooo," a throaty cry bellowed from the leeside of the ship. Taro turned her head to that direction.

"Maaaaaavoooooooooo." Its cries were slightly louder as if the distance was decreasing between it and the ship.

"What is it?" Stonewall asked Nox. The captain raised his finger to his mouth for Stonewall to lower his voice.

"It is a fog eater," he whispered. "Ancient beasts living in the fog banks of the ocean, relentlessly stalking prey. Often, they travel in packs. One will use their voice to flush out its prey so the others can attack its victim as it tries to outrun the sound."

"You don't recommend running away from it?" Stonewall whispered back.

"Just the opposite. It will hear us trying to get away. Because of the fog, their eyesight is poor, but their gift of hearing is great. Everyone must be perfectly quiet."

"What's going on?" Burbon yelled as he climbed on deck. Everyone motioned him to be quiet.

"Sorry," he answered, "I didn't know supper was over."

"Maaaaavooooooooo." The sound was almost on top of them. Burbon looked to Stonewall who nodded to remain silent. Burbon gulped, unsure of what was approaching. Captain Nox took the wheel and steered it slightly left of the wailing sound. The whole crew remained immobile, no one was making a sound.

"Maaaaawooooooo." The sound was slightly behind them now. The crewmembers relaxed and someone leaned on one of the crates. A loading knife fell off the crate and splashed into the ocean.

"Maaa..." the cry stopped and then silence. The crew scurried around the deck, picking up anything that remotely resembled a weapon.

"Draw your weapons," Nox ordered. The crewmember that made the mistake whispered to Nox, "Vas la nosga der..." his words died in his throat as huge set of jaws appeared from the fog and snatched him from the deck. His scream lasted short seconds before a sickening crunch was heard and then the ocean went quiet. The men grouped themselves together to form a circle, back to back, waiting for the monster to strike again. One man grabbed a hook and threw it toward an empty part of the deck.

"Clang!" It rang and almost instantaneously the monster emerged from the fog to grab at whatever made the sound. It shook its head from side-to-side, puzzled at the lack of fresh meat. The sailors threw their weapons at the head, aiming for its eyes. The weapons punctured the skin but nothing lethal. It cried and disappeared back into the fog.

Taro shifted her weight and a bolt in her quiver bumped against others making a slight tinking sound. The beast attacked from the other side, intent on swallowing her whole. Nox threw his dagger and skewered it between the eyes. It turned from Taro for a second to roar at Nox.

Before it could turn back to her, Taro yelled, "Conject iti!"

The flames shuddered through her body slamming down the throat of monster. It roared in pain and the smell of burning flesh was overpowering. Taro slumped down to the deck, exhausted from her exertion.

"Did we get it?" Burbon whispered. His answer came in the roar of pain from the fog eater. And then another roar from the left side. And then two more roars from the front. The burnt fog eater's cries have brought the rest of his pack. *The Dragon's Feast* was surrounded. Captain Nox and his crew scrambled, taking positions on the deck. Stonewall pulled himself up to Nox.

"Can we do anything to help?" he asked.

"Pray," Nox answered. "We've only ever beaten one of them. A pack is nearly impossible. But they won't take my ship without a fight!" Brave words but the sight that greeted us next would chill our hearts.

The fog was breaking. Before the ship rose the fog eater, taller than the highest mast. Its flesh was burned which intensified its anger. It was a huge water serpent, most of its bulk was hidden beneath the ocean. It coiled its head back, ready to sink the ship.

"The flames have made him mad. The next strike will be our last," Burbon sighed.

"We are not lost yet," Stonewall pulled the staff out of its sheath that Turbine gave him. He placed it down on the deck and pulled Taro up next to him. "I need you to use your powers one more time," he requested.

"I don't think I can," she replied and stumbled as the fog eater lashed at the deck.

Crash! It splintered the first mast. The sails came tumbling down, covering several sailors. The fog eater eyed the sailors pinned to the deck.

"Taro, please conjure your flame one last time," Stonewall asked.

"I will try." She weakly rose holding one end of the staff. "Conject iti," she squeaked. Stonewall shifted the staff at the advancing monster. Acting as a conduit, Taro's flame surged through the staff as Stonewall aimed it straight at the head of the beast. Stonewall yelled in pain while guiding the power of the flames as it hit the beast. The fog eater's head exploded, and its lifeless body fell and floated on the ocean.

"I think I swallowed brain," Burbon whined and spit it out. Stonewall was slumped on the deck and Taro rest against him. "Are you okay?" she asked.

"I am spent and so is this staff." Taro watched as the staff in Stonewall's hands turned to dust before her eyes. Burbon stood by Stonewall and slapped him on the back.

"You did it, Stonewall! You saved our lives. Now, what are you going to do about them?" Burbon pointed off in the distance, as two large fog eaters closed the distance between them and the ship.

"There is nothing I can do," Stonewall croaked and slumped down to the deck.

"Hard to port," Nox yelled to his crew. *The Dragon's Feast* veered toward the advancing monsters.

"What are you doing? You'll kill us all!" screamed Burbon.

"Watch me," commanded the captain. The fog eaters were twice as fast as the ship and race toward us in a head on collision. Five ship lengths, Four, three.

"Is this a game of chicken?" Burbon wondered over Nox's shoulder. At one boat length, both monsters veered right to their fallen comrade.

"Do they think they can help it?" Burbon asks.

"No, they go to feed," Nox replied. The monsters ravaged the flesh of their fallen as *The Dragon's Feast* disappeared back into the fog. Several other fog eaters' screams filled the air.

"If their need for flesh wasn't so great, they would have come after us. They hunger meat so badly; they will eat one of their own if it doesn't fight back." Nox looked at the bow of the ship. "Brace the forward mast —avast mon cratonlo," he ordered to his crew. He looked at Stonewall who had recovered slightly from the staff's blast.

"I don't know what magic you carry, warrior, archer. But your help is greatly appreciated. You have the gratitude of myself and my crew." He peered at Burbon. "What power does this little one carry?"

"He'll talk you to death," Taro raised her head while smiling.

The next several days proceeded uneventfully. The mists broke over the horizon and revealed the lonely Isle of Modan. The reefs protected the broken shores, making approach a hazardous venture. Nox peered at a rocky cliff through his spyglass.

"The three of you have been close-lipped about your destination. The Island of Modan is treacherous with countless dangers. Are you sure I can't take you instead to our next port of call?"

"No, Captain Nox, you have fulfilled our bargain admirably. Burbon, pay the rest of the gems to him," Stonewall commanded. Burbon made a face as he reached into his tunic to remove three gems. Nox put his hand on Burbon's to stop him.

"Your comrade's bravery saved my ship and my crew. It is I who am in your debt."

"Take us to the island and consider our debt fulfilled," answered Taro. Burbon stared at Nox.

"Can I have my other gems back?" he asked. Stonewall swatted his head. "Ow, I was just asking," Burbon cried.

The dory cast off the beach and headed through the reefs. Captain Nox waved goodbye while the sailors rowed steadily back to the ship. The three pondered their next step. Taro pulled out the living map which squirmed at her touch.

"Sorry we haven't taken you out sooner," as she unrolled the map. "Here, toward the tip of this mountain. There lies the next piece." The three scanned over the island's thick jungle. Sheer cliffs, jagged rocks and dark hills welcomed them. Burbon walked ahead while turning to his two comrades.

"Come on. Somewhere on this desolate rock lies the third stone."

17

The Guardian of the Island

The wind rustled through Sunder's feathers as he flew high above the fog-shrouded ocean. Sunder heard the distant roar of the fog eaters swirling in the ocean currents. The griffin's keen eyes found it difficult to make out shapes among the shadows below.

"Maaavvvvvoooo!"

Sunder flew higher to avoid the cause of the sound. The fog broke and Sunder stared into the eyes of a mammoth fog eater. Its neck reared, ready to fling its razor-sharp mouth at Sunder's body. The bird tensed for the oncoming collision.

"Bllllassssttttzzzz." An energy bolt boiled the left eye of the fog eater. It sizzled sending the beast into throes of agony. It dropped to the ocean surface, writhing in pain. The smell of sulfur permeated from Darkmoor's specter.

Filthy beast. I wish my magic could banish their kind from this world.

The fog eater is not a creature to be trifled with master, thought Sunder.

Enough! Concentrate on the task at hand. My spies in Amir told me of three travelers whom left on The Dragon's Feast, but that vessel is nowhere to be found.

Darkmoor scratched under his helmet at his disfigured face. The scars always reminded him of his father.

The pain I have endured will be nothing like the pain the three will feel when I find them.

"How are we going to get there?" whined Burbon as he crossed the sand bar.

"We walk. If we could get there by talking, you'd already be there by now," commented Taro.

"The land becomes more solid once we cross these shells," Stonewall pointed out.

Blue mussel shells lay with their mouths open, glued to the rocks. Years of salt and fresh water have cemented them to the ground. Burbon went first.

"Crunch!" his feet stepped on the shell skeletons. "Ouch, these things are tough."

"*Then you better watch where you step.*"

"Hey I'm trying," Burbon replied.

"Who are you talking to," asked Stonewall.

"Didn't you tell me to watch where I step?" questioned Burbon.

"I did no such thing," he replied.

"Sounds like you're losing your mind," commented Taro. "Not that you would have far to go."

Burbon looked back to his comrades.

"Oh, I get it. Play another trick on Burbon again. Since the cactus, I don't believe anything the two of you say." He continued walking while the Taro and Stonewall shook their heads.

"Be careful, these shells have existed for hundreds of years, their pieces can be sharp." Stonewall warned as shells crunched under his soles.

"*Actually, we have been here thousands of years.*" Stonewall stopped.

"Taro did you just say something?" he asked.

"You're starting to sound like the trader. No, I didn't say anything. Maybe Burbon is throwing my voice," Taro answered.

"Not me! I'm not going to sink to your trickery," Burbon replied. "At least not right now," he whispered.

"*That's not the way to act.*"

"Will you two cut that out!" Burbon yelled back.

"Stop playing around Burbon," Taro answered.

"Maybe he's telling the truth."

"Who said that?" Taro scanned around them. All three of them stopped and looked down at their feet. The voice that has talked to them individually now talked to all three.

"You should go back. You don't belong on this island." The voice was louder but was not spoken, only heard in their thoughts.

"Who are you and what do you want? Stonewall commanded.

"We are nothing and we are everything. We guard this island allowing the residents to live in solitude. You are not welcome."

"What are you going to do, scare us?" laughed Burbon.

"Nothing so crude, but we will urge you to return to your ship."

One of the mussel shells spit saltwater into Burbon eyes.

"Ouch, cut it out! The saltwater stings," Burbon cried.

More shells sprayed their salty water at all three until the water hits with the force of sharp rocks. A cut formed on Stonewall's forehead and blood dripped down his wet face.

"I have had enough! I mean you no harm, but you have tried my patience." Stonewall took out his broadsword and slashed huge groups of shells. Burbon and Taro joined him by jumping into the air and smashing down on the mussel shells. They ran against the wall of spraying water, almost like kids running through a sprinkler. The spray clanged against their armor. Then as suddenly as it started, the mussels closed, and the water spray stopped.

"You have proven that you will not be deterred. Continue on your task but be warned that there are others that live here that won't be as gentle as us." The voice vanished from their minds.

"Gentle! One of those water shots gave me a black eye. Why don't you come out and I can return the favor?"

"The spirit is gone Burbon. Don't fight a battle that doesn't exist," Taro walked past him. A shell opened its mouth and sprayed water at Taro's butt just as she stepped into the tall reeds.

"Ouch!" she yelled. Burbon laughed.

"Way to go, spirit. Good to see you have a sense of humor." Stonewall put his massive arms around both Taro and Burbon and pulled them up to higher ground.

"Be on your guard. The challenges to come will be much more severe then this subtle warning." His blade hacked a way into the forest.

As they make their way to solid ground, the woods opened into a grassy plain. The center of the field were rock formations that formed a circle. They looked at the structures and to decipher the glyph symbols scrawled in the rock. Taro placed her hands on a winged four-legged beast. Below the statute was writing in a strange language.

"All around us are statues of animals, some of which I have never seen before," commented Stonewall. "Are you familiar with some of these from your hunts?"

"Not many," Taro answered, "but I feel there is common thread among them. I wish I was blessed with more than the ability to create flames." She received condolences from an unexpected source.

"Give yourself time. Your flames may be the first ability that has manifested itself," added Burbon.

"The trader speaks good advice. You have many natural abilities. If other magic abilities appear, be ready to use them wisely," Stonewall pointed out.

"But what if this is the only power I will have?" she asked. Neither Burbon nor Stonewall could answer. The sound of scrapping stones carried across the field.

"Who's there?" Stonewall questioned. Silence was his only answer.

"Maybe it is an animal," Burbon stated.

"It sounded heavier than wild game," mentioned Taro as she walked over a large mound of stones. Burbon tripped and fell face first, narrowly missing a rock statue.

"Do you need some help with your feet, Trader?" inquired Taro. "Remember what we discussed, left, right, left, right."

"And I didn't think elves had humor in their culture." He stared up at a rock and an eye blinked at him. The rocks shuffled and a living creature formed from their mass. Burbon backed up and tripped over the same piles of stones.

"Stonewall, Taro, we have company!" The stones stood up. The creature's head swirled on its neck. Its body was easily several heads taller than Stonewall. Two eyes gazed upon them and a huge rock fist came smashing down, narrowly missing Burbon.

"I have never seen such a creature. What is it?" asked Stonewall. He watched from behind as a third eye appeared in the back of its rock head. Taro pulled out a bolt and aimed.

"It's a Triclops, a guardian for other beings. Impossible to sneak up on and nearly impossible to disable." Her bolt bounced effortlessly off of the monster. Stonewall drew his broadsword and the sun gleamed off its sharp blade. The Triclops was drawn toward its light like a moth to a flame. Stonewall swung, his blade cut two inches into the rock monster's body before being stopped by the monster's rock body. Stonewall was picked up effortless by the triclops and sent flying into the bushes. Seconds later, Stonewall's sword came flying after him.

"I have never seen anything pick up Stonewall like that! I'm not going near that thing. Is there anything we can do, Taro?" Burbon asked.

"Just one. Run!" She past Burbon to meet Stonewall on the other side of the plain. She bent down to Stonewall. "A hasty retreat is in order," she advised. Stonewall was hesitant.

"I never run from a fight. Ever!" He grabbed his sword and advanced toward the Triclops. Burbon put his hand on Stonewall.

"I agree with Taro. Sometimes you have to pick your battles."

"Warrior, trader, follow me, if you want to live," Taro disappeared into the foliage of the forest.

The Triclops lumbered through the forest, squashing everything in its path. It could not speak, but pursued with purpose. It rounded a corner and hesitated for a moment, as if a hint of intelligence crossed his mind. It moved forward through the grass and then tumbled to the ground, falling over a trip wire. Its massive weight caused it to roll on the ground until it sailed over a cliff into the water far below. Burbon came out of the thicket and watched the water splash.

"Rock head wasn't so tough after all," commented Burbon. A seagull shrieked overhead, and the cliff reverberated, almost knocking Burbon down. He peered over the cliff to see the triclops pounding its fist into the granite wall to make its own handholds.

"I spoke too soon, it's heading back."

"It can try." Stonewall grabbed a nearby boulder and threw it down, hitting the Triclops square in the chest. It stumbled and fell back into the water. Seconds later, it clawed its way out the water again and resumed its climb.

"Stonewall, brute force is not going to kill it. How do you stop something that doesn't breathe, feel pain, and has an eye in the back of its head?" Burbon quizzed, his finger jabbing in the air. "Yes, that has to be it. Come on you two, follow me back to the rock statues." Stonewall and Taro shared a puzzled look but followed Burbon while the Triclops continued climbing up the cliff face.

Minutes later, the Triclop's arms came over the edge and it pulled itself onto the top of the cliff. It had no ability to smell, but examined a set tracks in the grass and pursued back to the plain of rock statues.

"It's got to here somewhere. Examine all the statues," Burbon asked.

"Are you sure about this?" wondered Taro.

"No, but I remember acquiring an ugly statue in the shape of a large hairy beast. It sat on my shelf for years until a hunter told me that it was magically sealed to control the beast it was shaped in. Apparently, he found the beast in the hills around the city and used the statue to control it for protecting his farm."

"So, you sold these creatures in slavery," Taro growled.

"I only knew afterwards, and besides I couldn't try to take back or be crushed by his protector."

"Burbon, get to the point!" demanded Stonewall.

"Find a statue the same shape as the triclops and we can control it!" yelled Burbon as he madly searches the rock platform.

"Better find it fast," answered Taro as the Triclops rushed across the plain toward them.

"I'll slow it down, you two keep searching." Stonewall jumped on the Triclops, pulling it down to the ground.

Taro scrambled through the rock statues, birds, centaurs, bears, but no triclops. "Burbon," she howled.

"I don't see it!" he yelled. Stonewall went flying by and smashed into a tree. He was dazed momentarily and the Triclops turned its attention toward Taro.

"Burbon, keep looking. I will distract this monstrosity!"

Taro yanked a bolt out of her quiver and aimed for the Triclop's head. It's one eye on the back of its head blinked and then turned around. The triclops tilted its head and caught the bolt straight in it eye. It made a gurgling sound with its mouth and then yanked the bolt from its rock head, like a child removed a splinter from its hand.

"That was ineffective," Taro commented as the Triclops reached for her. She evaded its grasp and swung onto its shoulders. Taro squeezed her legs tightly around the triclops neck to try to cut off its air. That would work fine for something that breathed. The triclops slammed Taro back into a tree and she slid off to the ground.

"Why isn't the statue here?" Burbon exclaimed and then looked up to see that he had the full attention of the monster. He backed away until he felt a marble pillar blocking his exit. The Triclops advanced quickly and raised its fist as if to squash Burbon in one mighty blow. Burbon closed his eyes and raised his hands above his head. *I didn't think this is the way I would go.* He stared up as the fist swung down at him.

"Stop it!" he cried in frustration and cowered. One second past and then another, and still the killing blow did not land.

Hello, did time stop? Burbon thought. He opened one eye and saw the monster's fist inches from his face. He closed his eyes again as if the monster was teasing him.

He opened both eyes and saw the Triclops standing perfectly still as if frozen. He moved to the right expecting the triclops to move but the creature remained still.

I don't understand. One second this thing tries to tear us apart and the next it can't move. What caused it to stop? Suddenly Burbon realized his last choice of words before he was about to be struck.

"Walk forward one step," he commanded. The triclops moved forward one step and then stood still again. Burbon could barely contain his excitement.

"Triclops, jump on one leg." It hopped on one leg over and over again. Burbon was giddy and laughed at his cleverness.

"Triclops, stand on your head." The Triclops bent down and put one arm on the ground, then its head and became an upside-down statue. "Okay, Triclops, dance." It stood on its feet again to do a jig. Burbon was not impressed. "Not like that, like this," Burbon danced next to the Triclops to teach it the proper jig etiquette. Taro and Stonewall walked slowly over.

"I thought the little traveler might be hurt and instead the two of them are dancing."

"I'm still trying to figure out which one of them is brainless," Taro added.

Burbon whirled around to greet his friends.

"Isn't this great? The Triclops doesn't work from a statue, it takes commands. See, watch this."

"Triclops, lift me on your shoulders." The large monster put Burbon on one of his shoulders; Burbon dangled his feet down. "Now I can ride to wherever we're going." Taro had an idea.

"Drop rider," she commanded. The Triclops remained motionless.

"Hah, I guess it doesn't listen to elves. This thing is smarter than it looks. Stonewall, try giving it a command."

"March forward," he ordered. The triclops almost raised its foot to move but remained in its spot. "The creature seems to be attuned to the resonance of a voice like yourself, Trader," Stonewall commented. Burbon shook with excitement from his upward perch.

"From now on, the two of you listen to me or my triclops will take care of you. Isn't that right?" He slapped the back of the Triclops, the motion made him lose his balance and he fell onto the ground.

"You should coordinate yourself a little more with your newfound friend," Taro teased.

The four of them journeyed toward the highest point of the island. The day was hot, and the humidity did little to cool the travelers. They pressed on as morning turned to afternoon. Far in the distance, they saw a tall wooden tower and the outline of a village. Burbon sat on a rock while eating rations.

"What do you think the villagers will be like? Do you think they will be friendly?" he asked with his mouth full. Stonewall stared at Burbon trying to decipher his speech.

"The sailors made more sense than you, little trader. I expect the worst and hope for the best. My main concern is persuading them to give up their piece of this crystal," Stonewall answered.

Burbon threw a chicken bone towards the Triclops. The rock monster examined the bone but with no mouth, the bone was a puzzle.

"After our travels thus far, I am not hopeful," she answered. The Triclops balanced the bone on its stubby rock fingers.

"I hope they have some good grub because our rations aren't going to last forever." Burbon threw a chicken bone into the woods. An animal roared. All three stood up, ready to draw their weapons. From the distant trees, there was the sound of animals running.

"We should run for the village. We're close and hopefully they can keep at bay whatever that is," Burbon recommended.

"I could track the animal and find out more about it," Taro offered.

"Burbon is right. We have battled enough for one day. Let's march quickly to our destination. Hopefully there we will find respite."

For the next hour, they travelled hard and fast, the hoofed stomping never far, but never close enough for them to get a good look at the cause. Burbon sat on the Triclop's shoulders the whole time, always looking back but glimpsing nothing more than running shadows. Soon they arrived at the village. From a distance it looked normal, but in close proximity the buildings appeared strange with doors wider than usual.

"Don't exert yourself too much, Trader, but can you see anyone from up there?" asked Taro.

"No, the village is completely deserted. No sign of life."

The pathway opened up to a clearing with well-trodden ground. A large wooden tower with a long dangling rope stood in the middle of the village. A nest of branches cradled the apex of the tower.

"The path shows many hoof marks yet there is no corral for livestock," Stonewall examined the ground. Taro tiptoed to a thatch door, which was wider than normal, but the height was shorter than Stonewall. She walked in, searching the living area, but it seemed odd. Although sparsely furnished, everything was widely spaced as if the residents needed greater space to move around. Burbon and Stonewall stepped behind her.

"Everything about this village creeps me out. The spacing of furniture isn't right, it's as if they all have big bellies that makes it awkward to move around," Burbon mentioned.

"There are hoof marks on the floor inside, in all of the rooms." Stonewall knelt to examine the prints.

"Do you think whatever trouble has occurred, is the cause of the villagers' disappearance?" asked Taro.

At that moment, a loud reverberation of feet surrounded the house, their dark shapes whirling around. They moved so fast; it was hard to see their forms through the window.

"What did you do with the Triclops?" wondered Stonewall.

"I left him by the tower, but I can't even see him thorough the mass of shapes," Burbon responded. He was agitated and ran outside to confront their pursuers.

"What do you want?" he yelled. "What have you done to the villagers?"

A large shape separated itself from the herd and sauntered toward Burbon. The creature was half man and half beast. The top half was a man to his waist, the rest of body was a horse like animal with four legs. His face grimaced with anger. Hanging from his neck was the missing third piece of the gem.

"We are the villagers, you two-legged buffoon! And you are trespassing on our village and our island. The price for trespassing is your death!"

18

The Attack of the Four-Legs

Superior numbers surrounded them. Burbon's first reaction came naturally to him. He tried to bargain.

"Now, we got off to a bad start. We came to your island strictly for business. I have gemstones to trade, perhaps for the one around your neck?" Burbon asked.

"You are a greater fool than I thought two-legs. I am Magnus, leader of a great people, superior to any of the two-legged races." Magnus spit on the ground and tapped his back hoof.

I'm getting the distinct feeling that they don't like our two legs. I wonder what his problem is? Burbon thought.

"Magnus the Minotaur?" Burbon responded not realizing his insult.

"Minotaur! That two-legged obscenity! We are centaurs. My people have been subjugated for centuries by two-legs to be their slaves, their workforce. We escaped to this island, to create our own culture away from creatures like you," Magnus proclaimed.

"We should be off then. Real sorry to have bothered you," Burbon tried to walk through the door but Magnus's arm barred the way. Stonewall unsheathed his broadsword. Three centaur archers aimed their bows at his head.

"Enough. Unlike the way your kind has treated us, I will give you a chance. Follow me," Magnus motioned and stepped out from the house. They trailed slowly and saw dozens of centaurs. They passed a gauntlet of male and females who regarded them with mistrust. A small male centaur kicked dust at Taro as she walked by. His action pushed her past her anger point.

"The elf people have never used another race as their slaves. Try that again and you will find a bolt in your hide," she yelled at the little centaur. Stonewall gently pushed her forward.

"None of us have ever subjugated the centaur people, but they cannot see past their racism. They relate all two-legged creatures as the kind that enslaved their race. They will not be an easy people to talk to," Stonewall commented.

Burbon hopped on one leg hoping to glimpse the Triclops to give a command for help. Magnus looked amused by Burbon's antics.

"If you are looking for the rock monster, you will not find him. My people have moved it to a safe location. For decades it has acted as our guardian and has served its purpose well. I don't understand what magic you used to control it, but you won't use it against us." Magnus stopped before the wooden tower and motioned for the three of them to look up. "Once we lived in the colonies as slaves to the two-legs to be sold and traded like common goods. This tower is a symbol of that past life. All the clothes we wore, tools that we used, were burned to symbolize the end of our slavery. We have no reminder left of those dark days except for you. You have trespassed on our land."

"Which we did not know," answered Stonewall.

"Ignorance is no excuse," Magnus responded, "but our people, unlike the two-legs, will give you one opportunity to save yourselves. If you fail, you will become our slaves. If you succeed, you will get your freedom. Do you accept?"

"I don't see any choice. You speak of honor but prevent us from leaving. You make the same mistakes of those who owned you," Taro spoke.

"You're wrong. I'm giving you a chance that I, that my people, never had," Magnus paced back and forth, his massive hooves sending dust into the air. His fellow centaurs watched him with respect. "I will set the wick now. This will ignite the fire in the tower exactly when the twin suns set. You have until that time to evade my hunting party and me."

"What is this, hide and seek? How can we avoid your superior numbers on an island we barely know and that you have spent your entire life on? You know little about honor," spit Taro.

"Take my challenge or I will shackle you now," Magnus glared.

"We accept, on the condition that we have a head start," Stonewall replied.

"Granted! Now be gone from my sight! If the three of you aren't tied and bound under this tower by the time the fire nest ignites, I will allow you to leave the island."

The three hiked away from the center of the village toward the peak of the mountain. They felt the glares of the centaurs as they disappeared into the thicket.

"How long do you think he will give us?" asked Burbon.

"Not long. All of his talk of honor speaks volume by his actions," answered Taro.

"Magnus is wrong, but I do understand his pain. His people have been abused and he sees us as his former masters," mentioned Stonewall.

"Feel sorry for them later, warrior. Now we run for our lives. I will use my tracking abilities to make our path as difficult as possible to follow," replied Taro taking branches from a tree.

Magnus and his hunting party trekked closely behind. Although his people would follow him anywhere, some voiced concern with his decision to let the travelers have a head start.

"Why let these two-legs have a chance when we centaurs never had a one," a young centaur named Oglie asked.

"Because we are better than the two-legs. We will show this when we return them to our village to the cheers of our people. What's this?" he stopped to inspect the ground before them. The dirt was clear of footprints, yet the ground looked tidied over as if swept over.

"I expected better than this. They have tried to cover their tracks. They are heading toward the river," Magnus declared as the centaurs galloped towards the water.

"Shouldn't we have caught up by now?" asked Oglie. "We are much faster than them."

"Patience young centaur," commanded Magnus. "The two-legs are running for their survival. You will be amazed at how fast they can run when they are scared. We will catch up with them soon. Come, they are using the river to obscure their trail." Magnus and the main party chased, crossing the distance quickly. Oglie was in the back of the pack and was surprised by a falling leaf. He watched it land on a nearby rock. Motion caught his eye as he looked up. Oglie had no time to raise an alarm as his world went black. Burbon stepped over the fallen centaur. Stonewall and Taro dropped down from the trees as well.

"No one ever looks up," Burbon mimicked Taro speaking. "This little centaur looked up and it was my quick thinking that prevented him from raising the alarm."

"You acted wisely, Trader, while Taro bought us time to think," answered Stonewall.

"Our time is short. It won't be long before they discover no tracks further up and double back," Taro answered. Stonewall picked up the unconscious centaur and deposited him under some bushes, out of sight.

"Then we have only one choice," Stonewall suggested.

"What's that?" asked Burbon.

"To return to the village."

"I agree," answered Taro.

"Are you two insane?" exclaimed Burbon. "Aren't we supposed to be running away?"

"Yes, but it will be unexpected. They know this island too well to hide from them. But finding a hiding place near the village may buy us enough time before the fuse is lit."

"I hope were not running into the arms of the centaurs," commented Burbon.

Sometime later, they lied under a small cluster of trees by the village as dusk was approaching.

"Have you seen the Triclops?" Stonewall asked Burbon.

"No sign. Wherever they have hid it, I haven't been able to see it in or near the village."

The fire on the rope wick had reached two thirds of the way to the top.

"If we can hide a bit longer, we may win our freedom yet," commented Taro. The sound of hooves in the distance caused them to turn their heads.

"You spoke too soon. Look!" Burbon pointed. Magnus and his herd were galloping over a rise not far from their position.

"Do you think they can see us?" asked Burbon "We have no more places to hide."

"Then I will battle them to my last bolt," snarled Taro grabbing one from her quiver. Stonewall placed his hand on hers.

"There is another way. Head to the lower part of the village and stay hidden. I will buy us some time." Stonewall charged towards the centaurs.

"Stonewall!" Burbon yelled but his voice was lost in Stonewall's battle cry. He flung his massive frame at the centaurs and the ground became thick with dust.

"Come, Burbon," Taro grabbed his arm. "He has sacrificed himself in order for us to continue. There isn't much time left. Follow me," commanded Taro. Her elfin body ran as fast as a deer and Burbon struggled to keep pace. Together they circled around the village, the fuse on the tower burning close to the top.

"Taro, it is only a matter of time before they find us. You should go on without me. You're the fastest and the least likely of us to get caught," said Burbon.

"No, I will not abandon you," she replied.

"Great, I'm trying to get rid of you and you're getting all noble. I'm not trying to sacrifice myself. We can still win if one of us is free before the fuse burns out."

"Okay, but I'm not sure if we can delay capture much longer."

"Then you go one way. I'll go another." Burbon laid his hand out to Taro. "I'll see you at sunset, after we have won."

"After we have won," she sprung away from the village. Burbon circled down to the lower edge of the huts, closer to the ocean. He heard a sound behind him and hid in a hut. A small centaur boy trotted past with a pot of hot water. Burbon scanned the buildings around him in search of his prize. *Somewhere out there, is that rock monster. If I can find him and give him one command, I can fight these centaurs myself. If I were a Triclops, where would I be?*

Suddenly, an idea came to him. Burbon turned into the opposite direction. He crashed into the hairy wall of a large centaur. The last thing he remembered was a large fist coming at his head.

Taro dashed through the forest, trying to head to higher ground. She arced around the town, putting some distance between her and the village but still keeping the tower in view. *I hope Stonewall and Burbon are still okay, we three have come too far together to be stopped now. And the stone, I wish there was someway to get the stone off Magnus's neck.* She hesitated as her keen ears heard a branch break in the woods.

Taro raced to the field of tall grass away from the sound. Several centaurs appeared and tried to block her entrance to the field. She heard hoof sounds all around her.

Trapped! She pulled a bolt from her quiver and prepared for their approach. A dark shape hurtled toward her and she steadied her crossbow to engage. The centaur charged at her; his horns prepared to strike her body. Before she fired, a fist sailed through the air knocking the centaur into the ground. Captain Nox stepped out of the grass and bowed his hat toward her.

"Could you use our assistance?" he asked. His men streamed through the grass.

"Your timing is appreciated," as Taro kicked another centaur in the face.

"We would have been here sooner if it hadn't been for some talking shells."

"Why did you come?" Taro questioned.

"You and Stonewall saved my ship. We came to repay our debt!"

"Come with me, we must free the others," Taro cried. Captain Nox and his crew raced toward the tower.

Pain rattled Burbon's head as he realized that his wrist and feet were bound. Next to him Stonewall sat, similarly tied.

"I was worried that you weren't going to wake up," Stonewall asked with concern.

"Considering the headache I have, I almost wish I was still unconscious," Burbon wished he could rub his skull. "Where is Taro? Have they captured her?"

"No, but there is a lot of noise from the fields to the south of the village. Hopefully they haven't found her yet. The suns are almost down, and the tower nest is almost lit; if she can hold out just a little bit longer."

"Look, she's still free and she has brought reinforcements!" Burbon noticed activity away from them. Captain Nox and his men streamed into the village to meet the centaurs head on. Magnus galloped into the center of the chaos.

"Where did these two-legs come from?" yelled Magnus, flinging a crewmember into the trees.

"They came from the ship. What do you want us to do?" a male centaur asked.

"Make these two-legs wish they had never left it," Magnus charged, and bodies flew everywhere. Taro jumped through the confusion, toward Burbon and Stonewall. She landed beside Burbon while cutting his and Stonewall's bonds.

"Go!" she yelled. Burbon ran toward a church steeple. "Captain Nox and his men have bought us some time, but they are outnumbered.

"We should even the odds." Stonewall charged into the fray, heading toward Magnus's hulking frame. Stonewall leapt at him without any hesitation.

"You could not escape us. Your two-legged friends have only delayed the inevitable. Your treachery negates our deal," Magnus punched Stonewall in the chest.

"You talk of honor, yet you said nothing in our pact about help for us. In your arrogance, you just assumed that we were alone."

"It makes no matter; I will still dispose of all of you before the sun is set."

The crewmen's numbers surprised the centaurs, at first forcing them into a defensive position. But the centaurs were strong willed and knew their island intimately. Although Captain Nox and his men were brave, the Centaur's numbers were wearing them down. The Centaurs gradually surrounded the sailors herding them together. Stonewall stood back to back with Nox.

"Your men fight bravely. I'm sorry that we brought you into our mess," Stonewall replied.

"No matter, warrior. My men make their own decisions. We fight together, we die together!" Nox's sword bounced off a centaur's steel spear.

"Enough!" roared Magnus. "You two-legs have lost, surrender to us now!" His people marched closer, ready to finish the battle.

"I am an elf. Our people have surrendered to no race in our entire history," screamed Taro.

"Then prepare to bow to me!" Magnus exclaimed as he advanced towards her. Before he could attack her, a fist sent him crashing to the ground. Behind him the smiling face of Burbon hung in the air, his feet dangling over the shoulder of the Triclops.

"I found him in the church. They were using him as an idol," he yelled. "Fight the centaurs!" The Triclop's fist punched a hole in the crowd of centaurs. Bodies went flying as Stonewall, Taro and Nox renewed their attack. The battle ended as the tower's nest ignited in flames.

"Look, the fuse has burned to the tower. We have won!" Burbon yelled. Everyone watched as Burbon danced on the shoulders of the triclops. Nox's men raised their hands in victory. The centaurs turned to Magnus for his decision. He advanced to Stonewall.

"Will you keep your promise?" Stonewall asked.

"We will keep our deal. The centaurs are an honorable race, unlike you two-legs. Be gone from our island and never return." Taro eyed the stone around Magnus's neck, looking for a way to secure it when her thoughts are interrupted.

"Magnus! Come quickly, one of your boys has fallen from the cliff," a female centaur rushed to him.

"What? That area is forbidden, what was he doing there?" Magnus galloped towards the cliff with both centaurs and two-legs following behind him.

"He was scared, Magnus, the fighting made him run away, I could not stop him," she cried.

Magnus ran to the cliff. Part way down the cliff face lays the scared centaur barely holding onto a rock ledge.

"Hold on, Johswa. I will come get you," Magnus tried to step down but sent a flurry of rocks down on him.

"Stop!" commanded Stonewall, "you will kill the boy. Taro, do you have enough rope in your quiver to reach the boy?"

"I think it is too short, but we can try." She pulled out the rope and Stonewall tied one end around his wrist. He dangled the rest of the rope over the edge, but it was short of reaching the little centaur.

"There must be another way," said Magnus.

"There's no time," answered Taro, "the ledge is unstable, and it could give under him at any time."

"Wait, I have an idea," suggested Burbon. "Tie the rope around me. I'll go down to catch him."

"You! Why should I trust a two-leg?" snarled Magnus.

"Because this two-leg is the only one small enough! I won't send the whole cliff down on your son but I'm strong enough to pull him up. Are you going to help lower me down or will you let the two-legs do all the work?" Burbon took the rope from Stonewall and tied a knot around his midsection. Magnus held the rope firm.

"If you do anything to hurt my son, I will drop you in a second."

"Now that would be extremely stupid of me wouldn't it. Stonewall? I want you right behind him holding the rope."

"With pleasure, trader," he replied.

Burbon looked down the cliff face.

"Well, here goes everything," he commented as Magnus and Stonewall slowly lowered the rope and Burdon down the ledge. He looked below and saw the terror on the little centaur's face. *I don't know if he is scared of me or if I will knock the cliff face down on him.*

"Hurry," Johswa cried, his four legs scrambling to hold on to the ledge. "I'm slipping."

"Hold on, I'm coming," Burbon replied. "Magnus, he's going to fall. Drop me faster!" Magnus and Stonewall lowered more rope over the edge until the last of it was in Magnus hands. Burbon was still ten feet short.

"Lower me more, I can't reach him!" he yelled.

"I have no more rope," responded Magnus and turned back to his people. "Vascra, finds us more rope," Magnus commanded as a strong centaur dashed back the village.

"There is no time," yelled Stonewall, "your son can't hold on much longer. Lean down, I will hold you." Stonewall reached his massive arms around the centaur. Magnus front feet dangled over the edge of the cliff as they lowered Burbon farther down. Magnus was completely at the mercy of Stonewall's grip. Burbon's fingers barely grasped the young Centaur's torso.

"Stop squirming or I can't grab you," he directed. The ledge under Johswa broke away and the centaur hung motionless in the air before gravity hauled him down to the jagged rocks below.

"Not on my watch," Burbon stretched his little frame and grabbed the centaur. Somewhere above, both Magnus and Stonewall hung precariously on the cliff before centaurs and ship members lent their strength by dragging both away from the edge.

"I want my Dad!" the centaur cried, his little legs kicking Burbon.

"Then stop moving or your dad can't bring us up." Burbon was strong for his size but the child squirmed, bearing his full weight.

"Hurry up, I can't hold on much longer," he screamed. Their last pull was so strong that both Burbon and Johswa were pulled high into the air over the edge. Johswa fell back to land on Magnus's back. Burbon went up and then fell straight back the way he came.

"Stonewall, catch me!" as Burbon journeyed downward. A strong elfin arm pulled him from oblivion.

"Stonewall's busy, can I help?" replied Taro as she grabbed him away from the cliff's edge.

"My arm may be out of my socket but that has to be the sweetest thing you have done for me. I forgive you now for the cactus trick. How about a big kiss?" Burbon requested.

"Your gratitude is enough for me," Taro blushed from Burbon's unusual affection. Two strong arms lifted Burbon off his feet and put him on his shoulder.

"You did good, trader. It's good to see you concerned for something other than currency," congratulated Stonewall.

"I'm not so sure that was a compliment," questioned Burbon. Magnus stood in front of Burbon.

"Come with me to the tower," he commanded. His fellow centaurs marched with him to the village center.

"He's going to let us go, right?" posed Burbon.

"If he has any honor in his four-legged body, he will," said Taro. The three accompanied Nox and his men to the flaming torch in the center of the village. Magnus stood before his people as they watched Stonewall and the others walk.

"Today, a two-leg has saved my son. I have always hated the two-legs for their slavery, but maybe all of them aren't the same. The one they call Burbon, please come forward," Magnus motioned toward him. Burbon hiked to the front as the centaurs made a path for him to walk through. As he stepped toward the altar, Magnus knelt on his front two legs.

"I honor the one named Burbon. Your friends may choose to be escorted safely off our island or to stay as guests of my people. I will gladly accept any of your requests." Taro motioned her head towards Magnus's necklace. Burbon understood.

"Uhhhhh, I do have one request. My friends and I have come a far distance for one object, a gem with the power for great good or evil. We ask for the gemstone that hangs around your neck," Burbon gulped, worried about the response. He was right to worry.

The rest of the centaurs released a collective gasp.

"How could he?" said one.

"That has been in our keeping for centuries," replied another.

"It brings good luck to our crops, what will we do without it?" answered a third.

"Enough!" commanded Magnus. He stared straight at Burbon. "What you ask for is a treasured item among my people. It is a good luck totem for our families. It brings life and love to our island. Could your need be any greater?"

"Much greater!" responded Taro as she pushed herself to the front of the centaurs.

"We are on a quest to unite the four pieces of this gemstone before true evil can control it for its use. Yours is the third piece. If you do not give it to us; then an evil being called Darkmoor will come and take it from you. Many of your centaurs will be hurt in the process."

"I have heard of Darkmoor and his growing power. But surely, he does know not we are here," replied Magnus.

"If we found you, then so can he. The three of us can never return home in peace until the four stones are reunited. Please, give us a chance to bring good to our world," Stonewall marched through the crowd to stand before Magnus. The centaur leader looked to his people who were quiet, almost holding their breath, awaiting his decision.

"The two-legs have done tremendous harm to my people. Only on this island, separate from them, have we finally found peace. Yet today you have shown an act of kindness that makes me rethink our feelings toward your people. Darkmoor could hurt both our races, I would be negligent not to offer our help." Magnus lifted the gemstone necklace off of his chest and handed it to Taro. "Use this wisely," he instructed.

"You have my word," answered Taro. She pulled out the other two pieces and placed the third next to the jagged edge. The connection was instantaneous. The gems merged to form a larger one. Sizzling red energy emanated from the stones. The Seer's facial features appeared and became more defined than before, as if the growing stone gave him strength. His ancient eyes stared out of the gem.

"Are you going to congratulate us or tell us where the last stone is," asked Burbon.

"*Neither,*" the Seer replied, "*I bring a warning that Darkmoor is closer than ever. You must leave this island now or face losing all three stones. Follow the living map to the last location and merge the stones before Darkmoor catches you. He who combines the four stones controls their power. Now hurry, before your presence endangers the inhabitants of this island!*" The Seer's voice vanished as a red light shimmered in the stone with a one jagged piece missing. Captain Nox approached the three of them.

"I can grant you safe passage to our next destination, if you can reach it by sea.

"At this point, I don't think we have any choice," answered Stonewall.

"We can't lose the stones now. Too many lives hang in the balance," Taro replied.

"Then come, you have a journey to complete and a world to save!" Nox beckoned.

19

Return of the Gobtrolls

Nox's ship sailed away from the island as Burbon waved to the centaurs and the Triclops. A tear filled his eye from losing the rock monster. Stonewall put his arm around his small friend.

"He is in good hands, Trader. The Triclops responds readily to the young centaurs."

"Funny how that creature responds to childish voices," mentioned Taro. Burbon made a face at her.

"Bring out the living map," Stonewall asked, "I want to know the location of the remaining stone." Taro reached into her tunic and took out the map. It unfolded on its own as it yawned. This time it did not cringe from Burbon's touch.

"It likes me, it really likes me," he exclaimed.

"It tolerates you; I won't say it actually likes you. I think it is still asleep," Taro answered as she stretched out the map. All eyes rested on their next location.

"The settlement of Cumus, the city of clouds," Stonewall's large finger pointed on the map.

"The city is at a high elevation?" asked Taro.

"Correct," answered Stonewall.

"How are we going to get there?" Burbon wondered.

"I can tell you how you won't get there. By land is nearly impossible. The magma swamps spew poisonous gas into the air while a fiery liquid flows that will burn a wooden boat up in moments," answered Captain Nox walking up from below deck.

"Lovely. Couldn't one of these locations have been an oasis?" whined Burbon.

"What kind of boat can navigate these dangers?" asked Taro.

"One made of rock, which will not burn in the waters," Captain Nox added.

"Rock! Do you have rocks for brains, Captain? A rock sinks," Burbon demonstrated by dropping a rock overboard and watching it sink to the bottom of the ocean.

"Not all rocks, Trader. You don't know much about rocks that are not precious stones. Pumice or volcano rock is full of air holes. It's actually quite light and floats on magma rivers. Unfortunately, the rock boats are tippy and are tough to navigate for any distance."

"So, what do you recommend, Captain?" Stonewall asked.

"I will take you to the seaport of Varna. From there you will have to travel north by land to bypass the swamps. It will add days to your travel, but it is the safest way. Once you reach the mountains, go east and you may find a way to Cumus." Nox walked across the deck and talked to his crewmembers.

"Can we afford to take this long route around?" Taro asked.

"There may be another way," answered Stonewall. "When we get to Varna, I have an idea for an alternate method of travel."

After several days of turbulent seas, the three stood on a dock and watched *The Dragon's Feast* disappear into the horizon. Taro held a note from Nox.

"Nox believes a caravan will be traveling north by next moon that will can us to the mountains."

"We can't wait that long. The Seer said Darkmoor may only be days behind us. We don't want to be captured when we are so close," said Stonewall.

"I'm with you," answered Burbon. He watched four shoremen push a huge harpoon gun on wheels into one of the warehouses. *I'd like to see the fish they catch with that thing.* He turned back to Stonewall. "What exactly is your plan?"

"Have you ever been to a museum, Trader?" Stonewall guided the three of them up a narrow street to the center of town.

"Museum?" Burbon's voice faded in the distance. "That doesn't sound like a lot of fun…"

Behind them, a warehouse door closed, and a large green hand scrawled a message onto a piece of cloth. Seconds later, a black crow flew off. The orange eye of a gobtroll blinked as it closed a wooden shutter.

Taro gazed up into the sky, the clouds were gray and hazy. She shivered. The climate was much cooler than her elfin home. *Home. I hope my family is well. It seems like forever since I left them.* Her feet splashed as she trudged through the muddy streets.

"Forever," answered Burbon, "That's about the last time I walked into a museum. What exactly are you looking for Stonewall?"

"I'll know it when I see it," was his reply as he marched up the granite steps to the museum.

"I'll know it when I see it," mimicked Burbon in a deeper voice. "Let's see this mystery object." They entered the museum through its double oak doors. Some school children giggled and ran by them. Burbon watched them as they left.

"Probably the last time I was in a museum was when I was their age," he commented.

"Bet you tried to bargain your way out," teased Taro.

"No, but that is a good idea," he grinned. They walked by a sea exhibit, bones from a huge whale hung from the ceiling. Burbon peered up.

"Now that's a big fish!" he joked to no one in particular. Burbon almost ran into a janitor while trying to catch up with Stonewall and Taro at the next display.

"Wait up, what's the big hurry…" his words caught in his throat as he stared at the huge apparatus in from of him.

Massive pulley ropes hung from the ceiling to hold it in place. Made mostly of wood with some light metals, a translucent shell dominated the object. A heating engine was affixed to the bottom. The engine warmed the air within a basket that carried its occupants. Burbon's jaw dropped open.

"You brought us here for a flying machine! How do you know if it even works?" Stonewall pointed to a sign describing the machine.

Built by the inventor Turbine Van Cans during the sea battles of '49. This air machine is capable of flight for several days. It was used primarily to spy on incoming ships to assess their battle readiness.

"I don't trust anything that inventor built," commented Burbon.

"What about the staff?" asked Taro.

"Okay, so the staff worked, but who knows if this machine is still able to fly now?" he answered. Stonewall pointed to another sign. *The air machine is flown once a year for the annual flight festival during the warm season.*

"Is every question I ask answered by these little signs?" Burbon questioned.

"All except one. How to fly such a machine?" Stonewall pondered.

"No one flies that but the mayor," a voice replied behind the bone exhibit. An old man with long scraggly hair, wearing overalls pushed his cart around the exhibits. He took his mop and wiped the wooden floor. "And he doesn't fly it very far. Just the length of the town so all the children can fly their kites in celebration.

"And does the mayor take any others with him on the voyage?" asked Stonewall.

"Voyage? It's just a trip across town. He takes a number of towns-people. They throw candies down to the children. The whole town lines the street to see the air machine. Quite a sight."

"Is the air machine easy to handle?" asked Taro.

"Easy to handle? Heck I've watched it enough times to know a tree monkey could handle it."

"Guess that leaves you out Taro," Burbon commented. The old man walked up to the exhibit.

"This engine creates heat that fills the sphere causing it to rise above the ground. The cloth sails," the old man pointed to the back, "steer in the wind currents. Can get tricky if the wind is strong and blowing the wrong way, but it works a lot like a ship."

"Would this machine fly to the City of Cumus?" asks Burbon.

"The City of Cumus?" the old man answered.

This old guy likes to repeat himself thought Burbon.

"This contraption would probably get you around the world and back, assuming you didn't spring a leak. Then you'd probably sink like a stone. Splat," he slapped his withered hands for effect. "Enough of my gabbing, I've got a floor to clean. Now scoot while I do my job." He mopped around Burbon who jumped backward to avoid the slippery floor. They passed the janitor and look up at the glass atrium that housed the exhibit.

"Are you thinking what I think you're thinking?" Taro asked Stonewall.

"You're crazy. What if we puncture a hole over the magma swamp?" Burbon replied.

"We have no choice," Stonewall answered.

In the waning suns, the three strolled down one of the town's narrow streets. "Provisions," said Stonewall pointing at their bags.

"Now you're talking my language," as Burbon rubbed his stomach and went to the next store. Before he could enter, the owner locked the door, closing the curtain a moment later. Burbon caught a hint of fear in the storekeeper's eyes.

"Not a friendly lot in this town, are they?" as he counted the remaining gems in his pouch.

"I don't think they are scared of us, just scared of having us in their stores. In the last two stores, they moved so fast I felt like they were rushing us back into the street. By the way, Stonewall, you sure bought a lot of candy at that last store. You have a sweet tooth?"

"They're not for me," he answered. Before Burbon could question him further, a shadow passed in the alleyway behind them. Orange eyes gleamed in the murky darkness. The travelers continued unaware down the street. All around them doors locked and shuttered close as the residents hid for the night.

"What happens at night that everyone locks their doors to keep us out," said Burbon.

"Not us, them!" pointed Taro. In the distance, three large gobtrolls stood at the end of the street, their eyes and teeth gleaming in the darkness.

"I thought we left their kind back at the caves," commented Burbon.

"Their kind lives everywhere," stated Taro. "We beat them before, we can beat them again."

"Taro, these gobtrolls are tougher than the ones we faced before." Burbon looked up at Stonewall. The three gobtrolls were as large as Stonewall and their faces scarred from many battles.

"We'll separate and meet in the alleyway of the museum. We fly off at first light. It is too dangerous to leave when it's still dark. Whatever you do, don't be followed!" Stonewall put his massive hands on both Taro's and Burbon's shoulder. "Be careful."

"You as well, Warrior," answered Taro.

"No gobtroll is going to catch me," yelled Burbon and he ran away from the gobtrolls toward the harbor. The largest gobtroll in the center motioned his head to the right gobtroll. He pursued after Burbon down a parallel street. Taro leapt onto a crate and jumped to a rooftop. The left gobtroll advanced to a building and climbed up a reed drainpipe with amazing speed. The last gobtroll smiled at Stonewall with ragged teeth. He lumbered toward Stonewall with silent confidence.

"I never run away from a battle." He pulled out his sword and swung it back over his shoulder. "Prepare to lose your head!" The gobtroll's eyes watched his blade.

"Damn!" Several blocks away, Burbon tripped and fell into the mud. *I hope that thing isn't right behind me.* He jumped up. Burbon heard heavy shuffling from two houses over. *I'll lose this beast at the pier and double back to the museum before the moons are half high.*

To his left he felt the salt air and stepped on the wooden planks of the pier. The dock was deserted. Its many laborers had gone home for the night. The only sound was the sloshing of the water against the boats. *I won't expect any help from the townspeople.*

He scrambled around a corner and ran down a long pier. It ended suddenly and Burbon shifted his weight to prevent from falling in. He leaned backward and grabbed a wooden post to stop from falling into the ocean.

"Well that was close," he muttered and watched the gobtroll marching towards the end of the pier, unaware of Burbon's location. Burbon peered around the end of the pier. *There's nowhere else to go.* He stared down at the icy coolness of the ocean.

Clunk, clunk, Taro's head turned slightly to see the gobtroll several rooftops behind. Her feet stepped noiselessly along the thatch roofs. *I wonder what the villagers think is crossing their rooftops,* as she leapt to another roof. *It won't be long before I outrun this ugly brute. He is foolish to even chase me. An elf is faster than his people could ever dream.*

She took two steps forward and then her third step meet thin air. She stopped immediately. Before her was the town common, a park with a fenced in garden. She turned behind her and the gobtroll had halved the distance between them, intent on his prey. Taro surveyed her options. *I can attack the gobtroll on the rooftop or try to lose it in the park.* The arrow that scraped the side of her face made the decision for her. It imbedded itself into the chimney beside her. She turned toward the source.

Another one! She saw the orange eyes of a gobtroll in a park tree as it notched another arrow. She had seconds to make her decision. She leapt towards the first gobtroll on the roof. It was surprised by her approach. She listened to the air and heard the arrow released behind her. She ducked down in front of the gobtroll who took the arrow dead in the chest. It gurgled and then fell off the roof to the ground below.

I have to find a place to hide. I'm a sitting target up here. As she ran, the gobtroll set another arrow in its bow. It had Taro in its sights and prepared to loosen the arrow in her chest. Before it could release the arrow, it watched the elf charge straight at a stone chimney and disappear through the solid structure. It shook its head, unaware of any magic an elf had to produce such a feat.

Taro slipped though the stone chimney to the other side. The chimney hid her from view. *I have moments before that creature figures out where I went.* She watched the park tree shake from anger after missing its target. Several seconds past before she saw a body part to aim her crossbow. A hand broke through the brush to grab another arrow from its quiver.

That's all I need. Taro moved fluidly, grabbing the bolt, aiming and firing it in one motion. The bolt pierced through the gobtroll's hand. Startled, the gobtroll tumbled out of the tree landing headfirst. *He's not shooting another arm at me.*

She dropped down from the house and proceeded ahead to the museum. She fingered one of the portal balls that Turbine had given her. *Science he called them. Maybe magic isn't the most powerful force after all.* She ran towards the museum. *I hope the others are okay.*

Crash! A large mace bounced harmlessly off of Stonewall's sword. Stonewall swung back with his broadsword but the gobtroll blocked his blow. *This beast is hard to defeat. Its body is well armored, the chain mail covers most of its flanks.* Stonewall pushed the gobtroll back two paces. The creature lifted its mace, a mangled bloody tool and smiled a broken grin. Stonewall punched it in the mouth.

No armor there. The gobtroll staggered back. Suddenly, a blow slammed Stonewall on the back of his head. If not for his helmet, his head would have been crushed. Stonewall turned to face a second gobtroll, smaller than the first. *These beasts always come in packs.* He slashed at the mace of the second creature and send it sailing into a nearby building. The gobtroll lunged and caught Stonewall in the chest, momentarily knocking the air out of his lungs. Stonewall stumbled back against a wall as the gobtrolls advanced, one carrying a fish net. The first one swung its weapon, Stonewall's blade blocked its blow. The second charged while Stonewall kicked it in the gut.

Stonewall sheathed his broadsword as he spied a pile of crates placed against a building. He leapt onto the crate, turned through the air and double punched both gobtrolls in the face. Both creatures crumpled to the ground. Stonewall walked over the fallen bodies and looked at the net full of fishhooks. *I glad I didn't get caught in that net.*

Its feet rattled off the wooden planks of the pier. The gobtroll stared at its blurry reflection in the water at the end of the pier. The only sound was a distant bird flying overhead. The gobtroll turned back up the pier when a bubble in the water attracted its attention. It drew its face closer to the water's surface.

Splash! Burbon broke the water's surface and grabbed the gobtroll, dragging it into the water. They both thrashed as Burbon reached for the end planks and pulled himself up onto the pier. Burbon watched the gobtroll as it struggled to get out. *The heavy armor will keep it struggling for a few minutes.* His clothes dripped onto the pier as Burbon ran back to the harbor buildings. *I'll be at the museum in no time.*

He rounded the corner of a small fishing sloop and stepped back in time to see two more gobtrolls coming toward him. *They'll see me if I try to dive in the water. There is only one option.* Instead of turning around, Burbon ran straight at them, decreasing the distance in seconds. The gobtrolls were surprised but stood their ground, blocking the end of the pier. Burbon made his tiny frame as tall as he could stretch it. The gobtrolls raised their clubs to knock Burbon off his feet. He landed in between them, curling his body and rolling on the pier. Both creatures swung their club, missing Burbon and knocking each other into the water. Burbon rolled to his feet and continued running, not bothering to look back. *Sometimes you don't have to be big to be effective.* The moons were halfway up in the sky as Burbon zigzagged to the museum.

After an hour, Burbon slipped into the alley behind the museum. *It took me forever to get here. Every street corner had those stupid gobtrolls looking for me. It's a wonder that I ever made it here at all.* He spied a wooden garbage container and hid behind it. He was alone in the alley. *Where are Stonewall and Taro? I can't be the only one that escaped?*

As he pondered this, a large hand pulled him through an open window. He suppressed his scream as Stonewall placed him gently on the floor. Taro silently closed the window.

"You both made it! Guess what? I took three of them out. You both would have been proud of me. Not bad for a little trader." Burbon excitedly explained his last few hours.

"You made sure you weren't followed here, didn't you?" asked Taro.

"What do you take me for? No one saw me enter here, although you could have called me instead of pulling in."

"Sorry, we thought we saw torches, and I wanted you in here before anyone saw you," answered Stonewall. Burbon dusted off his clothes.

"All right, what's next?" he followed Taro's outstretched hand and saw the massive air machine unroped from the wall and pushed into the middle of the huge hall. The dome above the room was partially dismantled to allow the machine to exit.

"I imagine the mayor had the machine disassembled and reassembled outside, but we don't have time for that. Somehow, we have to fit out the roof," mentioned Taro.

"Is there enough room to exit?" Burbon asked.

"Barely, but we have no choice. We must fly out of here by dawn otherwise we risk detection by the museum staff.

"How can I help?" Burbon asked as Taro pointed to the rooftop.

Hours passed as Taro and Burbon shimmied up ropes to fully dismantle the rooftop. It was painstakingly slow, since dropping anything from this height would cause unwanted noise. Stonewall labored on the heat engine. He adjusted and oiled the apparatus that caused the machine to rise and fall. Burbon yawned as the sunlight filtered through what's left of the glass dome. He leaned back and closed his eyes for a few seconds. *Just a few minutes of sleep and then I'll finish.* A poke by a sharp bolt jolted him awake.

"Youch! Okay! Show me what's left," he yelled.

"We're done," answered Taro. "Slide down and load the last of the provisions into the bottom platform." The platform was a wooden ring that gave the riders a full 360-degree view as they walked around the heat engine. Hooks and baskets enabled them to stow gear safely.

"How are you making out, warrior?" Taro asked.

"Good. We should be ready to fly shortly. Watch the main entrance to make sure we have no early arrivals." Taro strolled to the oak doors and watched out the window into the main square in front of the museum. A few farmers pushed carts to the local market and a couple of boys ran along the cobbled stones headed for school. There was no sign of their gobtroll pursuers. She stepped back to the main hall and noticed Burbon's back pressed to a large window. Something glimmered from a distant rooftop. Taro only had seconds to react.

"Burbon, move out of the way," she screamed, leaping towards him. Burbon followed her gaze out the window to see the deadly arrival of large boulder. He fell as Taro hit him and the window shattered as the rock crashed into the wall.

"They found us. Get this machine into the air!" commanded Taro. She watched a dozen gobtrolls run through the courtyard scrambling for the main doors. She loosened two bolts quickly the broken window, disabling one gobtroll, while the others smashed at the door.

"Stonewall, hurry up!" cried Burbon.

"I'm almost ready!" he yelled. "Delay them!" Burbon ran to the main hall as several gobtrolls bashed their way through the front door. They lumbered towards him. He looked to the wall and spied the rope holding up the whale exhibit. He sliced the rope and the bones crashed down pinning the creatures to the floor.

"How you are doing, Stonewall?" Burbon questioned.

"Not ready yet!" A gobtroll barged through the broken door and around his fallen comrades. He headed straight at Burbon; his mace aimed squarely at his head. Burbon tripped against an exhibit podium and fell to the floor. Burbon watched as the gobtroll lifted his large boot over his head. An iron spike was set in the heel, poised to slice him to ribbons. Burbon was pinned and had no room to move. Before the killing blow could land, the gobtroll slumped backwards, a crossbow bolt sticking out of his back. Taro pulled Burbon up.

"Come on!" she demanded. They ran back to the main hall but stopped dead at the sight before them. The air machine was floating in the air, the main engine spewing flames to heat the sphere. Its basket hovered above the ground, too high to reach. Several ropes dangled down.

"Grab hold," Stonewall yelled down. Both Burbon and Taro reached onto the ropes. Taro effortless scaled the rope in seconds and maneuvered herself into the basket. Burbon climbed but froze as the air machine exited through the rooftop. There was little space to spare as the sphere barely cleared the dome. As Burbon climbed the rope, a spear sailed past him. Another gobtroll grabbed the end of his rope and climbed after Burbon. Burbon kicked his feet to knock the beast off. Taro aimed her crossbow at the gobtroll. She saw Burbon's frightened eyes.

"Don't shoot, you'll hit me!" The air machine cleared the museum and set off over the city. Townspeople pointed up at the sphere. Children chased after it.

"Awfully early for the festival this year," one storekeeper said to his client.

Burbon looked down, the gobtroll was gaining on him. He was too far to reach for the basket.

"Help!" he yelled.

"Taro, grab this mechanism and keep the flame steady," Stonewall commanded.

"What are you going to do?" she asked.

"Help," he answered. He seized Burbon's rope Burbon and yanked with all of his might. Burbon flew up in the air past the basket and fell down onto the platform floor.

"Next time tell me what you're doing," he shouted at Stonewall. "I almost lost my grip!"

"You're welcome," Stonewall answered. He pried out a small knife and cut the rope that the gobtroll clung to. It had several seconds to realize that it was no longer attached to the balloon before it fell to earth. The gobtroll landed in the fountain at the center of the town square.

"Perfect shot!" yelled Burbon.

"Actually, I was aiming for the statue," pointed Stonewall.

Minutes later, the air machine caught the prevailing winds, pushing it eastward.

"Taro adjust the sail. We need to be flying northeast," shouted Stonewall. She pulled the sail, angling the balloon with a slight turn to the right. Burbon stared below.

"I don't think the gobtrolls have given up yet." Coming up from the dockyards, three gobtrolls pulled a cart with a large harpoon affixed to it. They steered the harpoon to the center of town where no buildings would block their shot at the air machine.

"They are too far for my crossbow. Do we have any weapons that can stop them?" Taro inquired.

"No weapons, but something else might slow them down," Stonewall held several small bags of candy. Burbon realized Stonewall's plan.

"Stonewall, you're brilliant. Here let me drop them." He slices open the bags, spilling the sweets onto the streets below. It took several seconds before the townspeople realized what the machine was dropping. Two kids running to school were the first to notice.

"They're dropping candy. Come on, let's get some." The cry multiplied and soon kids flooded the main street, collecting their treasures. The gobtroll's cart came to a complete stop, unable to proceed further. They took a side street to detour around the commotion.

"We're not clear yet." Taro pointed to a large cliff that overlooked the town. It created a natural barrier preventing people from leaving the town by ground to the north. The air machine caught a gust of wind and sped towards the cliff.

"We're awfully close to the peak of the hill. Could you get us a little higher?" Burbon wondered.

"I'm trying. We are carrying more weight than this machine is used to," Stonewall replied.

"Want to volunteer to jump off?" sneered Taro to Burbon.

"Then who would you have to pick on," Burbon answered.

"Stop bickering. Look!" Stonewall pointed.

The gobtrolls found a clearing in the town and turned the harpoon around. They cranked one of the cogs and raised the height of the weapon until it was pointed directly at the sphere.

"If they hit us, we're going to drop like a rock," shouted Burbon.

"Then we better make sure they don't hit us," Taro stretched her hands out and yelled," Vachus mon dale!"

"It's too late, they released the harpoon. Are you trying to burn it?" Burbon asked.

"No, I can't reach it! But I can reach this," flames jut from her finger adding to the heat generated by the flames of the motor. The additional hot air sent the balloon up quickly and the three of them stumbled in the platform, losing their balance. Burbon looked over the edge.

"Good news, the harpoon will miss the balloon. Bad news it's coming right at us!"

The distance decreased in seconds as the steel of the harpoon approach Burbon's head.

Clang! Stonewall's massive broadsword smashed the harpoon and it fell harmlessly to the ground below. The gobtrolls danced in anger.

"You did it, Stonewall! You saved us from being skewered like a pig on a spit." Burbon jumped for joy. Stonewall grabbed him.

"Settle down, trader. After all that I don't want you falling out of the balloon."

"Excuse me for me being excited about having my life saved."

"The two of you may want to save the celebrations for later. Look," Taro pointed.

The air machine cleared the mountain and the three of them examined the plains on the other side. The ground was black with ash and criss-crossed with red inlets. The air was hot and reeked of poisonous gas. Nothing lived below because of the extreme heat and lack of solid ground.

"We have just entered the Magma Swamps," proclaimed Stonewall.

20

To Become a Man

Three days had passed. The travelers had been flying and breathing in the stink of the swamps. They were tired. The heat and smell prevented everyone from getting a good night's sleep. Below them a geyser spewed magma into the air, Stonewall adjusted the balloon to avoid the spray.

"I'm sick of this place!" Burbon complained while looking to the horizon. "Do we know how much farther to the city of Cumus?" Taro examined the living map.

"At least another day of flying according to the map." It fluttered nervously in her hand, sharing their discomfort of the terrain.

"I hope that map is right. If we have to stay up here more than one day, I'm going to jump," Burbon warned.

"Don't tease," replied Taro. She peered below and watched the swirling red liquid turn in a spiral. She thought of their destination. "What type of city is Cumus, Warrior? Will the people there welcome our arrival?"

"That would be nice for a change," added Burbon. Stonewall relaxed from adjusting the primer on the engine.

"The City of Cumus is shrouded in fable and hearsay. Few have ventured to the city and fewer have left its borders. What I have heard is that the city is built on a mountaintop, where the air is thin and one can touch the clouds. The city is ancient by any standards. It has rock turrets that cover the four quadrants of the city. You are supposed to be able to see the approach of any armies from their heights.

"Sounds like they don't like folks getting in," mentioned Burbon.

"Or getting out," added Taro.

"Whatever their reason, the city has isolated itself. And because of the treacherous lands around it, no one has much reason to visit."

"I can see why it's not on my list for leisure spots," Burbon commented.

"What about the people? What are they like?" Taro inquired.

"Maybe they are different than us to handle the higher altitudes."

"Will we be able to breathe the air?" Burbon asked.

"You'll adjust, trader," Stonewall said with confidence.

Roar! A geyser burst from below spewing its magma into the air. Once again, Stonewall adjusted the mechanism banking the air machine to the right. Burbon grabbed a handle to stay in the balloon.

"That was a close one," remarked Burbon.

"Too close, look at the balloon," pointed Taro.

They looked up and there was a slight smoldering on the surface of the sphere.

"If that burns though," commented Stonewall.

"Then we're up in smoke," finished Burbon.

"Get up there. You're the lightest," Taro pointed at the rope.

"I've got to learn to eat more," he murmured. Burbon seized the rope and ascended up the balloon where the magma spray hit. It had already begun to eat away the material.

"Hurry up, Burbon," Taro yelled up.

"I'm trying!" He reached the spot and unsure of what to do, he tried to blow it out.

"Stop that, you're feeding the fire," Stonewall yelled. The damaged area grew from the added air.

"Try to beat the flame out," directed Taro. Burbon strived to extinguish it with his hands but the flexible balloon material makes it difficult to stamp out the flames.

"This isn't working!" Burbon replied.

"Put some water on it," Taro called up.

"With what, I don't have a canteen with me."

"Well improvise. How else can you produce liquid?" Burbon looked down at his waist.

"You want me to water the balloon," he unclipped his belt.

"No, you buffoon, spit on the balloon, use your saliva." Stonewall shook his head.

Burbon frantically spit, rubbing his saliva on the growing hole. Seconds later, the burning stopped.

"You did it, Burbon, good job! Taro congratulated. Burbon eyed the small hole and the air that was slowly escaping out.

"Save the cheers, we've sprung a leak!" Stonewall noticed that the air machine was slowly sinking. He compensated by adding more flame to increase the hot air.

"Be careful, warrior, if you make it too hot, you'll melt the balloon," Taro reminded.

"True, but if I don't increase the heat, then we'll burn up when the basket hits the magma." Taro searched down at the sea of red.

"What are we going to do?" she asked.

"Hand me up some candy!" yelled Burbon.

"Burbon this is not the time to develop a sweet tooth," cried Taro.

"I'm not, I need something sticky to fill the hole." Taro ran to the bags and searched for the candy. She scanned the wrappers. *Hard candy, Sweet candy, wait this should do the trick.* She pulled wrapped toffee from the bag.

"Catch," she threw two pieces up. Burbon caught the first one but missed the second. It continued its downward arc until the parchment ignited in the magma.

"This stuff really melts in your mouth," he said after a few chews.

"Don't eat it, trader, or we will all perish!" Stonewall yelled.

"Look over there!" Taro pointed off in the horizon. The magma swamps ended, and blackened brush and groundcover appeared. "We won't make it to Cumus but we're almost to the flatlands and out of this swamp."

"Burbon, plug that hole. Our lives depend on it," Stonewall commanded.

Burbon took the toffee out of his mouth and placed it over the hole. *Perfect, it covers everything.* He moved his fingers away and they stuck to the toffee. *I don't believe this.* He pulled a little harder and finally broke his fingers free from the candy. A slight ripping sound echoed. He had pulled more fabric off and now more air was escaping.

"How is it going?" Taro asked.

"I need more candy!" Burbon yelled. Below them the magma had grown closer and its gaseous fumes more powerful. One of the ropes dipped into the magma and ignited, unnoticed by the crew.

Burbon chewed more toffee, applying it to the new rip. Moments later, he was able to secure the leak. He swallowed another piece of candy as a reward before he realized the next problem. The heat of the hot air was making the candy soft and it was dripping off the balloon. He feverishly chewed more candy.

"Keep plugging, Trader, the flatlands are coming up. If we can stay elevated, we can make it," assured Stonewall. Taro peered down and noticed the flaming rope that had burned up to the basket.

"Fire," as she tried to stamp out the flames.

Splosh! Another geyser sprayed the air with liquid fire. Several globs landed on the balloon. Burbon chewed even faster as he saw two new spots on the fabric smoldering. He placed sticky toffee on one hole, spit on another and beat out the flames on a third. Stonewall felt the basket lowering. The approaching flatland still looked too far away.

He increased the heat on the engine to get more height.

"Ouch," yelled Burbon while rubbing his hands. It's getting hot up here!"

"It's hotter down here," said Taro as she desperately beat out several spots of flame. Stonewall motioned to her.

"Throw anything out that we don't need. We won't make it with our current weight." She scrambled through their belongings; she tossed out the remaining candy out first. It melted into a pile before being swallowed by the magma.

"Hey, I wasn't done with that!" yelled Burbon.

"Sorry, we've got to jettison some weight."

"How about the anchor?" Stonewall pointed. Taro dashed over to anchor, cut the rope attached to it and dumped it into the swamp. It disappeared with barely a splash. The balloon dipped up slightly, leveled, and then began to sink again.

"Way to go, elf! At this rate, if we dump everything including ourselves, we might make it," Burbon commented. Stonewall spied a vulture flying above them, catching a thermal to higher heights. It gave Stonewall an idea as he steered towards a geyser.

"Warrior, what are you doing? Those magma geysers caused the problem to begin with!" exclaimed Taro.

"Are you taking us down with the ship?" Burbon posed.

"Trust me," Stonewall's replied as he focused on his destination. The geyser erupted again, and the magma flew into the air. A burst of warm air continued to erupt from the ground. Stonewall steered into it and the air machine was caught in the updraft.

"All right, Stonewall that will buy us some time!" cried Burbon. "Man, that gas stinks," as he plugged his nose. Now, there were too many fires on the air machine for the crew to contain. Stonewall steered toward blacken trees along the edges of the magma swamp.

"Are we going to make it?" asked Burbon to Stonewall.

"You will," Stonewall said as he threw him over the edge. Burbon's scream froze in his throat as he sailed over the magma onto boggy ground. He faced the balloon and received a bag of goods in his face.

"Catch!" Taro yelled as she shot a bolt at a tree. As it hit, she swung from the balloon down to the ground. The air machine was on fire and it landed in the magma as Stonewall jumped out to roll onto the ground. As he stood, he nearly slipped into the nearby magma. Burbon grabbed his hand.

"Not so fast, Warrior. We're not going to lose you like this," he grimaced as Stonewall's massive weight yanked on him while he regained his balance. They both moved to firmer ground. All three watch the entire air machine ignite as it sank into the magma swamp. Burbon took off his hat.

"I guess the museum is going to need a new toy for its parade next year."

"We're lucky it got us as far as it did. Taro, where are we on the map?" Stonewall asked. She reached for the map. The parchment felt dry and cracked under her fingers. Even it had been affected by the extreme conditions.

"The city is northeast through the blackened forest and over the foothills. Burbon moved over to get a look.

"That's a long journey by foot. Are you sure that our provisions will last that long?"

"They'll have to," she answered. "If not, I'll hunt."

"Could be difficult," he picked up charred dirt. "Doesn't look like a lot of things live here."

"Things could be worse, Burbon," Stonewall added. "Let's head to that high ground with those rocks and get away from the magma.

"Be vigilant, there are still soft spots where the magma pools. You don't want to step there," Taro motioned. Burbon stepped aside and beckoned to Taro.

"Ladies first."

The suns were low in the sky by the time they reached the small rise. As they camped for the night, Burbon searched for wood to start a fire. He doesn't watch his step and narrowly sidestepped a small pool of magma bubbling by a large rock.

"Somebody should mark that," as he dropped the wood within a circle of stones made for the fire. "Archer, work your magic and create some fire for us," as he pointed to his pile of wood.

"Absolutely," she picked up one branch and waved her hands over it to conjure up her magic. "Brandaxus" she commanded and then dipped the end of the stick into the small pool of magma that Burbon missed. Within seconds, the end of the branch ignited, and she tossed it into the pile.

"Sometimes common sense prevails over magic," said Stonewall as he sat next to Burbon. All three rested before the fire watching the magma swamp in the distance. Every few seconds a burst of flame erupted and illuminated the sky. The view would be more breathtaking if hadn't almost taken their lives. Burbon placed dried meat on a stick and heated his supper.

"Well one good thing did come of this. I'm sure Darkmoor couldn't have followed us through that."

"I wouldn't be so sure," Stonewall spoke." From what I've heard, he has no flesh left to burn in these swamps.

"My father knew very little of his history. How did he become so powerful?" Taro asked.

"For once I know more than the two of you," Burbon interrupted.

"Go on, you have our attention," commanded Stonewall.

"Well, it all began when I traded with a woman from the shadow lands. She told me about the time that Darkmoor ascended onto the throne of his Kingdom....

A cold wind blew through an open window and a hand covered with many rings tapped on the sill. Dirty snow reflected off the ground from the light of the moon. Villagers scrambled to get out of the cold and into their homes for their meals. He stared at the glass window and two cold eyes reflected back at him. He ran his fingers down his chin, caressing a scar from a fight with his father. He smiled, dark thoughts filling his mind. *Tonight, is the ceremony of my entrance to manhood, the day where I leave boyhood behind and become a man.*

His father had prepared him for manhood, teaching him how to fight, to endure extreme hardships, and to inflict horrible pain. In some ways, he had become stronger than his father. He was young and lean while his father had grown old and fat. Yet no one dared oppose his rule or they would suffer the consequences. When someone was pronounced guilty, punishment included all of the offender's family members as well. Citizens had long ago learned to accept their ruler's cruel ways.

But tonight was about him - when *he* became a man. It would be many years before his father ever surrendered the crown, but at least now in the eyes of the law he was old enough to accept the title. Tonight, Lord Darkmoor began his manhood!

Darkmoor proceeded down the rock stairwell, exiting the turret to the main dining area. Seconds later, he was joined by his squire, Toed.

"You look elegant, my lord," he spoke and bowed his head out of respect. Darkmoor looked down at his servant, so utterly obedient. He could send him to his death and Toed wouldn't hesitate to complete the request.

"Have all the guests arrived?" he asked. Toed knew who Darkmoor was interested in.

"Lady Gentra is here with her family, my lord," he answered.

"Good. All should be here on my day," replied Darkmoor. Gentra was a lovely, intelligent girl, everything that Lord Darkmoor was not. Her family had been coaxed to bring her in hopes of pleasing him. Her family had suffered several unfortunate financial problems lately that could easily be resolved by a courtship with the prince.

Huge oak doors opened before Darkmoor. The room was alive with conversation, a gathering of the King's friends and his military. All types of food and drink were laid out on several tables. A large red carpet ran down the center of the room and ended at the head table.

"His Lordship, Prince Darkmoor," the attendant announced to the room. Several nobles reached out to shake his hand as he walked by.

"Just like your father."

"Happy Birthday, Prince."

"You'll make a wonderful King someday."

He reached the head table where his father laughed a little too hard at a soldier's joke.

"Started drinking a bit early tonight, Father," Darkmoor commented to the group. The soldiers laughed nervously as Darkmoor sat down. His father said nothing to the prince. Suddenly his father stomped his foot on top of Darkmoor's. His heavy boot was sharp and hard. The linen hung over the table preventing others from seeing the King's cruelty.

"You'd best treat me with the proper respect, boy. I'd hate to see your special night end in tragedy." His father smiled, evil to Darkmoor, but to others around him a fatherly gesture towards his son. His father removed his foot and he began talking to his soldiers again.

Darkmoor's face was red with anger, but he knew his place. *My father grows old. Soon my time will come. Until then I will hold my tongue and my blade.*

"Prince Darkmoor, let me congratulate you on your party. You will make a fine future King to your people," Lord Arnur approached Darkmoor with his daughter Gentra in tow.

They wasted no time making their presence known, thought Darkmoor.

"Thank you for attending, Sir Arnur, and for bringing your lovely daughter tonight."

Lady Gentra didn't blush. Darkmoor felt no love directed toward him, just the obligation of a daughter to her father. *If only he had such a bond with his father.*

"The honor is ours, Prince Darkmoor," she answered automatically. Obviously, she had been trained to give the correct response.

"I hope you will reserve a dance for me later?" the prince asked.

"I look forward to that," she curtsied and disappeared back into the crowd with her father. *So much to look forward to and so little time*, thought Darkmoor. The entire room fell silent as the King stood to make his speech for Darkmoor's ceremony.

"It is a father's privilege," the King began, "to be the gatekeeper to his son's entrance to manhood. There is a time in every boy's life when he must step through that gate and become a man. My son has a lot to prove with a father a great as I." Someone laughed in the background as if thinking the King was joking about his greatness. The voice stifled as the rest of the room nodded and voiced approval with the King's statement. The King raised his hands to quell the support played out for him.

"I have done my best to show my son the way to manhood," the King looked over to his son. "I'm sure he would tell you that I am too tough on him, that I pushed him too hard. I say obstacles make us stronger, and those that overcome them become men." The King stared into Darkmoor's eyes. "Remember that, even though you have reached the age of manhood, you still have to prove to me that you are a man." The room was silent, the crowd waited to see if the King would say more.

"Congratulations, Prince!" a soldier yelled out. Others joined in with their greetings until the room went quiet, as everyone waited for the King's next ritual.

Even on this day, he talks more about himself than about me. Darkmoor looked across the room at the soldiers. The captain of the guards marched up to the King with a sword laid across a red pillow. The King reached over and placed it in his hand.

"Son, kneel before me," the King commanded. Darkmoor stepped before his father looking into cold eyes. The King inhaled and continued his speech. "Only through sacrifice and pain can our victories be accomplished in life. The food on this table, the horses in the stables, and the metal in my sword all come with a price. All of us are here because someone was willing to sacrifice a part of himself. My wife, god rests her soul, labored many hours bringing my son into this world. Through her death, her sacrifice, my son was given life. I can hope that my son will find the right sacrifice in himself when it is time to give to his loved ones." The King placed the sword over Darkmoor's right shoulder.

"Through death there is life," the King recites and all in the room repeated his mantra. The King stared down expecting the obedient stare of his son. He saw only Darkmoor's pure hatred, an evil that matched his own. For a moment, his heart went cold as if an icy dagger had sliced his soul.

"Like father like son," whispered Darkmoor, "Like father like son."

Hours later, an attendant escorted the inebriated King back to his room. He leaned against his attendant, his bloated frame staggering into the wall. The attendant reached for the door to escort the King in. His hand was pushed away.

"Fool, I'm not too drunk that I can't undress myself. Be gone!" the King yelled. The attendant bowed and scampered down the stairs. The King opened the latch and entered the dark room. A cool breeze blew through the window.

"Why isn't my fire burning? I will make sure that worm of a servant returns and fixes this." The King turned to bellow at the door. He walked forward and a steel blade sliced through his chest and out his back. The King's eyes widened, unable to comprehend this attack. Darkmoor stepped from the darkness, his grin wide on his face.

"Through death there is life. Your death, my life!"

The King disappeared that night. The only clue was a small droplet of blood found by the window. Many of the guards suspected Darkmoor of killing his father, but no body was ever found. Some said his body was buried in the snow and was swept away in the spring run off. Others said Darkmoor walled him up in the castle and feed him to the rats. After a week's worth of searching, the captain of the guard had no choice but to crown young Darkmoor as King. Once the ceremony of manhood had taken place, the son could legally take the crown. Darkmoor relished the role as he ran his Kingdom into the ground. Like father, like son.

"How truthful do you think that story is, Burbon?" Taro asked.

"I'm pretty confident. She knew him very well during his reign as King," replied Burbon.

"What else did she tell you?" asked Stonewall.

"There's a reason he wears full body armor and a helmet. Magic has eaten away whatever humanity he had."

"Magic always has a price. It takes a little piece of you each time you use it," replied Stonewall.

"The two of you don't complain when I create fire," Taro commented, her arms at her hips.

"When it saves my life, I don't tend to complain," Burbon yawned. He pulled covers over him and laid his head down. "I'm getting some sleep. Hopefully we won't burn up in any magma pools tonight."

"That's what I like about you, trader. Always an optimist." Stonewall placed a pack under his head. Taro pulled out a bolt and sharpened it with her blade.

"Aren't you tired?" asked Burbon, raising his head.

"After your campfire story, I'll think I will stand watch for a little while," as she continued sharpening. Both Burbon and Stonewall lie down to sleep. The dark sky was intermittently lit by bursts of flame from the swamp. Behind their campfire, channels of magma rushed down a hill. Shadows flickered among the trees and a cloaked figure paddled closer to their camp.

21

And a Guide Shall Lead Us

Burbon felt massive hands shaking his shoulders, interrupting his sleep.

"Wake up quietly. We have company," Stonewall whispered. Burbon peered around, their camp illuminated by the morning suns.

"Where's Taro?" he asked.

"She's circling behind our visitor. Someone who paddled a boat in these swamps."

"How could anything live out here? Let alone paddle around this steaming magma?"

"That is what she is trying to find out."

"Without success," Taro replied from behind them. "But I did find this," she dropped a small rock. Stonewall examined it closely.

"Pumice, volcanic rock imperious to the magma. How did it get here? I've seen no evidence of it."

"I found it floating in a magma stream by those large trees. One side is jagged as if broke off a larger object."

"Taro, that rock could have been floating for days, big deal. Why did you think that someone is out there?" Burbon posed.

"I know someone is out there. I can track anything that lives. I noticed scrapes along the rocks as if a heavy staff had pushed against them.

"It could have been there for ages."

"They're fresh."

"Stonewall. Do you want to wade into this conversation? Do you think there's someone out there?"

"I know there is."

"How can you be so sure?"

"Because he's behind you."

Startled, Burbon turned around into the face of the arrival. The being was tall with a cloaked body and huge reptilian eyes. A tail thrashed under its cloak like a third arm ready to strike. Stonewall drew his sword. The creature was unimpressed as it reached into a pan on the fire pit and took out a piece of meat leftover from last night's meal. His mouth crunched on the dry remains.

"Yourrrrrr foood is tasty," the creature lisped, "pity you had to heat it up. The best dishes are served cold."

"State your business before my sword sinks into your flesh," commanded Stonewall. The creature surveyed him.

"Yessss, youuu look like you could do that," his tongue flicked out. "But I have come to help you. You are strangers in a strange land. I assumed you would need a guide."

"Wait just a minute. You show up out of nowhere and you want to sell us your services?" Burbon looked over to Taro. "Now this is this the type of creature I can understand."

"How did you find us in this desolate land?" Taro asked.

"Raattther easssilly actually. Your fire is a dead give away, even from quite a distance."

"Am I missing something?" Burbon pointed off in the distance at the bursts of fire from the swamp. "Fire is a pretty common commodity around here, friend. You'll have to come up with a better explanation than that."

"Nooo neeeeed," it responded. Magma bursts last for seconds, and then vanish, never appearing in the same place twice. Your fire was constant, never moving or wavering from its location. Easy to find for a trained voyager.

"And who are you exactly?" Taro asked. The creature's tail swung in amusement.

"I am Varden. My race ussssssed to be plentiful here before the magma swamp eruption, sending our villages closer to the ocean. Fewer and fewer of us venture this far these days. You three are lucky to find me."

"Yes, I am overjoyed by our good fortune," replied Taro. "Can you take us to there?" she pointed to the living map." Varden stared down at her finger.

"Yesssss, it is only a day's travel by boat. I can help you."

"No one does anything for nothing. What do you want for your services?"

"Surely you have ssssomething vvvaluable for trade?" Both Taro and Stonewall looked at Burbon. He was nervous by their stares.

"The two of you would trade me," he stammered.

"No merchant, the gems from the dragon. How many do you have left?" Stonewall asked. Burbon momentarily brightened.

"No problem, Burbon to the rescue," as he searched his pouch. His face sunk as he pulled the last gemstone out his pocket. "But this is my last stone," he whined.

"Which will do nnnnicely," Varden's tail extracted the gem quickly and placed it in the recesses of his robe. "Grab your belongingssss, we will leave shortly." Varden headed back to the swamp. The three hastily threw their packs together.

"Do you think we can trust him?" Burbon questioned Taro.

"I don't see we have much choice. We don't know this land. But if I suspect he is leading us astray..." Taro let the words die in her throat.

Sweat dripped down Stonewall's face and he wiped his sleeve over his forehead. Magma streamed by as their vessel sailed through the hot liquid. Black trees formed a canopy overhead making it difficult to see the distant mountains. Varden paddled with a pumice stone oar, gently guiding a boat made of the same material, impervious to the magma's heat. The boat was carved out this floating volcanic rock.

Burbon observed movement on a distant outcropping. A small creature with long ears sat scratching its back with long hind legs. Its eyes locked onto Burbon and hopped closer, bouncing from stone to stone. It cocked its head as if trying to communicate with Burbon. He reaches his hand out as if to touch its cute nose.

"I wouldn't do that. Rock rabbits are sssscavengers feeding on the flesh of the dead. No telling what it would do will a living creature," warned Varden. Burbon retracted his hand as the rock rabbit showed a double row of nasty teeth.

"Okay, I trust you now," Burbon gulped. Varden's forked tongue flicked out. Burbon watched the rock rabbit scamper to a cave opening. It hopped in following the magma flow into the darkness.

"Where does that lead to?" Burbon questioned.

"The lava cavesssss, their openings are everywhere. You don't want to go there. The dangers are many," Varden replied.

"Sorry I asked," Burbon shook his head.

"What is your businesssssss in the City of Cumus?" His yellow eyes gleamed with a hidden knowledge.

"They have something we want, and we intend to retrieve it," Stonewall answered bluntly. Varden nodded his head.

"The people of Cumus don't leave their city and they don't welcome visitors. They have talked to no one outside of their city for centuries. You won't be welcome."

"Why does that not surprise me?" chuckled Burbon.

"What do you know about them?" urged Taro, watching the steam rise. Varden studied her before responding.

"The city is sssssurrounded by huge mountains allowing only two means of access - flying down from the peaks above or climbing the walls from beneath. The Cumunian people are solitary and ssssself-sufficient. Our people are not welcome to mix with theirs. I have heard stories of a city inside of those walls made of stone cathedrals, temples, and fountains. But the people are the greatest mystery. They are supposed to be of great intellect, yet they fear anyone different than themsssselves. Once my boat journeyed by their walls. There were slots in the walls through which dozens of blue eyes watched. I spoke several timesssss but I received no response from them. They wouldn't talk to me."

"Or they weren't allowed," offered Taro.

"Either way, no one knowssss what they truly look like," Varden completed his tale and paddled the boat. Burbon gazed off in the distance, his eyes were tired.

"Don't look so glum, Burbon." Stonewall sat beside him. "We have made it this far. Taro and I will protect you from the dangers ahead."

"And that's the problem. I just can't understand why I am with the two of you. Stonewall, you are a great fighter and warrior," Burbon looked over to Taro. "She is a great tracker and magic user. And what do I offer? I'm just a trader. I sell and trade goods. Why am I here in the first place?" Stonewall put his arm on Burbon's shoulder.

"You have been as important on this journey as any of us. Don't let your small stature diminish your contributions." Stonewall smiled at his friend. They both turned to Taro awaiting her response. She remained silent while looking at the two of them. Finally, she spoke.

"Elves are not a social group; we don't tend to share friendships with other races. It is a bias of my people." She walked to Burbon putting her hand on his shoulder. "But I echo the warrior's comments. You are invaluable to this journey, whether you realize your talents or not. I don't approve of all of your methods, but you have helped us get this far."

"Thud!" Varden's oar smashed against a rock.

"We are in trouble!" Varden cried. "There are problems coming up ahead. Many problems." Varden pointed off in the distance.

"What are those?" Taro motioned to the swirling bodies ripping up the ground in their path.

"Devils," replied Varden. "Steam devilsssss, at least a dozen of them. They form as small waterspouts, grabbing debris from the ground and dragging it into the sky. Cold ocean wind currents merge with the hottttt magma air. From sssssskinny to large they range in size, but they are all dangerous at their core."

Burbon watches the devils whirling around like mini tornadoes. One devil spun over a piece of ground and yanked a rock rabbit into the air. It landed with a smoky hiss into the magma.

"Hope it got a bite out of that," Burbon remembered its double row of teeth.

"Can we outrun them?" Taro asked.

"No, there are too many of thhhhhem. We have to find ground with something to grab on to."

"How about the large elder tree to the right?" pointed Stonewall.

"We'll ttttry," as Varden steered toward it. Burbon raised his eyebrows.

"We'll try? You're not instilling a lot of confidence in me. You should meet a captain friend of ours."

"Not now, Burbon," scolded Taro.

One of the steam devils veered west, spinning magma into the air. The magma landed on a tree; the dry wood ignited into fire. Like a blazing torch, it's a warning of what could happen.

"Maybe heading toward that large elder isn't such a good idea," commented Burbon.

"It doesn't matter, were not going to make it. Look!" Varden pointed. Two steam devils have merged, doubling its girth and speed. Its size making them unavoidable.

"We will have to ride this out and hope for the best," Taro pounded a bolt into the boat's side as a handhold.

"There is one other optionnnnnn," said Varden as he directed to a cave opening in the underground.

"You told Burbon earlier that it was too dangerous to go into the underground caves," Stonewall answered.

"Dangerous yes, but the steam devils will either rip us apart or toss us into the magma to burn. We might survive the dangers in the caves." Already the magma churned as an after effect of the rapidly approaching steam devils.

"Then do it," replied Taro. The others nodded in agreement. Varden steered away from the elder tree and turned towards the cave entrance. The steam devils decreased the distance between them in seconds.

"Are we going to make it?" Burbon cried.

"Barely, yessssss," Varden hissed as the smaller steam devil spun around them causing a wave of magma, which threatened to capsize the boat.

"Here we go!" Varden yelled as the darkness of the cave swallowed them up. The funnel of the steam devil slammed into the rocks behind them. The gusts threw small stones at their back. As the boats sailed deeper into the cave, the wind from the outside world died away. An occasional burst of magma illuminates the cave every few seconds giving a glimpse of what lies ahead.

"You can slow the boat, Varden. We are beyond the reach of the steam devils," Taro's voice echoed.

"I'm not paddling anymore," he replied.

"The boat's speed has increased, what's moving us?" Burbon asked.

"The current," answered Stonewall. "Listen!" In the distance a dull roar grew louder.

"What is that?" Burbon wondered.

"Hold on!" Varden commanded as the boat careened over the edge like a roller coaster. Gravity dropped the boat down through the air for an eternity until finally splashing at the bottom of the cave. The boat popped up from the magma like a cork and floated forward. Flame ignited revealing four sets of shocked but living eyes.

"Can we go back and get my stomach?" Burbon asked. He stepped to the other side of the boat and disposed of his last meal into the magma. It burned like fuel and illuminated, adding embarrassment to his prone position. "If that was the best route, I hate to see what would have happened if we had stayed with the steam devils."

Burbon felt a long hard bony arm on his back. "Can you leave me alone for a few minutes," he asked, not wanting his friends' pity. When the hand doesn't move, he turned and almost swallowed his tongue. "Ahhhhhh," he yelped and almost falling into the magma.

"What's eating you," Taro yelled in the darkness. A burst of flame illuminates a dead skeleton hanging upside down from the ceiling.

"Don't worry, Trader, that creature hasn't eaten anyone for a long time," commented Stonewall. "Don't be so fearful."

"Silly me. What's to be scared in a dark cave with dead bones reaching for me and flames that can incinerate me? I don't know where my head was," Burbon added sarcastically.

"Keep your head on for a little while longer. Varden, can you we get back to the surface?" Taro asked.

"Eventually, but the tttttrrick is finding the right path. If we go the wrong way, we could go deeper into magma core until the temperature is too hot for any of us to survive."

"Oh, I feel better now," Burbon answered. "I don't understand how we can get back to the surface. It seems like we went down quite a distance."

"Your point is trueeeee, we must fund a magma lock," replied Varden.

"Like a river lock?" questioned Stonewall.

"Corrrrect," Varden lisped, "Certain chambers fill with magma and then spill onto the surface. Such chambers can take moments to fill while others can take days."

"I'm all for the moments," Burbon interjected.

"How can we find such a chamber?" Taro asked. Varden tapped his nose.

"By the smellllllll, the magma gases will be strongest at the eruption point. It also means they can be lethal if the poisonous gases are too strong."

"You've sold me. Let's find the stinkiest, vilest odor and if the nauseous smell doesn't kill us, the erupting magma will," responded Burbon.

An hour past and the heat from the magma was stifling. All four had stripped down to the barest of clothes, lashing their weapons and packs to the boat's floor. With the exception of Varden, sweat poured down their bodies.

"How do you deal with the heat, Varden, the temperature is unbearable?" Taro asked. He turned and stared with cold eyes. "My speciesss has adapted to these lands for centuries, we are cold blooded and can take extremes of heat. But even though my skin doesn't sweat, I still feel the heat. None of us will last much longer down here if we don't find a lock soon."

"What's worse is that this place stinks the whole time we have been here. How are we going to know if we are near a lock?" Burbon asked.

"You'llll know," as he pulled the oar back. The soupy red liquid swirled around it. A squeaky murmur came from the distance.

"What is that?" posed Stonewall. Varden was alarmed and stopped paddling.

"Blood bats!" he whispered. "They sleep during the day and come out at night, sucking the blood of small animals. Their ears are attuned to the slightest sound. Do not speak another word until we pass beneath them."

"You overrate the danger of blood bats. The blood they would take from you would only be equal to an insect bite," stated Stonewall.

"It is not your blood loss that you have to worry about. The diseases their dirty little bodies carry are horrible. Some can drive a creature mad. We are far from any medicinessssss. A bite could destroy your mind before we can find any help."

Burbon tugged at Stonewall's arm. "I vote for being quiet," he gulped.

The boat sailed silently through the cave. The only sound was the constant burst of flame from erupting pockets of magma. Slowly the gibbering of sleeping bats echoed along the walls, their dirty bodies hanging upside down from the cave ceiling. There were dozens of them, their waste dripped down into the magma below illuminating their clumped bodies. They breathed slowly as if in a deep sleep. A fluttering of wings created a small breeze. The sleeping bats continually adjusted themselves to prevent from losing their grip and falling to their death. As the boat passed underneath, Burbon felt an uncontrollable urge to retch again from the overwhelming stench. He looked at the others who also expressed a similar reaction.

Gurgle, his mouth uttered before he can cover it. A bat's eye opened at the noise. It chirped as if to signal its brothers to wake from their slumber. Burbon's face was horrified if he could imagine the bats biting at his flesh. All of them were silent while watching the bat. Its eyelids fluttered, and then its mouth stretched wide in a long yawn. It closed its eyes and returned to a fitful sleep. Gradually the boat sailed away from the colony of bats. No one dared speak for several minutes.

"We are far enough now for them not to detect us if we whisper but please," Varden said, looking at Burbon, "no loud sounds."

"Is there anything else in these caves that we should know about?" asked Taro.

"The blood bats live on the higher levels, I am not familiar with anything that lives closer to the magma core," Varden answered.

"Which is another way to say *I don't know*," added Burbon. "Those blood bats were hideous; I can't imagine anything worse living down here."

"Don't tempt the fates," scolded Taro.

"Wait a second, what is that sound?" Stonewall heard a distant rumble.

"I believe it is what we are looking for. We will know shortly," answered Varden. Several minutes past as the roar became louder and the magma fumes were stronger.

The bats didn't smell as bad as this, Burbon thought.

The boat steered into an open cavern with large waterfalls of magma streaming down, changing direction as they hit various rock outcroppings. Burbon watched as bursts of steam gusted from holes in the rock wall. Pieces of rock laid smashed in the pool, blown apart from the explosive pressure.

"Varden, this doesn't look like the safest place to be. Where is your lock?" asked Burbon.

Gouts of magma surged into an opening with a thunderous roar and Varden only needed to point.

"Use these," as he handed out small leather straps with flaps to cover their nose. Burbon tied it behind his head thinking. *Why didn't we use these before?* Varden steered and the boat was swallowed up into the opening. Inside the hole, magma surged against the wall. Taro deftly avoided spillage as it splashed off the wall. The red liquid puddled and smoked in a small hole beneath the boat.

"Beware of the splashing magma. We are like a cork in the ocean. Keep your faces covered." Varden closed the hood over his face.

"Have far do we have to float up before getting back to the surface?" Taro asked. Her voice almost drowned out by an incoming wave.

"Look up," pointed Burbon. She looked up the sheer walls to a distant pinprick of light.

"At the rate the magma is flowing in, it shouldn't be too long before we float to the top," commented Stonewall.

"If we don't burn to death first," Burbon sidestepped another spurt of magma, but a splash got on his tunic. He patted out the flame using a cloth wrapped around his hand.

Taro was the first to hear a familiar chirping sound. Before she could ask the others, they all turned left toward the opening.

"What is it?" she questioned Varden. He immediately covered every piece of exposed skin.

"It's the bats. It must be close to their feeding time. At dusk, they go to find what little water exists in this realm."

"Any chance they might not be flying out this particular passage?" Burbon asked.

"I'm afraid not. Look above!" Varden pointed. A huge hole gaped out of the rock cliff near the top of the lock. Bat droppings oozed down the cliff face. "If they come out before we reach the top, they will descend upon us like locusts. We'll be sitting ducks with no escape," Varden stated.

"Great, dinner is served," as Burbon evaded more splashing magma.

"We're still minutes from the top but I don't think the bats are that far away," as Taro wrapped everything but her eyes and mouth.

"We have to get to the top now! Taro do something!" Burbon yelled.

"What do want me to do? Make us float faster!" she answered in anger.

"No, Burbon is right," Stonewall spoke. "Use your power, Taro, heat the magma with your flame, the eruption will send us to the top.

"Or burn us in an explosion of magma," she replied.

"Better to burn than die by the diseases those bats carry," stated Varden.

"Thanks for your support," Burbon answered.

Taro extended her hands to the fire. She concentrated and mumbled the words to herself. The flames burst so strong from her hands that it knocked her down onto the boat. Her flames blasted off the wall and ricocheted back, narrowly missing Burbon. Stonewall rose over her.

"Burbon, help me stabilize her," he commanded. Burbon stood

behind her and held one of her arms pointed at the magma. Stonewall was beside her, holding her other arm down. "Try again!"

"Volita shay!" as her flames charged the boiling magma. Her flames sunk deep and the magma boiled, releasing gases at an unbelievable rate.

"Longer!" Stonewall yelled. Taro strained a few moments longer until the color drains from her face and she fainted back onto Stonewall.

"Hold on," Varden screamed as they dropped to their backs and grabbed hold of the boat.

The gases exploded. Heated magma had nowhere to go but up, confined by the walls of the tunnel. The boat was sent hurling up, riding the top of the magma wave. Burbon saw the night sky hurtling towards them. The geyser erupted, spraying the magma into the air and for a few moments, Burbon was flying with the boat. Seconds later, he tumbled off the boat and crashed to the ground on his back. He sank into a warm liquid that embraced his body and a relaxing sleep trying to overcome him.

In seconds the magma will burn me, and all my worries will be gone. Moments past and his consciousness remained. He looked up and a mass of bats exited the cave and surged into the sky. Without thinking, he ducked his head to avoid their bites. *Why am I not burning up?* Burbon's head broke the surface and Varden's hand yanked him onto solid ground.

"I see you have found one of the hot springs," he said, "its heat powers many of the windmills in my village." Burbon surveyed his surroundings. Even in the dusk he could tell the land has changed. Rivers had replaced the streams of magma and green foliage had changed from blacken terrain. Far in the distance, a huge walled city surrounded by moats of water beckoned them. A large mountain in the center extended into the sky and was surrounded by clouds.

"We are close now," Varden replied. "In the morning you will be at the City of Cumus."

22

Speak No Evil

The four of them were silent as the boat sailed slowly toward the city walls. Huge fortifications lined the top of the mountain slopes with sentry posts. No activity stirred. A griffin flew overhead and disappeared into the brightness of the sun.

"Any chance the residents packed up and left?" asked Burbon.

"No," answered Varden, "They are there. I can feel their presence. They will make themselves known when they are ready." Taro sharpened a crossbow bolt in anticipation of battle.

"Are you going to fight the whole settlement?" questioned Stonewall.

"I believe in being prepared, warrior. No one has just handed over their piece of the gem. I expect nothing different here," she responded. Burbon glimpsed a distant motion at the top of the mountain walls. The movement disappeared like heat mirage. *Maybe my eyes are playing tricks on me.*

"How do you think they climb these walls?" Burbon asked. "The walls are smooth and polished; I don't see any climbing apparatus to use."

"We will find a way," answered Stonewall.

The boat meandered around a turn and a huge pyramid tower jutted into the sky. Its white alabaster stone reflected heat from the morning suns.

"Wow, I'd like to meet the people who built that," remarked Burbon.

"Be careful what you wish for," Taro responded. Several sets of blue eyes stared at them through peepholes in the wall. Burbon danced on the boat.

"Hello! Can we come in to visit?" he shouted.

"Burbon, be careful or you'll dunk us all in the water," Taro commented.

"I'm trying to get their attention. It's better than trying to aim a crossbow at them. Varden, you have met them once before. Is this how they acted?" Varden stared in the blue eyes through the wall as they blinked at him.

"The same. They provided no means of communication to speak with me. They were curious but not inclined to talk," Varden confirmed.

"I will create an invitation," as Stonewall directed his booming voice to the wall. "I am Stonewall," he yelled, "we mean you no harm but wish to visit your city. Will you grant us entry?" Many eyes blinked, but if his words are understood there was no response to confirm.

"I believe that the Cumunians think they are superior to our races and refuse to communicate," stated Varden.

"I second that thought," Taro piped in. "We are trying to communicate with them and all they do is look at us."

"Maybe they are too simple to talk," said Burbon.

"Doesn't explain the architecture. Only an advanced race could build a wall as tall as this without it collapsing on itself," commented Stonewall.

"Well, I'm fresh out of theories. We aren't getting in without an invitation," Burbon answered.

Stonewall unsheathed his sword and sunk it into the rock wall. All forward motion on the boat stopped. His left hand reaches for a rock handle and he pulled himself up. He ripped the sword out of the wall and slid it back in, higher up. His hands searched for another handhold. It was a slow and arduous task.

"You'll be doing that all day Stonewall. There has to be an entrance to this place," Burbon commented.

"Every journey begins with a single step. If the Cumunians show you a way in, come get me," he grunted pulling himself a few inches higher.

"You can stop now, warrior. The Cumunians are coming to you," Taro pointed. The four of them watched a fluttering motion at the top of the wall. Four distinct figures came into view. Three strong males covered in silk robes with a similarly decorated female. Their most remarkable feature had nothing to do with their physique or their clothes, it was their wings. Beautiful white wings, twice the span of their bodies. Taro pulled her crossbow out and aimed it at one of the Cumunians.

"No," commanded Stonewall. "We do not know their intent."

"For the amount of trouble, it took to get here, I'm preparing for their intent. I hope I'm wrong," Taro gritted her teeth. The Cumunians covered the distance to the water in seconds, their mighty wings drumming in the air.

"They're coming in pretty fasssttttt." The first male scooped Burbon off the deck and into the air. Taro loosened a bolt that missed its target as the female Cumunian tried to grasp her by the shoulders.

"Taro, they mean us no harm. Look!" The two males lifted Stonewall up under his shoulder and gently glided him into the sky. "Let the woman carry you," he yelled. Taro scanned the woman; her face was devoid of emotion. There were no traces of malice or warmth. Taro relaxed her stance and allowed the woman to lift her into the air.

"What about Varden?" Burbon asked as his carrier pulled him higher.

"Don't worry about me," Varden answered, his voice fading. "They aren't here for me. They have revealed themselves for a purpose. Good fortune with your quest." The guide and his boat disappeared as they were carried over the wall and into the city. The sight that greeted them was breathtaking.

The city was an architectural marvel. Huge stone temples with majestic statues radiated from the center of the city. The streets ran diagonal from the center, like the rays of the suns spreading out to the edges of the walls. The air was thick with fliers. A multitude of blue eyes watched their approach. A flock of young boys followed behind them. An adult gave the boys a cross look and shoed them away. The city amazed them, but Burbon was impressed with the Cumunians themselves.

Except for the fluttering of the wings, the city was perfectly quiet. No talking, no yelling, no laughing. The Cumunians did not speak. The three were gently lowered to the town square. Other Cumunians gave the three travelers a glance as they flew by. Stonewall greeted one of his carriers.

"We mean you no harm. Why did you bring us here?" The largest of three males merely stared blankly and motioned his hand toward the temple. The female watched Stonewall, curious about his appearance. Burbon walked over to Stonewall.

"Stonewall, these people are mute. How are we going to communicate with them?"

"Not everyone has to open their mouth to express their intentions," stated Taro. "Look in the sky!"

Glancing up, they saw dozens of carrier pigeons flying from building to building. One of them landed near him. Burbon spied a metal clasp on their legs with a tube to place a message.

"You mean they use those birds to talk to each other?" asked Burbon.

"For long distance messages, the military has used the same methods for scouts to send messages back to their commanders," explained Stonewall.

One bird landed on the shoulder of the female Cumunian and she unrolled a message tucked on its leg. Taro and Burbon peeked around her shoulder but the writing was unfamiliar. If these creatures communicated in this manner, it was not in a form of writing that she was familiar with. The female wrote several symbols onto the paper, rolled it tightly and returned it to the tube. She lifted her arm into the air to signal the bird to fly. Taro may not have understood the language, but it did give her an idea. She motioned to one of the male Cumunians.

"Could you look at this?" she asked not expecting him to understand her words but perhaps her body language. She unfolded the living map, which gave an illustrated drawing of the city with the location of the last gem. The four Cumunians gathered around Taro, amazed by the drawn representation of their city. One dared to touch, and the map cooed like a dove to his touch.

"That's an endorsement of these people if I ever saw it," commented Burbon. He placed his stubby finger on the center of the map pointing to a flashing symbol of the gem. "We want to go here!" The large male nodded to Burbon and motioned to the female. He created a several different hand shapes, the female nodded her head and flew off to a distant building. The lead male gestured with his hand for them to follow him.

"Do you think they understand and can help us?" Burbon asked Stonewall.

"They seem like an intelligent race with no signs of harm toward us. Their silence would seem to cut them off from communicating with any other races. Perhaps this explains why Varden and his people have never met them."

"Seems convenient that they just happened to come down and pluck us into their city." Taro suggested.

"No offence to Varden, but he isn't from the most attractive race. Maybe we just look friendly," as Burbon licked his fingers and curled the end of his moustache, "or handsome?"

"Yes, Burbon, the Cumunian people just had to meet you," laughed Taro as she stepped through a huge metal door. Inside the building they were impressed by the sheer size of the room. Huge windows in the ceiling allowed light to shine below on mammoth shelves. The shelves were latched to the walls with ropes and could only be accessed by the winged beings that fluttered between rows looking for scrolls. There were thousands of scrolls varying in sizes and colors. Most Cumunians continued to read, although a few younger readers stared at them.

"For an isolated culture I expected more worried looks than this," replied Taro.

"Perhaps we are not the first culture to have visited their city," answered Stonewall.

"Whatever the reason, this is better than any library we have at home," commented Burbon.

The group past through the large amphitheater, there was fervent scribbling as notes were written and exchanged. At the end of the room, another larger door stood before them, awaiting their entry. Burbon eyed the oversized doorknocker shaped as a sculpted face. He examined it from all sides.

"Checking for demons?" Taro asked. The doors clanged open as two Cumunians on each side pulled the door's massive weight with huge ropes. The doors revealed a wide room with a large window with a view of the city. In the center of the room sat a huge wooden pyramid that reached the ceiling that was many stories tall. The pyramid was built like a wooden exoskeleton with beams that brace the entire structure together. The beams were lashed loosely together allowing light to flow through. Inside the pyramid was an elaborate maze with one entry point at the bottom. At the center of the pyramid, in plain sight, sat a very important treasure.

"The fourth stone. We have finally reached it!" exclaimed Stonewall.

"But how are we going to get to it?" asked Burbon as he stepped to the right of the pyramid. The three-dimensional maze had vertical and horizontal paths. The entrance was a narrow opening at the bottom. The center of the pyramid was open with the fourth stone in a cage, but the openings were too small to pull it out. Burbon rubbed his chin as if contemplating his options as Taro stood behind him.

"Stonewall could smash the structure with his broadsword and we could pick up the gem from the rubble," she commented.

"Not practical," Stonewall answered. "That wood is strong. Even if I could knock a hole into the center, the wood above it would crush the stone before we could retrieve it."

"I doubt the Cumunians would let us get that far. Excuse us as we demolish your important monument and take the valuable gem from its center," Burbon mocked.

"No, but you give me an idea," replied Taro. She took the three combined pieces and placed them on her hand for all to see. The Cumunians immediately reacted. All four that had accompanied them, now bowed in unison before Taro's hand in religious fervor. Then they pointed at the gem in the monument.

"I didn't expect such a strong reaction," she replied. "They obviously regard these gems as important pieces of their culture."

"Which will make taking the last stone that much more difficult," answered Stonewall.

"They let us in on their own free will. They may not be able to talk but their actions speak volumes. Now how are we going to get this last stone?" Burbon asked. The Cumunians watched the three of them as they investigated the structure. Stonewall checked the solidness of the framing. Taro examined the master chamber looking for a way to reach the gem. Burbon examined the small opening which is the entrance to the maze.

"Looks like only one of us going to fit into this opening," he pondered. Taro joined him at the entrance.

"You have a little extra around the middle. Are you sure you can fit?" she patted his stomach. Burbon pulled away.

"I case you haven't noticed, due to the lack of good food and being attacked constantly, I have lost a great deal of weight," Burbon stated.

"The space is tight. Are you sure you want to attempt this?" asked Stonewall. Burbon reached up to his full height.

"Yes. I can offer something that the two of you cannot."

"We could ask the Cumunians to send a child through there instead," Taro asked.

"They aren't too good at communicating with us. Besides the wings on even a child's body would get stuck in there. I'm the logical choice," Burbon said with an air of authority. Taro stared into the narrow opening.

"You're going to need a guide to help you see ahead," she climbed onto the wooden pyramid and held on with one hand. "I'll help you from the outside." Burbon peered back at Stonewall.

"You don't feel left out, do you warrior?" he asked.

"I will stay back and keep an eye on the whole monument. I'll let you know if any surprises are coming up," Stonewall smiled.

"Why? Do you think there are traps?" Burbon was concerned.

"If there are, I know you will handle them." Stonewall patted Burbon on the back. The compliment gave Burbon a burst of confidence.

"Well, here goes everything," as he climbed into the narrow opening. He took note of a small symbol cut into the corner of the wood. The Cumunians observed Burbon's entrance into their pyramid structure, but their faces remained neutral. Only their bodies betrayed an interest as they moved closer and watched Burbon climbing. He scaled the wooden tunnel cautiously. Despite the slats allowing light to shine through, Burbon felt claustrophobic. He reached a fork allowing him to veer right or left. Taro matched his steps by climbing on the exterior of the pyramid.

"Which way should I turn?" he asked Taro. Stonewall interrupted as he walked over to the right side.

"The structure seems less complex on its right side. That could make it easier to navigate," Stonewall offered viewing the entire pyramid. Taro nodded her approval.

"Right it is," said Burbon and turned to the right at the fork. He noticed more symbols cut into the corner of each entrance. Similar to the front entrance, it has a symbol of a lightning bolt followed by several sun symbols. He peered back at the other entrance. The symbols of the sun are also described followed by a sword-like symbol. He switched back to the thunderbolt, which reminded him of something he had seen before.

"Why did you stop," asked Taro. "I thought you were going right!"

"Patience," he answered. "I'm noticing a code in the corner of the turns, like the symbols on the Cumunian's paper. Too bad they couldn't explain to me what they mean."

"What do you see?" posed Stonewall as Burbon crawled into the right entrance.

"Thunder bolts on one side, swords on the other," he answered.

"Do you think it represents a type of trap?" Taro questioned.

"Anything is possible. Burbon be careful," Stonewall commanded. Behind him, the female Cumunian watched intently.

"Like I wasn't already," he answered as his foot caught on a wooden switch. Burbon's foot flinched as he peered back.

Taro climbed to look at the lever.

"It's connected to that!" she pointed. The bar pulled down a wooden door that latched shut behind Burbon, closing the entrance to the fork. Burbon backed up and kicked the new door. The wood was solid and his foot had no impact.

"Ouch! I'm not going out the way I came," as he wiped his forehead.

"Let me climb ahead of you, Burbon, so I can see if anymore switches will get in your way," Taro ordered. She scanned the nearest crawlspace. "Looks clear. Take your time."

"Easy for you to say," replied Burbon. "You're not in a space that feels like its going to close in on you." *I must have been crazy to volunteer for this.*

He climbed up and down encountering numerous forks, each requiring a decision. Burbon saw many symbols, three, four, sometimes all the same, sometimes all different. Several times Burbon encountered a dead end and had to turn back. Burbon crossed one passageway and felt his weight shift. Something moved and he stopped in his tracks.

"Can you hear that? I hear a creaking sound," Burbon questioned. Taro climbed further ahead.

"I see a rope moving on a pulley, but I can't see what it is attached to," she answered.

"I can!" stated Stonewall. "And you're not going to like it!" He pointed higher up to a wooden gate with sharp spikes on the front side sliding closer. "Burbon, find another passageway!" Burbon needed no further encouragement and scurried down. He fell feet first, jamming his body in tight.

"Ahhh, I'm caught," he yelled.

"Now is not the time, Burbon!" Taro climbed to dislodge him. The distance between him and the spiked wall was halved. Burbon pulled with his hands just as his legs popped free. He scurried to the next fork. On the right are two thunderbolts and a sun, on his left two spears and two scrolls. *What do these symbols mean?*

"Burbon!" Taro commanded. "Make your decision now!" He turned right and felt a wooden spike graze off of his shoe as it slammed into the wall.

One way to lose weight, he thought.

"Good job, Burbon, you're almost there," encouraged Stonewall. Burbon climbed thorough a narrow center and emerged into a small antechamber. At the apex was the fourth stone, lying on a dish surrounded by metal chains. *Why does this look familiar*? He slid around the dish examining it from all sides. Taro ascended above him and slid a bolt into an opening but encountered more wooden spikes. She scrambled down and found a similar bed of spikes below the antechamber as well.

"Taro look at the weight at the end of the rope pulley, it is to the left," Stonewall pointed.

"I see it. I also see what it will move. Burbon, get out of there!" Taro commanded.

"Hold on a second, this contraption hasn't moved in a long time. I think I'm safe as long as I don't touch anything."

"Or hit something by mistake," added Taro.

"This whole setup bothers me because I have seen it before," said Burbon. "It looks like a weight scale, similar to what I use in determining payment for goods."

"What do you mean?" asked Stonewall.

"When making change, it's important to exchange the proper amount of gold for silver or other precious metals. Gold is heavy, so more pieces of silver go in the scale to even out the exchange."

"And you think the gem is sitting in a scale?" Taro posed.

"I do," Burbon replied.

"Well if that's true, as soon as you remove the stone, both walls of spikes are going to meet in the middle."

"And I'll have holes in places I didn't know existed," Burbon said with an unusual calm.

"What are you thinking, Burbon?' asked Stonewall.

"The scale has stayed perfectly balanced because the weight is correct. If I can replace it with the exact weight, the scale should remain at the same position."

"You think you can do it?" Taro questioned.

"Taro, this is what I do. I can judge the correct weight of currency in a bag with my eyes closed.

"Burbon, this isn't currency, this is a gemstone," Stonewall corrected.

"Never mind, it is the same principle. I can do this."

"What can we do?" requested Taro.

"Just be quiet and watch." Burbon pulled out a number of silver coins from his pocket. He tossed them into his right hand and then tossed them into his left. *Seven or eight. Got to be sure on this one, if I want to stay alive.* He stared at the stone. It gleamed silently at him, ready to deal death without a hint of remorse. Burbon thought of all the customers he had dealt with, measuring and exchanging currency with the quickness of a sword fighter. *Go with your gut. Seven it is.* In his right hand laid the seven silver pieces while his left was ready to grasp the gem. Both Taro and Stonewall looked at Burbon but were afraid to utter a sound that might distract him.

"It's been nice knowing you," Burbon smiled and placed the silver coins in the plate at the same moment he took the gem. For several seconds no one spoke while Burbon stood frozen. He breathed a sigh of relief. The weight on the scale moved slightly.

"Burbon!" Stonewall yelled. The spikes on opposite sides were about to slam shut on the antechamber.

"Get out of there!" Taro yelled.

"No time! Only one thing left to do," he cried.

Stonewall could not watch helplessly and charged at the monument. He swung his sword in a desperate attempt to break open the chamber. His blade stopped inches into the wood as the spike walls ceased moving.

"Eight pieces of silver," Burbon commented having placed one more piece onto the plate to find the correct weight. Taro sunk down on her knees.

"You did it, Burbon. You did it!" Stonewall jumped for joy and hugged the female Cumunian. For the first time, her eyes projected emotion.

The doors behind them opened as several large Cumunians entered.

Behind them marched a dozen gobtrolls. Burbon stared out of his cage at the strange sight. As the gobtrolls split to stand on either side of the doorway, a tall armored figure walked between them, carrying an evil looking blade. *This has to be Darkmoor*, Burbon thought as his heart leapt into his throat.

My gratitude. A voice echoed loudly through all three of their brains. *You've finally delivered my prize.* Stonewall was the first to recover his senses.

"Treacherous villain! These stones are not for you. We journeyed to prevent you from acquiring them!"

Wrong on both counts, warrior, the voice exploded in volume threatening to overwhelm their minds. *The stone is for me and you have acquired its pieces because I needed you to. A feeble wizard told you the following prophecy:*

Once evil has divided the orb
Only the power of good can unite the broken pieces
To the bold and brave
Beware of deceit on the journey
Only strong shepherds will be your guides
Strength will provide protection
Magic will provide direction
Wealth will set them free
Prevent pure evil from claiming the power

If a piece is false, the holder will be punished

I could never collect the pieces. Only good could gather them. I never wanted to stop the three of you. I just needed to motivate you to push onward. You have fulfilled your part of the prophecy, now I will complete it!

"No!" yelled Stonewall charging at Darkmoor. Four gobtrolls intercepted him before he could cover half of the distance. "The Seer said they WE were meant to keep this power away from you!"

You pathetic fool! The Seer never existed!

Darkmoor conjured with his hands and the stones in Taro's pouch came to life. She placed them in her hand as a familiar voice resonated from the stones. A familiar image of an old man shimmered.

"*I am the Seer! Please follow the trails of the stones for all that is good. I will lead you...*" the voice trailed off. Darkmoor walked over and clapped his hands. The force blew the apparition of the Seer into dust.

I am the Seer! I always have been! You followed my commands because I could not gather these stones without your help. Now I will gain their power and bring this world to its knees. All because of your help!

Taro jumped down from the pyramid and put the stones back into her pouch. "You don't control us. You'll have to take these stones from our dead bodies!"

Darkmoor looked at her without any fear.

As pawns I don't expect you to understand what has happened. You have been my puppets the entire journey. Now is the time to cut your strings!

23

Evil Unleashed

Burbon was speechless, probably for the first time in his life. Never had he worked so hard toward a goal only to find out that he was lied to. Every step they had taken was a predestined march designed to deliver the stones to Darkmoor. He almost retched, sick of the thought that all their effort had been for nothing. He and his friends had delivered the world's most powerful magic to this evil. *What had they done?*

"Step any closer to me and these gems will be destroyed," Taro yelled as she moved towards the window. The building was high enough that their fall could damage them. Darkmoor appeared unfazed.

You'll do no such thing. I have anticipated your every move. I toyed with you, pushing you hard enough to run, but not hard enough to give up.

"We could have died," replied Taro.

Then I would have learned that you weren't the ones. Give me my stones. You have no choice. The outside window shattered. Taro was thrown against the wall by Sunder's winged body. The stones were tossed from her hand into the air, landing unharmed by the pyramid. Sunder roared as he attacked the archer. In desperation, Taro ushered a final incantation.

"Volanti Shaw!" She focused her fire at the mighty griffin, but he anticipated and swerved to the left. The flames singed his left flank as he grabbed Taro in his claws and took her through the window, down to her death.

Now they were two. Stonewall looked at Burbon's trapped form.

Don't worry about him, warrior, Darkmoor said to Stonewall. *I'll cut him out. Now it's time for you to join your fallen comrade.* A killing force of gobtrolls stepped away from Darkmoor and marched towards Stonewall. As mighty as Stonewall's strength was, he could not fight these odds. Stonewall turned to Burbon.

"I won't forget you, Burbon," he commanded. "I will fight you all to my last breath!" He charged and was swallowed up in the gobtroll mass.

"No!" screamed Burbon from his prison. His grief racked his body, putting him on the verge of giving up. *What can I do?* His fingers touched the potion bottle that Turbine gave him. *A way to even the odds.* He threw the small tube through the opening and it smashed on the floor. Brown droplets splattered on the granite like a dirty mud puddle. Burbon watched as the results were immediate. The drops grew like a tree before his eyes forming sturdy but small fighters, all in the image of the holder, himself. Ten shapes of Burbon grew before his eyes. Single-minded in purpose they waited for one command to execute for their short lives.

Burbon yelled, "Attack the gobtrolls!" The tiny army turned in unison and descended like an angry horde upon the gobtrolls. Some of the beasts turned from Stonewall to this new threat. The Burbons leapt into the air and landed on the heads of several of gobtrolls, knocking them to the ground. One of the Burbons was skewered by a gobtroll's mace. It turned into dust and scattered into the air. *I hope they can help Stonewall.* Burbon rotated his head as he smelt smoke coming from behind him. Looking around, he saw the flames from Taro's spell spreading quickly throughout the tinder dry pyramid.

Great! As if the other dangers weren't bad enough. He dove to an exit and to hurry out of the maze.

Taro felt the griffin's claws tighten around her torso as the wind raced at her back. She knew there were only seconds before her body would be hurled to the ground below. One thought came to her mind. *Why? Why are you doing this?*

How can you talk to me? A voice was returned as the griffin veered away from the ground, wanting a moment longer before smashing its prey.

I just can. I thought I could feel an animal's thoughts. You however are the first to respond. The claw loosened and she punched the griffin in the face, almost causing him to relinquish her.

That was foolish. If I let you go, you will fall to your death.

An image flashed before her eyes of a hunt when she was a girl.

Better to choose my own destiny.

Noble words for one about to die.

Then be honorable and make it quick. Unlike your master, who will cause untold horror for thousands of my people. The griffin snarled in anger as if his world had been challenged.

He has cared for me while others would hunt and skin my hide as a trophy. Taro remembered an old memory. She walked in the forest with her brothers and father following behind her.

Better to die a trophy than live as a slave. Taro spit in the face of Sunder. She knew she had seen this face before. Sunder saw the image in Taro's mind. A young elfin hunter who allowed a young griffin its life, watching it fly away, and Sunder looking back to her.

I know you, with the realization of the past event. *You let me live.*

That was my mistake and stabbed the griffin with a bolt tip. Sunder's claws released her, and she fell to the ground.

Stonewall was bleeding, he had cuts to his face and his arms stung with open wounds. He kicked two gobtrolls against the wall and managed to stand on his feet again. Even with the Burbon apparitions, the odds were still heavily stacked against him. He smashed a gobtroll in the mouth and its ugly black teeth went flying as its body crumpled to the ground. He turned as a gobtroll's blade was about to imbed itself into his heart.

A Burbon double leapt into the way, stopping the blade with its body before it disappeared into dust. Stonewall knocked the sword out of the enemy's hand and kicked the unfortunate gobtroll out of the broken window to its doom. Another jumped at him as his back was turned. Stonewall watched as the gobtroll's head fell forward, smashed by a shattered chunk of ceramic. The female Cumunian held a broken vase in her hand and stared at Stonewall. *Apparently not all of the Cumunians are watching from the sidelines.* Stonewall charged, his energy renewed at the remaining gobtrolls.

The smoke was overwhelming. It stung Burbon's eyes and made it hard for him to breathe. *There is no room for error on the way out. Make one wrong turn and the fire will overtake me.* He came to another fork, three moons and a thunderbolt on one side; two towers and a sun on the other side. *What do these symbols mean? I can't guess my way out. I have to know the answer now!* The flames were licking at his feet. He thought about the scale of the pyramid. *I swear that the maker of this pyramid dealt in currency. The chains and cup resembled a weighing scale.*

Suddenly an idea sprung to mind. *What if the symbols are immaterial, but it's the number of symbols that are important? Most of the world's currencies are grouped in threes to symbolize the customer, the seller, and the value of the product. Maybe the turns of three are the way out?* He stamped out a flame as it ignited his leather shoes and he dove into the tunnel of two towers and one sun.

Minutes past. Passages and forks flew by. Burbon choose the way of three each time, bringing him closer and closer to the exit and away from the flames. He climbed forward and fell out of the pyramid as it burst into flames.

"I did it! I made it out!" he coughed. He crawled across the floor to grab the stones left by Taro. As he tried to merge the stones, a cold armored hand took a stone away from him and Burbon's brain felt on fire.

Yes, little trader, you did it. The whole world will thank you some day. The thoughts resonated as Darkmoor stood over him. He took the remaining stone from Burbon's hand. Burbon was too exhausted to resist.

"Stop!" Taro climbed off the back of Sunder as the large griffin flew in from the window. Stonewall tossed the last gobtrolls against the wall as he, the female Cumunian, and the few remaining Burbons walked among the fallen bodies.

"Look around. You have lost. While the group of us fight together, you now fight alone," Stonewall wiped his bloody blade.

"And you will die alone!" screamed Taro shooting a bolt at Darkmoor's heart. At close range, there was no way Darkmoor could evade her killing blow.

The bolt disintegrated a foot before hitting Darkmoor, who howled in delight.

You are too late, archer. You and your friends will be the first to die as the power of these stones is now mine to control! He put the remaining stone in place, combining all four. The last piece resisted being merged. Then all four cackled with a red energy that licked Darkmoor's hands like vipers. *It was your fate to bring their power to me. My fate is with these stones. My nightmares will finally come to an end!*

The gems formed a black portal around his hands and a howling wind emanated from the core. Gusts caused the burning pyramid to crash down to the floor. Its flame spread around Darkmoor, but he was impervious to harm. The others scattered to a safer distance. Darkmoor felt the energy course through his blood. He sensed a thousand thoughts in a second as he realized the power he was about to attain. Only pure evil could control the gem's ultimate power. His mind flashed back to his life of hatred and death.

Images of slave torture
His father's death
Hurting his subjects
Darkness in his cell
Poisoning his enemies
Kicking a defenseless old man
Stealing the wealth of his subjects

His thoughts came to a halt. Momentarily, Darkmoor weakened and instead of feeding on the gem's strength, the gem began feeding on him. He fought, his mind full of evil images and hatred, knowing that only total evil could claim the gem's power. He relived his pain and treacherous acts:

Desertion of his wife
Taking from the weak
Slaying of his foes
The torture of his enemies

No! Something feels wrong. Why does the stone's power need my energy? Am I not the evil that is prophesied to wield this power?

The travelers watched as the gem slowly swallowed his body. Darkmoor's life force was drained into the stone. His armor fell to the floor and the gem dropped to the floor into three stone pieces and a small rock.

Burbon walked over and picked up the small rock. Stonewall rushed over to him while Taro retrieved the three stones.

"Are you all right? What did you do?" asked Stonewall. Burbon held the small rock for all to see.

"Remember the halo rock that Turbine showed us?"

"The one he told you not to touch?" mentioned Taro.

"I couldn't help myself. Even though I knew it wasn't real, I had to have it," declared Burbon. "I switched it with the real stone hoping that Darkmoor would only see what he desired—the fourth stone. I prayed that the prophecy was true. If a false stone was used, then the holder would be consumed."

"Your greed has saved us all, Burbon," stated Taro.

"Not yet," replied Stonewall. He pulled out the machine that Turbine gave them to neutralize the stone's power. Burbon withdrew the real fourth stone but as it came closer to the other three, a gust of wind blew from the merged stones. The wind spun in a circle like a cyclone. Their force almost made it impossible to stand. Taro pushed next to Burbon to help. Burbon reached out to his two friends.

"How do you know it will work? Everything the Seer told us was a lie!" he yelled.

"But everything Turbine gave us has been true. He was a pawn just like us," Stonewall answered, his words muffled by the wind.

"We need the machine closer!" commanded Taro. The female Cumunian grabbed onto Stonewall and pushed him towards his friends.

Stonewall placed the machine down while Taro extended the stones. All four beings grabbed one of the pieces. Burbon felt an incredible power rush through him and almost considered taking the stone for himself. He stared at Taro's eyes and saw the same internal battle waged. He put his piece towards the machine.

"Now!" Stonewall yelled as the four of them placed the four pieces in the machine at the same time. The effect was immediate as the machine flashed, absorbing the energy from the stones. In seconds, the machine melted, and the four pieces fell to the floor, vacant of any power. The howling winds stopped suddenly.

The room was quiet, and the fallen pyramid smoldered, its flame almost consumed. Burbon was the first to walk over to the remains; he kicked the empty helmet of Darkmoor.

Darkmoor did say something right, looking at the ashes of Darkmoor's body amongst the stones. *His fate was with these stones.*

24

Endings and Beginnings

Stonewall sat in a middle of the busy square oblivious to the Cumunians that flew over him. A small bird skittered towards him as if he was a statue to squat on. A shadow appeared behind Stonewall that caused the bird to launch itself into the sky. Burbon placed his hand on his shoulder.

"Warrior, why so glum? Despite being played as fools, we accomplished what we set out to do. We won!" Burbon smiled. Stonewall peered up into his face.

"Aye, we did win my friend and for that I am eternally grateful. But I have the feeling that Darkmoor might have told me what happened to my father," Stonewall spoke. "He planned all of this, including the metal stand in Turbine's home. Without him, I feel I have lost my only chance to find my father or to learn why he left." Behind both of them, one of the apparition Burbons walked by carrying a load of silk. Taro avoided the double as she juggled her amulet in her hand.

"I can't get used to those duplicates of yours, Burbon," commented Taro.

"I still have a few hours before the last one disappears; I might as well put him to work." He looked at Taro's amulet. "You know the power in the stone is gone now, don't you?"

"I do," Taro replied. "But I'll not give up my family heirloom." She pocketed the amulet. "The Cumunians have agreed to fly us to the seacoast so we can charter a ship home. Darkmoor was the first being that was able to speak to them through his mind speech and he duped them into thinking that we were the enemy."

"Fortunately, his actions quickly proved him wrong," Stonewall added.

"They owe us a lot more than some transportation. Who knows what damage Darkmoor would have caused to their city had he succeeded? Oh, by the way, I think the female Cumunian is sweet on you," Burbon commented as she flew by the three of them. "Let me see the stand." Stonewall handed it over to him. "Turbine said it was made in the region of Solvana."

"I have heard they are a warlike race," Stonewall commented. "I will go to these people. Perhaps they can help me with information on my father."

"You can't go alone; the region is hidden in deep woods. You will need a tracker to find them," Taro placed her arm on Stonewall's shoulder.

"Don't forget me. These people deal with goods. You'll need a good bargainer," Burbon offered.

"And what about your store?" asked Stonewall.

"What store? Last I saw, it was a pile of rubble. That rubble will be waiting for me when I return."

"I appreciate what the two of you are doing, but understand that the journey will be fraught with dangers...."

"That we can overcome together," Taro continued.

"Sounds like my kind of trip," Burbon turned his head and looked off into the distance.

"What is it, Trader?' Taro asked.

"I was just thinking. If we are heading to the Solvana, I know of a town along the way that sells priceless gold statues."

"Burbon!" Taro and Stonewall yelled in unison as the trio walked down the street.

ABOUT THE AUTHOR

James Kochanoff is currently in a four-book deal with Silver Leaf Books in Massachusetts. The series is a young adult dystopian fiction with the first novel "Drone World" exploring the life of a teenage girl who thinks she lives in a perfectly safe city patrolled by drones, until she tries to leave it.

He signed a contract with Toonz Animation, Asia's largest animation for an animated pilot of his novel "Men of Extreme Action." To see images from this pilot, please visit his website at www.adventurebooks.ca

It's tough to make a career as an author. About 1% can truly make a living at it. If you enjoyed this book, please leave a review on your favorite book retailers' site and tell others about the book.

256 - Jim Kochanoff

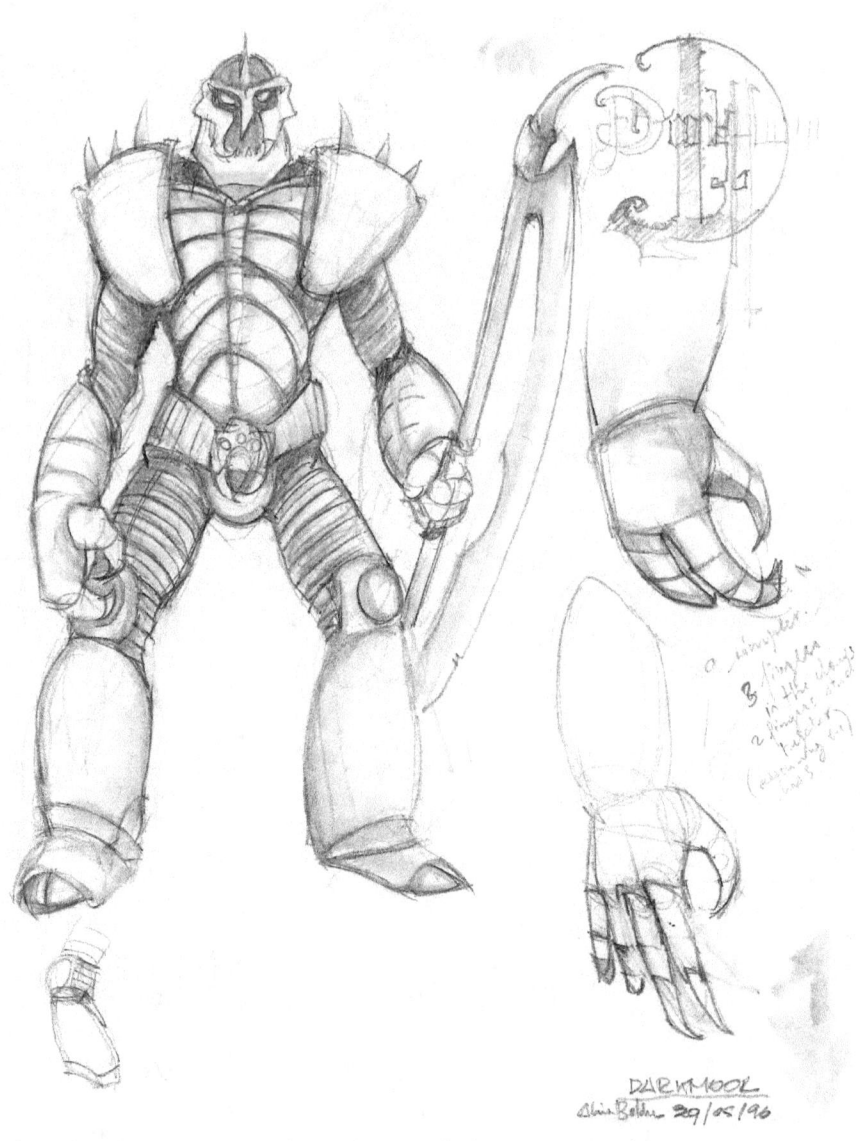

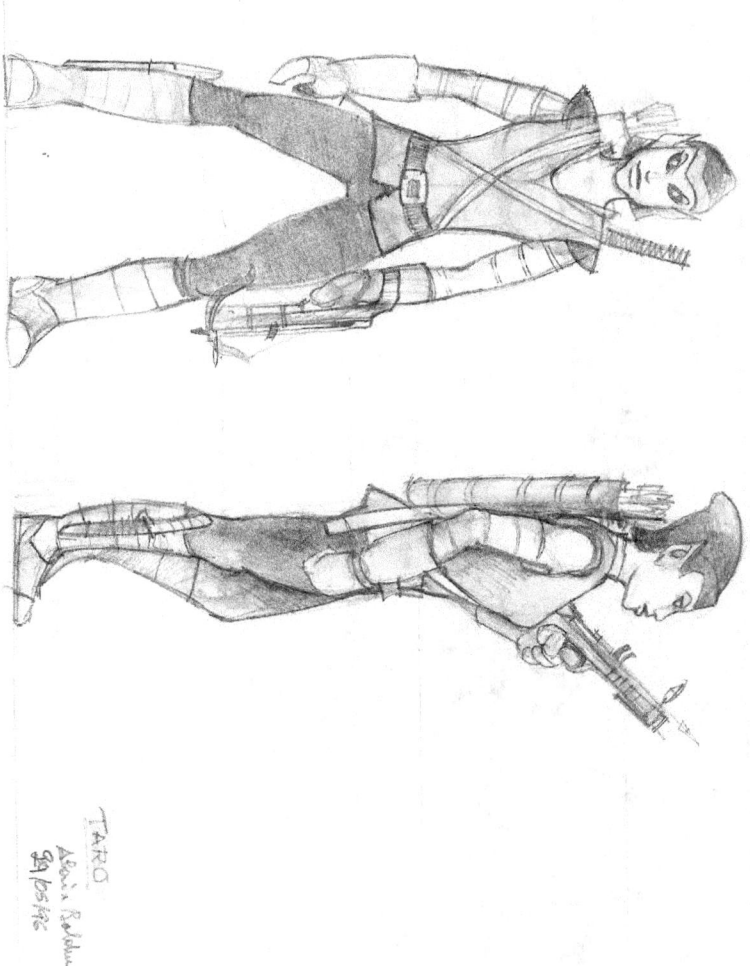

www.ingramcontent.com/pod-product-compliance
Lightning Source LLC
Chambersburg PA
CBHW070652120526
44590CB00013BA/921